Gender, Crime and Criminal Justice

Gender, Crime and Criminal Justice

Sandra Walklate

WILLAN
PUBLISHING

Published by:

Willan Publishing
Culmcott House
Mill Street, Uffculme
Cullompton, Devon
EX15 3AT, UK
Tel: +44(0)1884 840337
Fax: +44(0)1884 840251
e-mail: info@willanpublishing.co.uk

Published simultaneously in the USA and Canada by:

Willan Publishing
c/o ISBS, 5804 N.E. Hassalo St,
Portland, Oregon 97213-3644, USA
Tel: +001(0)503 287 3093
Fax: +001(0)503 280 8832

First published 2001
Reprinted 2001

ISBN 1-903240-41-7 (cased)
ISBN 1-903240-40-9 (paper)

British Library Cataloguing-in-Publication Data
A catalogue record for this book is available from the British Library

Typesetting and page layout by Willan Publishing. Text set in Palatino.
Printed and bound by T.J. International Ltd, Padstow, Cornwall

Contents

Preface and acknowledgements

This book updates and replaces my earlier book, *Gender and Crime: an introduction*, published in 1995. This was originally borne out of the support given to me by friends and colleagues in the Department of Sociology, University of Salford, and by the opportunity to develop my teaching interests by Ian Taylor, then head of department. Since then I have been Reader in Criminology, and since February 1998 Professor of Sociology at Manchester Metropolitan University, where I have been afforded the opportunity of developing a new degree programme in Criminology and Sociology.

Preparing a revised and updated version of this book has not been as easy as I anticipated. In some respects much has happened in the criminal justice world over the last few years. In terms of practice much is now in place in addressing the impact of crime (especially in relation to women) which was not there at the beginning of the 1990s. Moreover the MacPherson Report on the murder of Stephen Lawrence has focused the policy agenda on issues relating to ethnicity. I therefore constantly struggled with the questions of how much and under what circumstances did the question of gender still matter. However, that question now seems to me to be the crucial one. Clearly there are different lenses through which we might look at social life and gender is one of them. Without considering the centrality of this to us all (alongside race, class and sexuality) and some critical thought about how and when policies and practices might be differently informed, we shall be forever lost to sound bite politics.

This new edition, then, has been reorganised into three more clearly identifiable sections; roughly theory, praxis and policy; and each chapter has been updated to take account of more recent developments, both theoretical and empirical, in each of the relevant areas. My aim is not to offer a gendered analysis as an answer to the crime problem, but rather to lead students and practitioners alike to reflect upon how and under what circumstances the relationship between gender, crime and criminal justice is the salient one.

Sandra Walklate
Cheshire, June 2000.

Introduction: women and crime or gender and crime?

Introduction

Braithwaite (1989: 44) suggests that the fact that crime is committed disproportionately by males is the first fact that any theory of crime should fit. What facts like this actually represent, however, has not been subjected to detailed scrutiny within criminology until more recently. Indeed, some would argue that the maleness of criminal behaviour is actually a modern phenomenon, at least as far as officially recorded crime is concerned (Zedner, 1991; Feely and Little, 1991).

Before examining some of the questions that are raised by this empirical reality, it will be useful to construct a picture of what the patterning of criminal behaviour according to sex actually looks like. This will lead to a closer consideration of what kinds of crimes men and women commit, and what the differences might be between them in this respect. We shall be drawing on official statistics and other secondary sources to construct this picture alongside empirical studies that have relied upon such sources of data. First of all, then, it will be valuable to consider some of the inherent weaknesses in such data sources.

Making sense of criminal statistics

Official statistics on crime raise questions of reliability and validity for criminologists, politicians and policy-makers alike. Reliability refers to whether such statistical sources measure what they say they are measuring; and that they do this consistently and accurately. Validity refers to whether such sources actually measure what they say they are measuring. In some respects then it is more important to be assured of the validity of a data source, since without this it matters little whether or not the data is reliable. In the context of crime statistics it is important therefore to consider what is actually being measured by them. As these issues have been well discussed and well documented elsewhere (see for example, Bottomley and Pease, 1986; Coleman and Moynihan, 1997) we shall consider them here only briefly.

First it is important to remember that there is no necessary correspondence between the number of crimes recorded and the number of known offenders. More than one person might have been involved in committing an offence. One person may have committed many offences. Moreover, criminal offences are recorded for which there are no known identifiable offenders. So, if we are concerned specifically with who is committing crime rather than the total number of offences recorded we can already see that focusing on known offenders presents its problems.

The statistics on known offenders identify those individuals who have either been apprehended by the police, accepted a police caution, have admitted their guilt, or have been found guilty by the courts. Stated in this way it is easy to see the process from the moment a crime is committed and an individual apprehended for that crime, to the point at which any such individual receives a sentence from the court, involves a complex range of decisions. This decision-making process can produce wastage at any point within it. So, those offenders who become part of the official statistics only represent a part of all the crime known to the police.

In addition, to state the obvious, official statistics on known offending cannot reveal anything about those offenders who are not known or whose activities are not recorded in any way. As we shall see below, criminologists have endeavoured to employ other sources of information and data collection to overcome difficulties such as these. However, what is clear is that, presented in this way, acquiring an official criminal record is neither an easy nor a straightforward process.

Another way of trying to assess the nature and extent of criminal behaviour is to use criminal victimisation surveys. These are surveys of the general population in which people are asked what kinds of crime, if any, have been committed against them in the previous twelve months and whether or not those crimes have been reported to the police. Use of these surveys to establish a better picture of the nature and extent of the crime problem originated in the United States and have been conducted in England and Wales on a regular basis since 1982.

Victimisation surveys identify levels of victimisation as opposed to numbers of offenders. They reveal that on the whole the level of crime is about four times as high as that recorded by the police. In other words a good deal of criminal behaviour goes unreported and consequently unrecorded. What remains unreported, and thereby potentially unrecorded, varies. Thefts of motor vehicles are much more likely to be reported than vandalism, for example, because of the requirements of insurance companies.

Identifying who the victims of crime are as opposed to who the offenders are has been a very productive way of thinking about offending behaviour. This has especially been shown to be the case when the offender is known to the victim; though victimisation surveys vary in their effectiveness in revealing information on criminal behaviour which falls into this category. Looking at crime through the eyes of the victim has nevertheless had a significant impact on understanding the nature and extent of offending behaviour. Nowhere is this more the case than when we examine the nature and extent of sexual violence towards women (see chapter 4).

Finally, there are other sources of information on law-breaking behaviour. These sources generally come under the heading of self-report studies. Studies such as these endeavour to encourage people to disclose their own offending behaviour; a technique that has been used primarily in the study of juvenile delinquency. These data source also have their associated difficulties. People do not always tell the truth. This happens for a number of reasons; either because they are afraid of being found out or because they feel under pressure from their peers to say they do things when they do not. Moreover getting people to talk about serious offending behaviour is much more problematic. As a result such studies tend to focus on less serious law-breaking behaviour.

From this brief overview it is possible to see that different data sources can reveal different sorts of information about the nature and extent of law-breaking behaviour. None of these data sources are completely reliable or valid since they are all subject to the arbitrary effect of decisions made by other key actors in the process; whether that be the victim of crime who may be more or less willing to report a criminal offence, a police officer's discretionary decision to arrest, or a Crown Prosecution Service decision not to prosecute. What we finally know about who offenders are and the nature and extent of their offending behaviour is, consequently, limited. Caution is therefore appropriate. Having said all this, the question remains, what do we know about the sex differential in law-breaking behaviour from these sources of data?

Who are offenders?

In 1997 only 17 per cent of known offenders, that is, those cautioned or found guilty by the criminal justice system, were women (Home Office, 1999). In that same year 32 per cent of female offending involved indictable offences, 42 per cent summary non-motoring offences, and 26 per cent summary motoring offences. The equivalent proportions for men were 30 per cent, 28 per cent and 42 per cent. Theft and handling is the most common serious offence for females, accounting for 59 per cent of female indictable offences in 1997 as compared with only 35 per cent for men.

The prevalence of offending behaviour is greater amongst males than females, 34 per cent of men born in 1953 being convicted of an offence before the age of 40 as compared with 8 per cent of women; and only 3 per cent of female offenders have a criminal career of more than ten years as compared with 25 per cent of male offenders (all these figures are taken from Home Office data, 1999). This patterning of criminal behaviour has remained fairly consistent over time though Tarling's (1993) analysis does evidence some change in the ratio between male and female crime since 1955. He reports that the ratio of male to female offenders has fallen from 7.1:1 in 1955 to 5.2:1 in 1975 and has stayed at that level since then. Moreover, as the Home Office's own figures indicate these differences are not so marked amongst younger offenders.

This kind of patterning does not seem to be peculiar to the crime statistics of England and Wales. Wilson and Herrnstein (1985: 106) report that there appears to be some consistency in the propensity for males to be arrested more frequently than females internationally, a finding echoed by Harvey *et al* (1992). Reporting on a comparative analysis of United Nations survey data, they state that 'In all countries between 1975 and 1985, men greatly outnumbered women among those suspected, apprehended, prosecuted, convicted, and imprisoned'. They also report that in general terms women are convicted of less serious crime when compared with the kinds of crimes men are convicted for (see below).

Of course, as was established in the discussion above, official statistics represent only the tip of the iceberg when it comes to documenting criminal behaviour overall. It could be argued, and has been argued, that all sorts of bias enter into the criminal justice process consequent on the sex of the offender. Put simply, chivalry might work in such a way as to favour potential female offenders, thus resulting in more men appearing as known offenders. Classically, the work of Pollak (1950) articulates this kind of argument. The other sources of information commented on above could be used to support or invalidate such a hypothesis.

Evidence from self-report studies on criminal behaviour indicates that, whilst the sex ratio in relation to criminal activity narrows in such data sources, that activity remains predominantly male (see Morris, 1987; and Naffine, 1987, for a detailed summary of these findings). Moreover, victimisation survey data gathered in the United States has been used as a point of comparison with arrest statistics. Such comparisons suggest little variation between the kinds of incidents reported in which there was some knowledge of the offender and the kinds of incidents and offenders for which arrests were actually made. This suggests that at the arrest stage at least, police acted on available witness testimony rather than just in terms of chivalry.

Overall, then, there would seem to be some validity in the view that sex is a key variable contributing to law-breaking behaviour in and of itself. However, before we go on to consider where a statement like this might lead our analysis of criminal behaviour, there are a number of other questions on this issue worthy of further examination. For example, if sex is a key variable contributing to law-breaking behaviour overall, does that mean that men and women commit the same kind of offences to the same extent?

Do men and women commit the same kinds of crime?

As Heidensohn (1989) reports, women appear as offenders in all categories of offences from the most serious to the least serious. However, if we proceed to examine offending behaviour by offence type, we find that some types of crime are more dominated by males than other types of crime. Again looking at arrest rates, Wilson and Herrnstein (1985: 109) report that in 1977 in the United States males were most predominant in offences of burglary, drunkenness, auto theft, robbery, driving under the influence, possession of weapons, and sex offences. They were least predominant (though still clearly in the majority) in offences of vagrancy, fraud, larceny, forgery, embezzlement, disorderly conduct, murder; with females predominating in offences relating to prostitution. As the Home Office figures cited above suggest, there are differences between male and female recorded offending behaviour by offence type. Tarling (1993), reporting on data for 1990, illustrates some of these differences in ratio terms. For example, the male/female ratio for sexual offences was 105:1, whereas for theft and handling stolen goods, it was 3:1.

Heidensohn (1989) is clearly of the view that overall women commit less serious crime than men, and certainly the figures above would suggest that this is a reasonable conclusion to draw. So whilst female offenders do clearly appear in all categories of law-breaking behaviour, they appear much less frequently in some categories of offences that others. This requires closer examination.

If we take a closer look at the more serious crimes we find, for example, that in the case of murder, the sex-crime ratio is at its most clearly defined. Murder is predominantly a male activity. Men constitute the majority of the perpetrators and the majority of the victims of murder (Wilson and Daly, 1992; Buck and Walklate, 1993). In 1997 women constituted 35 per cent of all murder victims and in 79 per cent of these cases the perpetrator was known to them; 47 per cent of women were murdered by their current or former partners as compared with only 8 per cent of men (Home Office 1999). Indeed there again appears to be some international consistency to these findings. This does not mean, of course, that women do not commit such offences. They do. But when they do, the motivation appears to be different. Whilst there are female serial killers (Scrapec, 1993) and female terrorists (MacDonald, 1991), whose motivation to kill might be compared with that of men's, women who kill tend to be those women who have endured a violent relationship with a male partner (Jones, 1990).

Whilst it is clear then, that overall men and women commit all the same kinds of crime albeit at differing rates, women appear to commit the more serious crimes at a much lesser rate than men. The issue of crime seriousness, however, raises at least two further questions. First, it raises the question of the motivation for criminal behaviour as indicated above. If there is such a difference between the male and the female capacity to commit serious crime, does that mean that their motives for committing crimes in general are different? Second, this discussion also raised the question of what is meant by 'serious crime'? Does the term only refer to murder? As we shall see when more detailed attention is paid to who the victims of crime are, especially including those crimes which occur 'behind closed doors', the maleness of serious crime, in relation to personal assault, is sharpened. But the question remains, are men and women differently motivated to commit crime in general?

Do men and women offend for the same or different reasons?

In some respects this is the criminological question *par excellence*. Establishing an answer to this question would go a long way to answering the question of why people break the law; and, of course, if an answer to that question was found there would be little more need for criminology! The intention here is not to presume that it is possible to find an easy or a straightforward answer to it. Asking it, however, does provide an opportunity to consider a little more fully some other aspects of the sex patterning of law-breaking behaviour. Whilst the question of motivation clearly invokes an understanding of crime in terms of psychological processes, here the concern is not with individual differences, but whether or not it is possible to discern any other common features of men's or women's lives which might elicit a law-breaking response.

As has already been stated, females are to be found engaging in all kinds of law-breaking behaviour. It is also the case that as Carlen (1985) and others have shown, given the opportunity, women will engage in the same kind of criminal behaviour deriving the same kind of pleasure and excitement from it as their male counterparts. This is as much the case in 'white-collar crime' as it is for terrorism, for example. The official statistics discussed above, however, illustrate that the majority of people apprehended for law-breaking behaviour are so apprehended for property crime and theft. It is also the case that females appear more frequently as having been apprehended for this kind of criminal activity than any other.

That women tend to feature in this kind of criminal activity to a greater extent than they do in other types of criminal behaviour has been attributed to 'the feminisation of poverty' thesis (see for example, Wilson and Herrnstein, 1985; Currie, 1985). Put simply, a high proportion of female offenders steal in order to put food on the table for their children (for a much more detailed discussion of the interconnections between women, crime and poverty see Carlen, 1988). Indeed the tendency for women to engage in criminal behaviour for these reasons may be greater than official criminal statistics suggest, if the figures on benefit fraud were also included (for a fuller discussion of this and related issues see Cook, 1987 and 1988).

A survey of women in prison conducted in 1994 reported that the most common reasons for offending for mothers in prison were as follows: having no money (54 per cent); mixing with the wrong crowd (46 per cent); need to support children (38 per cent); drink or drugs (35 per cent); family problems (33 per cent); having no job (33 per cent). (Respondents could give more than one reason). It may also be the case, however, that male offenders engage in burglary and theft for some of these same reasons (see for example Campbell, 1993). Moreover, if we were to consider the interconnections between the use of hard drugs and prostitution and/or burglary, for example, we would, arguably, find similar motivational patterns for male and female law-breaking behaviour in these specific offence categories.

So whilst it would appear that there are some differences in style of offending behaviour between males and females, a search for an understanding of those differences in terms of motivation alone does not necessarily offer a full account of them. There are other features, potentially common to both male and female offenders, like poverty for example, which might elicit offending from both – although why poverty should produce this consequence for women, at a greater rate than men should, still remains to be explained. This does, however, lead to an important question. Are there any other variables associated with law-breaking behaviour that may override the effect of sex? One variable that merits some consideration in this respect is age.

Age as a variable

Young males comprise those who are identified for the most part as known offenders. This much appears to have entered political and policy consciousness. However, detailed empirical examination of the connections between age and sex and their relationship to offending behaviour is relatively under-explored. Tarling (1993) examined the criminal statistics for 1986 for England and Wales with these connections in mind.

The peak age of offending for males in 1990 was 18 and for females was 15. As offenders get older the ratio of male to female offenders declines (see Tarling, 1993: 16), though the peak age for offending for both sexes was reported as 18 in 1997. When type of offence is controlled for, there appears to be a remarkable similarity between males and females and the age at which they engage in offending behaviour. However, the absolute rate of law-breaking behaviour for different offences is also very different. If sexual offences are excluded, this leads Tarling (1993) to conclude that females are more likely to commit offences that are committed by older people and males are more likely to commit those kinds of offences committed by younger people. Thus it may be age rather than motivation which contributes to the differential patterning of criminal offences committed by males and females. Or it may be that if women are more likely to commit the kinds of crime associated with older offenders, this lends extra weight to the feminisation of poverty thesis. Given that the older women are the more likely to have family responsibilities, this phenomenon might be re-labelled a 'crime and responsibility thesis'!

So it appears from this analysis that it is possible that age, sex and criminal behaviour are related to each other in different ways for males and females. However, it may be that our criminological gaze is being distorted here with respect to these questions, because of the inherent limitations of relying on officially recorded crime data as our source of information for understanding these issues. Of crucial importance in this respect is, of course, Tarling's exclusion of sexual offences. Moving outside of the officially recorded criminal statistics and including sexual offences in the analysis, then, might lead us to a different conclusion concerning both the patterning of offending behaviour and its associated style. The inclusion of sexual offences also usefully returns us to the issue raised above; crime seriousness. We can best do this by reflecting on the data available, from a number of different sources, on patterns of victimisation.

Who are the victims of crime?

Criminal victimisation surveys, first conducted in the United States in the late 1960s, have become a veritable industry in their own right since that time. These surveys frequently focus on what might be termed conventionally defined crime; crimes against the person and crimes against property. In other words, they can be used as a direct point of comparison with officially recorded data sources on the nature and extent of crime.

The findings from these surveys can convey the message that, in these conventional terms (that is, referring to those offences which are directly comparable with officially recorded crime), not only are men more often the perpetrators of crime as indicated above, they are also more often the victims of crime, especially violent crime. For example, the 1992 British Crime Survey revealed that 53 per cent of victims of street crime were young males. The 1998 British Crime Survey reported that 6.1 per cent of adult men and 3.6 per cent of adult women had been the victim of at least one violent crime in 1997 (a figure which includes all types of crimes of violence).

However, if we move the victimological gaze away from crime as conventionally understood towards an incorporation of criminal behaviour which has traditionally been less visible in officially recorded crime rates – that is, towards including, 'domestic' violence, rape in marriage and 'date rape' – then we are left with quite a different picture of who the victims of crime are. This picture challenges the conventional view that men are most frequently violent towards each other and thereby the most frequent victims of such crime. In order to develop this picture it is necessary to draw on data sources which have largely been developed within, and have emanated from, work conducted under the umbrella of feminism.

Feminist-inspired work significantly enhances our understanding of the sex ratio associated with criminal behaviour in a number of ways. Not only does it draw our attention to the nature and extent of sexual violence towards women (see chapter 4 for a fuller discussion of this issue) but it also clearly conveys the message that when we consider that kind of criminal behaviour frequently hidden from view and consequently hidden from the criminal justice process, then the maleness of such behaviour is significantly highlighted. Thus the sex ratio of criminal behaviour, the question of styles of offending and motivation for offending behaviour, become questions which take on a different significance when the full range of law-breaking behaviour is included in the analysis – though it must be said that such evidence should not be accepted uncritically, as data from the 1998 British Crime Survey suggests. That survey, using a self-completion questionnaire, reported that 4.2 per cent of female respondents and 4.2 per cent of male respondents said that they had been physically attacked by a current or former partner in the last year, with the women more likely to have suffered injury and more likely to have been assaulted three or more times. Such figures are suggestive of some changing patterns here that are more fully discussed in chapter 4.

This brief overview is clearly suggestive of a number of themes. First, sex as a variable does seem to matter in trying to understand the nature of law-breaking behaviour, though how and under what circumstances is not clear cut.

Second, it is clearly not the only variable that matters. This discussion has also pointed to the importance of age. Other variables, like class and race, are also significant factors in contributing to those who are identified as known offenders. The fact that they are not discussed here does not imply that they are not important or not relevant. As this book unfolds it will become apparent that privileging one variable over another is more often than not a theoretical decision rather than an empirical one. The complex way in which sex, age, ethnicity and class interact is a common problematic theme in all the areas addressed in this book and will be returned to in the Conclusion.

Third, so far we have discussed the sex of offenders. We have not yet addressed the characteristics of the other actors who make up the criminal justice process: the professionals. We shall address this issue next.

Who are the professionals in the criminal justice system?

> Criminal justice professions are seen quite simply as male professions; it is man's work requiring the characteristics of men.
>
> (Morris, 1987: 135)

Both victims and offenders, if 'their' crime is reported, come into contact with the criminal justice system in different ways. That contact can often be crucial for how they both experience the workings of that process; whether or not they feel they have been treated fairly and equitably, for example. One striking feature of the criminal justice system and consequently how both victims and offenders experience it, is the way in which it is peopled. For the most part, as Morris rightly indicates, men people the criminal justice system. As we shall see in the chapters that follow, this has an impact on both men and women, as victims and offenders (complainants and defendants) who come into contact with it.

For example, in 1981 policewomen accounted for 8.6 per cent of the total police force in England and Wales. By 1989 this had only risen marginally to 10.6 per cent (*Social Trends*, 1991), but by 1998 this had risen to 16 per cent (Home Office, 1999). In 1994 three policewomen held the rank of Deputy Chief Constable and all Chief Constables were male though again by 1998 two Chief Constables were female. As far as the courts are concerned, in 1998, 26 per cent of barristers were female with 7 per cent of Queen's Counsel being female. In 1998 34 per cent of those qualified to practice as solicitors were female and in 1999 there were 30,260 lay magistrates, of whom 49 per cent were women. There were also 560 Circuit Judges, of whom 79 were women. In 1998 there were 7,208 probation officers of whom 55 per cent were women. In 1999, 14 per cent of Prison Officers were women, with 13 per cent of those operating at Governor grade being female.

These figures are telling in their consequences for the criminal justice system. Despite some small changes in the sex patterning of these professions they are for the most part both male-membered and male-dominated (Hearn, 1992). In other words, the majority of people working in the system are male, with the positions of power being almost exclusively male.

Again some similar observations could be made with respect to the ethnic composition of these various professions. Such a patterning is significant since it has consequences for both the men and the women who work within the criminal justice system. The message that criminal justice work is men's work (Morris, 1987) impacts upon not only the women who choose these professions but also on the qualities expected of their male colleagues. This is discussed in detail in the context of policework in particular in chapter 5. Second, entering such a male-dominated world implicitly, and often explicitly, structures the experience of that world for women who enter into it as either victims or offenders. Stereotypical expectations of appropriate feminine behaviour can pervade the judgements made about particular women who enter it. Stereotypical expectations of appropriate masculine behaviour can also pervade the decisions made by those working within the system. The impact of both of these processes is considered in later chapters in this text.

Ultimately, of course, how both victims and offenders (complainants and defendants) are dealt with, is, to a certain extent, framed by the law. The professionals working within the criminal justice system do not work within a vacuum, but draw upon the law and its interpretation in order to help them make decisions in particular cases. It is obviously, therefore, of vital importance to understand some features of how the law operates, and whether or not changing the law is likely to impact upon the way in which complainants and defendants experience its workings.

In this context too feminist work has made its contribution in encouraging us to think about the nature of the law and its domain assumptions. This work has raised the question of whose interests are best served by the law, and as a consequence whose interests are less well served by the central assumptions embedded within it. Attending to the impact that this final piece of the criminal justice equation has completes our picture of the criminal justice process as a gendered experience (see chapter 6).

So far then we have established some grounds for considering sex as an important variable for understanding the nature and extent of law-breaking behaviour, and furthermore for understanding how the criminal justice system operates in practice. In this discussion we have been careful to refer to sex as a variable rather than gender. This is important for two reasons. First, it is important to remember the distinction to be made between sex as a biological term and gender as an expression of psychological and/or cultural identity. In identifying the sex characteristics of crime statistics we are therefore making no presumptions about the behaviour that those statistics signify with respect to psychological or cultural identity. In others words the value of viewing them as an expression of masculinity or femininity has yet to be established. Second, making this distinction facilitates a discussion of why, for example, the title chosen for this book is *Gender, Crime and Criminal Justice* and not *Women and Crime*. What is significant about the difference in emphasis between these two labels for studying criminal justice?

The 'women and crime' debate

Several texts to date have seen it as their central task to address the 'women and crime problem'. Arguably this began with the seminal work of Smart (1977) and was continued by Leonard (1982), Heidensohn (1985), Morris (1987), and Naffine (1987). All these texts, whilst varied in content and theoretical approach, endeavoured in different ways to set the criminological record straight as far as women's relationship to criminal activity was concerned. They were concerned to challenge conventional criminological wisdoms concerning women and crime and in so doing were concerned to render women more visible within those criminological wisdoms. That each of these texts addressed this issue in a differently focused way perhaps goes without saying. They share, however, a number of common concerns.

First, they reflect a desire to move the criminological empirical agenda towards addressing a key, and what appears to be a constant, feature of the empirical data on crime; that is, crime is a male-dominated activity. So much this chapter has also been concerned to establish. Second, they reflect a desire to move the criminological theoretical agenda towards appreciating the diverse possibilities of feminist theorising and its potential contribution towards explaining that empirical data. Third, several of these texts reflect a concern to appreciate the fact that women's relationship to the crime problem needs to be understood not only in terms of their offending behaviour, but also in relation to women's experiences as victims of crime. Fourth, as texts they are all clearly suggestive of the view that the male-dominance within criminal activity might be better understood as a product of gender differences rather than a product of sex differences. What this means, however, not only for women but also for men, has until recently been relatively under-explored.

This text is in agreement with others written in this field that it is valuable to explore the operation of the criminal justice system from the starting-point of women's experiences of that system. However, there are inherent difficulties in solely concerning oneself with the 'women and crime' question. It is to some of those difficulties that we shall now turn.

Why not just women and crime?

There are a number of difficulties associated with a position that focuses solely on the 'woman and crime' question. Brown (1986: 35) has outlined some of these. One of the dangers presented by her is that:

> Crudely, the criticism they are offering is that the more one seeks to show that male criminologists take leave of their senses when the question Woman looms on the agenda, the more one implies that they are in their right minds when they talk about male crime.

In other words, Brown is clearly stating that the more that the woman question is treated as a separate and separable issue within criminology, the more that mainstream (read malestream?) criminology is left to its own devices, untouched by feminist criticism, and therefore presumed to be accurate when it talks about (male) crime. This is threatening for criminology for a number of different reasons.

- first, it leaves criminology and its domain assumptions untouched and unquestioned. Thus questions relating to women are always potentially seen as the 'other', second, marginal to the central concerns of the discipline.

- second, their behaviour is always likely to be measured against some masculine norms, which may or may not provide an adequate frame work for explaining crime for men, for women, or for either. Therefore, it does not follow that just because criminology has neglected or failed to explain female crime adequately, that it has performed better in relation to men.

- third, by implication, the 'women and crime' approach has for the most part failed to problematise men and their relationship with masculinity. This is important since not only has criminology implicitly paid empirical attention to criminal behaviour as being the behaviour of men, and thus failed to reflect upon the maleness of crime, but also the theorising which has guided such attention has been deeply rooted in masculine presumptions.

This last issue connects with a second danger that Brown identifies as being associated with the 'women and crime' approach to criminology. The 'women and crime' approach by its very label presumes two things. First, it presumes that it is possible to substitute the biological category of sex with the socio-cultural category of gender. In other words, women's criminality, for example, can be explained not by reference to biology but by reference to the ways in which women who fail to meet stereotypical expectations of femininity are stigmatised and fall foul of the criminal justice system. This approach presumes that it is possible to replace biologically rooted understandings (sex) with socially rooted ones (gender). Expressed in this way it is a position which hints at essentialism.

Essentialism refers to a way of looking at, in this particular instance, the differences between the sexes, and seeing those differences as given and immutable. So in some respects, a consideration of just women and crime takes us very little further *theoretically* in explaining those differences than a focus on sex differences might. This has happened in earlier writing about women and crime because the substitution of gender for sex has frequently still resulted in the presumption that gender equals women and not men. Moreover, it has also frequently been presumed that gender equals *all* women and not men. As we shall see, this is no longer a reasonable nor a sufficient starting-point for understanding the 'crime problem', or the response of criminology and victimology to it.

Nevertheless, it is without doubt that feminist-inspired empirical work and feminist theorising offers much to both criminology and victimology; and that includes that feminist work which has concentrated on and still does concentrate on the 'women and crime' question. This is despite the fact that both of these disciplinary areas have as yet to appreciate fully the implications of these developments (see chapter 1). Therefore, despite the potential problem of substituting one essentialist argument for another, without this shift in focus facilitated by feminist work, a re-examination of the relationship between, not only women and crime, but also men and crime, would not be possible. This brings us to the question of masculinity.

The expression of masculinity in its various forms constitutes a key feature of understanding the criminal justice process and all its related activities in gendered terms. An exploration of masculinity, its expression in criminal behaviour, the impact it has on men who are victimised, and its central presence in key professional areas within the criminal justice system, permits the development of a way of thinking about the crime problem which neither universalises men's experiences nor neglects women's. It is this perspective on the crime problem that provides a more accurate framework for thinking about gender and crime rather than women and crime or sex differences and crime.

So whilst there are significant difficulties in looking at the crime question from the perspective of the women and crime question, that question still constitutes a useful starting-point to not only understanding some features of the crime problem but also in explaining that problem and criminology's response to it.

Conclusion

The purpose of this text, then, is to introduce the student to the kinds of questions which feminist work, both inside and outside of criminology and victimology, has addressed and to explore how these questions have furthered an understanding of the crime problem. In so doing it will assess the ways in which shared feminist concerns like those outlined above, have contributed to criminological and victimological work (if at all). In addition it will explore ways in which thinking about the criminal justice system as a whole, from a *gendered* perspective, might lead to a better understanding of both women's and men's experiences of that system, as offenders, victims and professionals working within it. However we must note a word of caution.

As has been alluded to in the discussion of the empirical data cited above, sex is not the only variable that appears to be a constant feature of the crime statistics. Other key variables include age, class and ethnicity, especially when one focuses on those who are apprehended and processed by the criminal justice system. The way in which these variables interact with and relate to one another is not clear cut. Indeed, it is more a matter of theoretical perspective as to how such interrelationships might be read. The foregrounding of gender issues in this text is not intended to imply that other variables are not significant in producing certain outcomes for certain groups in their relationship with the criminal justice system. It does, however, reflect a view that when one examines the relationship between offending behaviour and the victims of that offending behaviour, across the full range of potential criminal activity, sex as a variable appears to be significant. What needs to be understood is how and under what circumstances does that empirical evidence warrants a gendered explanation in preference to any other kind of explanation.

Overview and organisation of this book

Each of the chapters following this Introduction addresses a key theme within criminology, victimology, and the criminal justice process. Chapter 1 offers a theoretical overview of both criminology and victimology. This overview is intended to offer an exploration of the key assumptions that underpin both of these disciplines and the impact that these key assumptions have had on conceptualisations of men and women as victims and offenders. This chapter also outlines the diversity of feminist thought and its potential and actual impact on these disciplines and their domain assumptions.

Chapter 2 offers a similar theoretical overview of criminology and victimology but in this case seen through the lens of masculinity.

Chapters 3 and 4 explore two substantive issues within current criminal justice policy; the fear of crime (chapter 3) and sexual violence (chapter 4). Exploration of these two substantive issues provides a vehicle for the further development and critique of the theoretical questions raised in chapters 1 and 2.

Chapters 5 and 6 deal with the nature of the criminal justice system and its response to both victims and offenders of crime. Chapter 5 pays particular attention to policework, and chapter 6 focuses on debates around the law.

The Conclusion considers what questions remain to be answered about crime and criminal victimisation in the aftermath of foregrounding the gender question. It is hoped that, at the end of this journey, the presumption that gender as opposed to sex is a key variable in helping make sense of the criminal justice system, will have been more than justified for the reader. It is also hoped that the reader will have developed an appreciation of both the strengths and weaknesses of the ability of criminology and victimology to see gender.

Suggestions for further reading

Anyone approaching this question for the first time should take a look at Smart (1977), *Women, Crime and Criminology*. This book made an important contribution to the development of criminology.

Heidensohn (1985) *Women and Crime* offers a good review of the literature, and sets the woman and crime agenda on the road to considering the more fundamental question of differential experiences of social control.

The chapters by Gelsthorpe on 'Feminism and Criminology', Jefferson on 'Masculinities and Crime', and Heidensohn on 'Gender and Crime' in Maguire, Morgan, and Reiner *The Oxford Handbook of Criminology* (2nd edition 1997) are also worth a look.

1 Criminology, victimology and feminism

Introduction

Paul Rock (1986: 72) has observed that 'a number of social sciences are lent a tenuous unity by their concentration upon a particular fragment of the empirical world'. Criminology and its sister sub-discipline of victimology are two such social science areas. These subject areas are peopled by academics from disciplines ranging from psychiatry to sociology and by policy-makers and administrators from backgrounds equally diverse. Such a diversity of approach to understanding and tackling the phenomenon of crime frequently poses difficulties for the person new to the area or for those seeking simple and immediate answers to 'the crime problem'. The purpose of this chapter is to seek out ways of making sense of this diversity through a critical examination of some of the underpinning assumptions associated with the different theoretical and analytical approaches found within this area.

An examination of these assumptions will reveal a certain consensus with respect to what Gouldner (1968) once called a discipline's 'domain assumptions'. These are assumptions so deeply embedded in the way in which the world is viewed that they are taken for granted as 'given'. One set of assumptions, which are embedded in many social science disciplines in this way, surrounds the question of gender. Criminology and victimology are no exceptions to this general rule. It is the purpose of this chapter to examine the way in which assumptions relating to gender pervade our understanding of crime, the criminal, and the victim. In other words we shall be exploring the ways in which the disciplines of criminology and victimology operate in 'gender-blind' terms.

Gender-blindness can be explored in different ways. As an idea it draws our attention to the particular ways in which any area of study makes fundamental assumptions about the substance of its concerns. Such assumptions are rendered more visible when we ask such questions as: who can know things, what it is that can be known, how can information be gathered, who is it relevant to gather information from? All of these questions, and the very way in which they are answered by social scientists, can privilege one set of interests at the expense of others. In other words it is important to understand the way in which any body of knowledge is put together along with the assumptions that encourage one way of thinking about the available information in that area in preference to another. Understanding the knowledge production process, as a process, has been a concern of many feminist (and other) writers. Their analysis leads to the conclusion that the result of this process is the presentation of the world as if it were a *masculine* world; even though the information and arguments presented may have been done as though they encapsulate a view of the world in *human* terms.

The human world, however, does not consist of androgynous subjects. It is made up of males and females who are attributed with masculine and feminine qualities. The failure to recognise this is a basic feature of gender-blindness; so, for example, it is of value to consider the question of how legitimate it is to make the assumption that the term human accurately conveys the views of male and females. One way of answering this question is to ensure women are made more visible, and heard more readily, in the way in which information and arguments are put together. However, asking this kind of question very soon leads to a consideration of issues beyond merely ensuring that 'women's issues' are given adequate coverage. As the discussion in the Introduction illustrated, substituting women's experiences for human experiences can sometimes result in the further 'ghettoisation' and marginalisation of those questions from mainstream academic work. Moreover a sole focus on women's experiences also reflects a view which presumes that women and men are essentially different in their make-up and consequently in their experiences, a view which at best confuses sex differences with gender differences and at worst constitutes biological determinism; that is, a view which presumes that biological sexual attributes explain all forms of both collective and individual behaviour. Questions such as these, as this chapter aims to demonstrate, ultimately lead to a consideration of much more fundamental issues as to what counts as knowledge itself.

Simply focusing on 'the woman question', then, cannot easily overcome the deep-rooted difficulties associated with the phenomenon of 'gender-blindness'. Such a position might encourage a recognition of women and an empirical examination of their potentially different experiences, but it does run the danger of over-emphasising those differences. Focusing on women, though, can take us a long way towards recognising some of the effects of gender-blind thinking. However, it is only through a consideration of the way in which deeply embedded assumptions about *men and women* structure their lives, and how we theorise about that process, that we can really appreciate the power that domain assumptions about gender possess.

'Gender-blindness' has been challenged across a range of knowledge production processes by what has been called the second wave of feminism (Banks, 1981). This chapter will explore the extent to which gender-blindness has informed the world views of criminology and victimology, the challenge that different strands of feminism has posed for those world views, and the impact that that challenge has had. But first it will be useful to summarise some of the key themes that underpin the academic disciplines of both criminology and victimology.

Gendering criminology

> The relative rarity of women offenders, on the other hand (like prevalence of motoring crimes), has for the most part been tacitly ignored by students of criminology, any clues suggested by this sex difference being generally neglected. Apart from the work of a few students who have interested themselves particularly in the offences committed by women the habitual reaction of sociologists and criminologists to the sex difference has been to eliminate the female subjects from their studies, on the ground that the number of available cases is too small to allow of any valid inferences being made. Yet if men behaved like women, the courts would be idle and the prisons empty.
>
> (Wootton, 1959: 32)

> Men as males have not been the objects of the criminological gaze. Yet the most consistent and dramatic findings from Lombroso to postmodern criminology is not that most criminals are working-class – a fact which has received continuous theoretical attention – but that most criminals are, and always have been, men. Instead of asking how the maleness of men connects with this result, with this hugely unexplained finding, we ask why women do not offend, as if even the criminogenic properties of maleness were normal compared with the cheerful and resigned conformity of women. This is because the *criminological* gaze cannot see gender; the criminological discourse cannot speak men and women.
>
> (Cain, 1989: 4)

These two quotes, separated by thirty years, stand as testimony both to how much and how little has changed in the nature of the criminological enterprise. Tellingly, they illustrate how gender-blindness has impacted upon criminology. These authors, separated as they might be by time and context, both exhort criminology to take the question of the maleness of crime seriously. Yet criminology still struggles with this demand. The question is, why? Part of the answer to this question lies in understanding the origins of the discipline itself, and the gendered assumptions that are embedded in those origins.

Many reviews of the origins of criminology begin by reference to the influence of 'positivism'. Whilst this is not the place to debate the various interpretations of what is meant by 'positivism' it is relevant to locate, historically, the emergence and influence of these ideas since they can reveal something about the gendered assumptions with which we are concerned here. Auguste Comte is largely attributed with having laid the foundations to the discipline of sociology cemented with the principles of positivism. Responding, as many of his contemporary writers and critics were, to the impact of the 'twin revolutions', the French Revolution and the Industrial Revolution, Comte viewed the role for social science as a positive one; that is, social science would constitute a positive influence on, and control over, the negative effects of the social upheavals taking place at that time. In this way, Comte not only laid the foundation for sociology (or what he first called 'social physics') as a science, but also as a science implicated in the policy process; that is in ensuring that social change occurred positively, without revolution. In this sense positivism became associated with particular ideas about the role of the knowledge-gathering process; that is, what we understand by science. The historical legacy of these ideas can be found in all the social sciences but they are particularly pertinent to understanding the nature and form of criminology and (latterly) victimology.

Taylor, Walton and Young in *The New Criminology* (1973) attempted to distinguish between different strands of positivism. Within criminology they state that positivism's major attribute is 'its insistence on the unity of the scientific method' (*ibid*: 11). From this they deduce three premises which frame much of empirical criminology: the quantification of behaviour, the belief in objectivity and the determinant nature of human behaviour. Roshier (1989) identifies the influence of positivism on criminology in more generic terms, though he too offers three key characteristics: determinism, differentiation, and pathology. Characterisations such as these delineate more precisely the impact that ideas of writers such as Comte had on the emerging social sciences and it is useful to explore them in a little more detail.

Determinism assumes that human behaviour, including criminal behaviour, is not rationally chosen. In the context of understanding criminal behaviour this is taken to mean that crime consists of actions merely responsive to social, biological, or psychological factors. Differentiation assumes that there is something measurably different about people who engage in such behaviour. In other words, they, as individuals, possess certain characteristics that can be clearly identified and that can clearly delineate them from non-criminals. Pathology implies that not only are such people different, but also that there is something abnormal about such differences. If we add to these features a notion of 'scientism', that is the concern to produce 'objective' empirical evidence to inform the policy-making process (Taylor, Walton and Young, 1973) we have some idea of the form of criminology that was to become so intimately connected with criminal justice policy (Garland, 1985).

There is, however, one further presumption associated with the influence of positivism on criminology that needs to be made explicit. That presumption concerns the desire to establish a universal explanation of crime and, thereby, a solution to the crime problem. This desire is clearly derived from the drive to emulate the natural sciences (hence Comte's first term for sociology, social physics), and from the desire to exert a positive influence (read 'control') over the processes of social change. Thus the search for a universal, all-embracing explanation of crime and criminal behaviour has dogged much criminological endeavour. It is within these deep-rooted conceptions of science – science as the search for universality and control – that we catch our first glimpses of gender-blindness, since these assumptions reveal much about what there is to be known and by whom. However, before developing a more detailed appreciation of these roots it will be useful to explore the way in which the positivistic views of science of the nineteenth century wielded their particular influence on the discipline of criminology, since that historical context encouraged criminology to view women (and men) in particular ways.

Sex, science and the criminal

Eagle Russett (1989: 63) states:

> Women and savages, together with idiots, criminals and pathological monstrosities, were a constant source of anxiety to male intellectuals in the late nineteenth century.

According to Eagle Russett, this anxiety was identifiable in the four principles that underpinned nineteenth-century 'sexual science'. These principles were: the law of biogenetics, the notion of the greater variability of the male of the species, the conservation of energy and the correlation of force within a species, and the physiological division of labour. Of these four principles, the most influential was the law of biogenetics. This law stated, 'ontology recapitulates phylogeny'. In other words, every individual organism re-visits the development of the species within its own developmental history.

This idea of the repetitive nature of biological history, or recapitulation, constituted one of the unifying and organising principles of anthropology, including criminal anthropology. Its influence on anthropological criminology is particularly crucial to understanding the way in which early criminologists strove to formulate a universal explanation of criminal behaviour and consequently how they viewed both male and female criminals. Its particular relevance to criminology lies in an idea derived from the biogenetic law, that is, the notion of atavism. This idea was constructed to overcome an empirical difficulty associated with the principle of biogenetics. The biogenetic law, as stated above, could not explain how it was that the process of recapitulation, guided by genetic inheritance, did not always work. In other words, its theoretic formulation could not explain how it was that sometimes individuals were produced who were 'abnormal' in some way. The notion of atavism was therefore introduced to explain why the principles of biogenetics did not always work to their full potential.

Atavism described a situation in which an individual member of a species could be identified as a throwback to an earlier genetic period. In this way the concept of atavism allowed the law of biogenetics to retain its universal status; aberrations were explained as reversions to earlier species type. The idea of atavism, or throwback, appealed to the criminal anthropologists as a way of explaining the abnormality of the criminal. It was an idea that was developed particularly by the Italian criminal anthropologist Lombroso.

Assuming that the process of recapitulation usually produced biologically normal individuals, Lombroso envisaged that the criminal was a throwback, an atavistic degeneration, to an earlier biological ancestry. Indeed, the tendency for criminals to mark themselves with tattoos led Lombroso to argue that this was evidence of their closer relationship with 'savages' ('savages' were deemed to be located at an earlier point on the evolutionary scale). Given that the same assumptions associated with the evolutionary process also applied to females and children, the idea of the 'atavistic criminal' served a double helping of inadequacy to the female criminal. It is worth spending a little time this in more detail.

In general terms Victorian science viewed women as a 'developmental anomaly' (Eagle Russett, 1989: 74). The biogenetic law presumed that the ultimate stage of development on the evolutionary scale was that stage of development reached by the white, caucasian male. Such a presumption facilitated the construction of certain views about women. In particular it allowed for the view to be developed that women, being less advanced in their biological development than men, stopped growing too soon; they were at best forever trapped in puberty. So if women in general suffered from arrested development, the criminal woman must be, as a consequence, a particularly problematic being. This is the conclusion reached by Lombroso and Ferraro in *The Female Offender* (1895).

There are two important elements to the biogenetic argument that led Lombroso and Ferraro to this conclusion. The first element is to be found in the belief that the development of women in general was arrested at an earlier stage of the recapitulation process. This made women closer to their species type. Such a proximity to species type rendered the female of the species, as an organism, more conservative than the male of the species. The second element is derived from the view that pathology (deviance) was explainable via the notion of atavistic degeneracy. Combining these two together the female criminal can indeed be seen as a 'monster', as more evil than the male, as she constituted both a throwback to an earlier species type as well as being arrested in her development as a member of her species. It is clear that there has been some dispute concerning the underlying explanation of criminal behaviour that led Lombroso and Ferraro to this conclusion. Indeed some would say that there has been a consequent misrepresentation of their views of the female criminal (Brown, 1986), so it is perhaps worth reviewing what Lombroso and Ferraro were trying to achieve.

Lombroso and Ferraro were searching for a universal explanation of crime driven by the influence of positivism. In their search for such a universal explanation they viewed female criminality as being problematic as a result of their conservatism rather than their deviance. Thus, Brown (1990: 50) is correct to assert that: 'the important thing about Lombroso and Ferraro's book is not biological determinism but the siting of women's conformity as the object of criminological analysis'. In other words, placed in the context of more general scientific ideas of the nineteenth century in relation to sex differences, they were concerned with a search for a causal explanation of criminal behaviour that could be universally applied to both sexes.

To summarise; the principles of evolution placed males and females (children and savages) on different points on the evolutionary scale. The greater development of the male (reflected in the greater variability in the male of any species) was likely to produce a greater variation in atavistic degeneration; whereas the greater conservatism (less variability) alongside the presumed arrested development of the female of the species, resulted in her degeneracy (in this case criminal behaviour) being all the more problematic when it occurred. Thus, the principle of the biogenetic law afforded Lombroso and Ferraro a theoretical consistency in their explanation of the male and the female criminal.

This search for a unifying explanation of criminal behaviour did not start and finish with the work of the criminal anthropologists, or biological positivists as they are more conventionally referred to. It is a recurrent feature of criminological theorising. What is particularly interesting about this biologically based approach, however, is the way in which ideas associated with it have persisted over time in relation to explaining offending behaviour. For example, the idea that female criminals are driven by their differently constructed nervous system (Thomas, 1923) or their hormones (Dalton, 1991) stand as testimony to the influence of this way of thinking about criminal behaviour.

Biologism, as these approaches are sometimes referred to – that is, explaining behaviour in terms of intrinsic biological make-up – was not solely confined to explaining the female criminal. Whilst the work of Dalton in the late 1960s is still debated by feminist critics (see, for example,

Kendall, 1991; Allen, 1984/1990) and still poses particular political dilemmas for practitioners (whether 'special cases' be made for female defendants or not), it should not be forgotten that what Hall-Williams (1982) labels the 'chemistry of crime', runs through a range of criminological work from twin studies through to chromosome studies. Many of these studies were focused either implicitly or explicitly on men, particularly violent men.

Such a concern is entirely consonant with a deep-rooted view of male offenders, of course, derived from a presumption of the greater variability of the male of the species. Thus whilst Dalton's work echoes the idea of the 'monstrous' effects of a woman 'at the mercy of her hormones' (Allen, 1984/1990), in a similar way a range of criminological work does an equal disservice to explaining male offending behaviour. If this is the case then biological determinism constitutes not only an inappropriate starting-point for an explanation of female criminal behaviour, but also has those same shortcomings in the understandings offered of male criminal behaviour. So, what is particularly significant about the influence of the nineteenth-century scientists and their biologically rooted explanations of the differences between males and females, is the way in which those ideas are carried forward into later work. This influence is particularly displayed in that work which presumes that the differences between males and females are 'natural', biological or given.

The criminal anthropologists (biological positivists) laid a particular foundation for the further development of criminological explanations. In drawing on the ideas associated with nineteenth-century science both in their commitment to positivism and in the biologically derived presumptions concerning the nature of sex differences, they provided a deep-rooted framework for thinking about and explaining crime. Moreover, the influence of nineteenth-century conceptions of the evolutionary process and the way in which these were applied to explanations of sex differences has, arguably, made a significant contribution to *cultural* conceptions of those same differences. In other words, they have framed the way in which thinking about males and females, and masculinity and femininity, has been constructed.

Whilst overt biological concerns were not necessarily present in all subsequent criminological explanations, few of these explanations lost the desire to search for a universal explanation of criminal behaviour. Later criminological work, for example, moved away from the purely physical and/or biological as causal factors of crime towards explanations that focused on mental and/or personality factors, emotional stability, child-rearing practices and/or deprivation of 'adequate' upbringing. None of this work was explicitly gendered but often presumed that the differences between the sexes were both natural and universal and in this way constitute a clear link back to criminal anthropology. Sexual differences in these studies, if not seen to be biologically given, were sometimes seen to be the product of sex-role stereotyping during upbringing. In this way biological difference is presumed to produce social difference. This latter view of the process of the production of sex differences influenced the more sociologically inspired sub-cultural studies of delinquency and deviance of the 1950s and 1960s.

Influenced by the sociological functionalism of Talcott Parsons a generation of sociologists proffered a range of studies specifically geared towards explaining juvenile crime. These studies presumed, for the most part implicitly (with the notable exception of Cohen, 1955), that the problem of juvenile crime was a problem of male juvenile crime. Summarising an earlier article by Millman (1975), Naffine (1987: 5) has this to say about this range of work:

> The overwhelming impression created by the sociological canon on deviance is that men alone are capable of standing up for their rights and defying convention, particularly when social rebellion is interpreted in terms of the 'heroic' qualities of bravery and loyalty to the oppressed. Deviant women, by contrast, are regarded as anaemic, as 'politically uninspired'.

Whilst females are not completely absent from these studies, hence the oft-quoted statement from Cohen (1955) that 'boys collect stamps, and girls collect boys'; they are studies which repeatedly focus on the greater criminal activity of the male and (implicitly) the greater conformity of the female.

In commenting on Sutherland and Cressey's work, for example, Naffine (1987: 31) states:

> Female behaviour and the female experience simply appear as significant exceptions to the central activity and ethic of modern society. Femaleness emerges as an anomaly. Female homogeneity contrasts with the general diversity of the culture. Female altruism or 'being nice' contrasts with egoism. The constraints of the female experience contrast with the limitless pursuit of gain of the rest of society.

The emphasis in this analysis on the female as anomalous, alongside the contrast proffered between female homogeneity and general (male) diversity, clearly echoes the tenets of nineteenth-century sexual science identified by Eagle Russett (1989).

Of course, what is embedded in much of this work is the structural functionalist sociology of Talcott Parsons. Such presumptions regard the acquisition of male and female characteristics as being given through the process of sex role socialisation. In other words, functionalist sociology presumes that sex differences are biologically given, and that these biological givens dictate the subsequent exposure to differential socialisation. For example, given that it is natural for women to bear children, their socialisation prepares them for this role; hence the presumed pre-occupation for girls in forming a stable relationship with a boy, and the pre-occupation for boys in actively creating their public identities as men to be reckoned with.

The ideas on sexual difference underpinning structural functionalism made it very difficult for the sub-cultural theorists to conceive of female crime as having the same motivational basis as male crime. If the female deviant was attended to, it was in relation to understanding the circumstances in which she was deviant from her expected, biologically given, sex role. In other words, work concerned with the female delinquent became pre-occupied with female status offences associated with the expression of 'deviant' sexuality, promiscuity and/or prostitution.

Of course, the threat posed by girls exploring their sexuality outside of the prescribed social rules and expectations is a very real one. The social control exerted over and by young working-class girls in their use and experience of the label 'slag' stands as a very real indicator of this (Lees, 1989). Sub-cultural theorists, however, did not view the impact of such status offences in quite these terms. Such offences were taken as illustration of the kind of criminal behaviour girls engaged in rather than such behaviour being seen as the product of the differential mechanisms of control which girls are subjected to. As theorists they failed to see their own contribution to the way in which women's relationship with law-breaking behaviour could be understood. The perpetual failure to see female crime in anything other than 'sexual' terms is reflected in the control theory of Hirshi (1969), the liberation thesis of Adler (1975), and, ironically, in the work of the labelling theorists. They all denude the female offender of any sense of agency other than that which fits with stereotypical/cultural sex role expectations.

Naffine (1987) offers the following summary of criminology's dealing with the female criminal. She argued that for the most part female crime has been associated with legitimate endeavours to find a mate or to sustain a relationship with a male. Women are not seen to be aggressive or violent because that is inconsistent with the feminine ideal. So, whilst there have been a variety of approaches to explaining crime since the days of Lombroso, all of which have dealt differently, and more or less visibly, with the question of female criminality (for discussions of this work see, for example, Naffine, 1987; Heidensohn, 1985; Smart, 1977), none of this work lost the deeply embedded assumption that crime was men's work, not women's (Jefferson, 1993). This is as true of that work emanating from the conservative voice of Eysenck as it is of the more critical and radical work of Taylor, Walton and Young. Later criminological work of the 1980s, whether that be administrative criminology or radical left realism, did little to rectify this omission with respect to offending behaviour (the contribution that this later work has made towards the study of victimisation will be discussed more fully below).

This summary of the criminological tradition has implicitly and explicitly drawn on feminist work of the last twenty years. In the context of criminology, as we shall see in later chapters, much feminist work in this area has been concerned to render the female criminal visible and as a consequence has posed serious questions for criminology, though not all criminologists would adhere to that view. For example, in appraising the importance of feminist work Downes and Rock (1988: 289) stated:

> Central as its role should be in the sociology of deviance we do not regard the significance of gender in quite such stark terms... it so happens that criminological theory has been crime led, and that the subjects around whom theorising has been formed have been predominantly white urban lower class and usually adolescent males in advanced industrial capitalist societies.

In a sense this statement both misses and makes the point. Whilst it may be argued that criminology has neglected to take women seriously as offenders because they were 'too few to count' or because those theories that did address female criminality did so with particular images of women in mind, there is still, as Scraton (1990) observed, a 'pervasiveness of hegemonic masculinity' within the discipline. This may 'be found overtly in the making, enforcement, and application of the law; it is also found covertly in the academic discourses which prevail within malestream criminology'. In other words whilst criminology might have thought a good deal about sex differences, it has roundly failed to think gender. The quote from Downes and Rock aptly illustrates this.

This summary has endeavoured to illustrate that there is a thread of gendered assumptions that link the early work of the criminal anthropologists with the later work of the sociologists of deviance. Nineteenth-century scientific work concerned with sex differences played a crucial part in constructing this thread. So too did the presumptions of positivism and the associated search for universal explanations. This has left us with a good deal of evidence concerning the maleness of crime; but evidence which has largely been dealt with in a very unreflective fashion by criminologists themselves. However, before developing our understanding further of the ways in which this process, in and of itself, produces a gender-blindness above and beyond the questions of who is made visible by whom, it will be useful to examine the extent to which victimology has been subjected to those same influences.

Gendering victimology

Victimology as a distinct area of study emerged much later than criminology. Its origins are usually located in the work of Von Hentig and Mendelsohn during the late 1940s. As lawyers-cum-criminologists, both of these writers were concerned to understand the relationship between the victim and offender and both endeavoured to construct 'victim typologies' as one way of achieving such an understanding. Each of them gave a very different focus to their typologies. Von Hentig was concerned with categories of victim proneness; Mendelsohn with victim culpability. Whilst neither of these writers intended to suggest that there was such a being as the 'born victim', they were nevertheless searching for ways of differentiating the potential victim from the non-victim which could be used in all victimising situations. A strategy clearly consonant with the work of the early criminologists.

Typologies, by their very nature do not lend themselves easily to empirical ratification, yet the construction of victim typologies has remained a key ingredient of victimology. Later versions of this kind of work are much more sophisticated than those of Von Hentig and Mendelsohn but they nevertheless share in the early criminological world view that if criminals could be identified in some way then so could victims. In this way it can be seen that victimology, unsurprisingly, also has a share in those fundamental tenets of early criminology: determinism, differentiation, and pathology. These are reflected in the work of those early victimologists whose typologies focused on either the personal characteristics of the victim (whether they were female, old, mentally defective, etc, for Von Hentig) or the contribution that their behaviour made to the commission of a crime (from being totally innocent to the criminal who became the victim, for Mendelsohn).

Arguably, this way of thinking about the victim reflects an underpinning view that there is a normal person, measured against whom the victim somehow falls short. In Von Hentig's work this normal person, given the categories of victim proneness which he identifies, is (implicitly) the white, heterosexual male, a clear parallel with the views of nineteenth-century sexual science discussed earlier. The presumptions underpinning Mendelsohn's work are, arguably, more legalistic. They convey notions of what might be considered reasonable or rational behaviour in particular circumstances. As we shall see as both this chapter and this text unfolds, the question of what is considered to be reasonable and/or rational behaviour is also a gendered one. However, it is not until the later development of Mendelsohn's work, when victim culpability became translated into a concept of victim precipitation, that the impact of what might be considered reasonable or rational behaviour for a victim is more keenly felt. As understanding this concept is particularly revealing in understanding victimology and its developments, we shall consider it a little more fully.

The concept of victim precipitation was originally formulated by Wolfgang (1957) in his work on homicide and later developed by Amir (1971) in his work on rape. Essentially this concept not only draws attention to the criminal act as involving two (or more) individuals, but is also concerned to understand the relative contribution of each party to the commission of that act. Derived as it is from a more legalistic understanding of the notion of culpability, its use has been seen to be particularly controversial when applied to rape and sexual assault.

Amir's (1971) study of rape provoked a strong reaction for a number of reasons. Not only are there empirical difficulties with his findings (for a detailed discussion of these see Morris, 1987), the associated connotations of attributing *blame* are very difficult to shed from a concept of victim precipitation, however carefully formulated. As a concept, it clearly encourages us to consider the contribution of a victim's behaviour towards crime, and whilst it has been deployed in a number of different contexts including, for example, burglary, its focus on the victim has contributed to what Karmen (1990) has called the move from 'crime prevention' towards 'victimisation prevention'. In the context of burglary, it might be felt unfair, though perhaps not unreasonable, to expect people to lock their doors in order to help prevent a burglary taking place. In the context of rape or sexual assault, however, the notion that somehow the victim could have engaged in more reasonable behaviour for the incident not to have happened to them, arguably, misunderstands the fundamental nature of an incident of that kind. In other words, the concept of victim precipitation presumes equality between participants where none may exist. This raises all kinds of questions as to what constitutes reasonable behaviour in situations where the individuals concerned do not possess, at a minimum, the same physical power with which to negotiate the situation (see chapter 3 for a fuller discussion of these issues). From this viewpoint this concept cannot therefore be applied to situations which are a product of power relations in general or gendered power relationships in particular. As a concept, it cannot see gender.

Although victimology, as originally formulated, was concerned with the relationship between the victim and the offender, the focus on the behaviour of the victim and the policy possibilities that that generates has been very influential, despite the associated attribution of blame. The same can be said for another influential strand to victimological work; that work centres on the concept of lifestyle.

The concept of lifestyle, in its original formulation, is largely associated with the work of Hindelang, Gottfredson and Garofalo (1978). Since victim precipitation as a concept was most useful when focused on individual victimising events but could not account for the regular patterning of criminal victimisation, these authors were concerned to develop a framework which could; hence the concept of lifestyle. Their framework was posited as a series of eight propositions all of which could be measured empirically. Influenced by functionalist sociology, these propositions largely directed attention to such factors as: how much time an individual spent outside their home, what activities they were engaged in, how they moved about, etc. This way of thinking about the risk of criminal victimisation, despite the definitional difficulties associated with the concept itself (for a summary, see Walklate, 1989, chapter 1), has fed significantly into the crime survey business (see chapter 3) and has also contributed towards a re-orientation of the crime prevention industry from crime prevention to victimisation prevention already commented on above.

The concepts of victim precipitation and lifestyle form the core of much victimological thinking. Fattah (1991), in reviewing the available data and explanations of differential victimisation, attempts to integrate a range of victimological work generated in this way into a general schema. In doing so he groups forty propositions about criminal victimisation under ten key headings; available opportunities, risk factors, the presence of motivated offenders, exposure, associations, dangerous times/dangerous places, dangerous behaviours, high risk activities, defensive/avoidance behaviours, structural cultural proneness. This listing, whilst evidently more sophisticated than the simplistic assertion of a notion of lifestyle or victim precipitation, still reflects the central influence that these concepts have had on victimology. They all, with one exception, direct attention to the victim's behaviour and they all presume some norm of appropriate or rational behaviour which the victim fails to adhere to in some respect.

The continued dominance of work influenced by these ideas illustrates what Miers (1989: 3) has called a positivistic victimology. This he defines as:

> The identification of factors which contribute to a non-random pattern of victimisation, a focus on interpersonal crimes of violence, and a concern to identify victims who may have contributed to their own victimisation.

Whilst Miers himself does not offer a definition of what he understands by the term 'positivism', the parallels with criminology are clear: the emphasis on measurement and identification added to differentiation, determinism and pathology, combining in that same effect of 'scientism' (Taylor, Walton and Young, 1973). What this effect illustrates with respect to the status of the knowledge produced within victimology will be developed shortly.

It is important to note that during the 1980s, the interests of victimology and criminology began to merge. The victim became 'politicised'

(Miers, 1978) and could no longer be seen as the 'forgotten party of the criminal justice system'. The victim became of equal significant interest to different strands of criminological work. Although feminists, for example, had long been concerned with the plight of women as 'victims' of men's violences, the criminological attention paid to crime victims arose rather more as a result of the increasing use of the criminal victimisation survey as a way of measuring the nature and the extent of the crime problem than it did from any deep commitment to the issues raised by feminist work.

As chapter 3 illustrates, there are differences in emphasis in the way in which what came to be called the 'administrative criminology' of the Home Office and that of 'radical left realism' utilised the criminal victimisation survey. However, their use of the victim as a source of information about crime, and their implicit acceptance of the lifestyle model on which such survey methodology is based, renders their adherence to the principles of positivism as characterised by Miers (1989) very similar. Whilst those of 'left realist' persuasion would argue that they have embraced the concerns of feminism and have challenged male presumptions of rationality especially with respect to the fear of crime (see chapter 3), they nevertheless face methodological difficulties in removing the positivistic stains from their work, a charge against left realism made by Smart (1990). The question remains, of course, as to how these victimological presumptions have contributed towards a notion of a gendered victim.

In one sense the process of understanding and identifying the influence of what counts as science and consequently what counts as scientific knowledge underpins the gendering of the victim in a very similar way to that which has occurred in gendering the criminal. These processes do not surface in expressions directly related to evolutionism within victimology but they do surface as having been influenced by the cultural legacy emanating from those ideas. For example, if we examine Von Hentig's typology of victim proneness we find that women (children, the elderly, people from ethnic minorities) feature as being particularly victim-prone. If we examine the concept of victim precipitation, it presumes some legal notion of reasonable behaviour which, when examined carefully, frequently means reasonable, white, male, entrepreneurial behaviour (Naffine, 1990). If we examine the work of Hindelang, Gottfredson and Garofalo (1978) we find that their propositions are derived from a highly functionalist view of the world, a world in which the concept of lifestyle presumes that individuals adapt to their structural location; and that they do this differently and passively according to the characteristics they possess: age, race, sex, etc. Such adaptations then become reflected in an individual's routine public life, that is, their daily street activities, thus implicitly accepting a sex role model view of gender issues and thereby accepting a very male view of what counts as a high risk place, that is, the street.

All of these examples arguably reflect a deeply embedded male view of the problem of victimisation; at a conceptual level in defining the scope of the discipline, and at an empirical level, in defining that which needs to be measured. At the same time these core victimological concepts have failed to take seriously or problematise some of the key findings which this work has itself generated. The lifestyle-exposure model, for example, as exemplified by criminal victimisation survey data, repeatedly reveals that young males are most at risk from violent crime and yet are least likely to express fear of it (see chapter 3).

However, it is not only victimology that has contributed to the gendering of the victim in this way. It has to be said that much feminist work, whilst developing outside of victimology both conceptually and empirically, has also contributed to this process. That feminist work, focusing as it did on the nature and extent of male violence, especially sexual violence towards women, has created the impression that only women (and female children) are victimised by such violence. This is not to downplay the political importance of all that was achieved by feminist academics and activists in drawing attention to campaigning against rape, 'domestic' violence, etc., nor is it intended to underestimate the importance of the feminist focus on the concept of 'survivor' rather than 'victim'. Neither, it must be said, should this be read as a denial of the overwhelming evidence that women and children suffer most at the hands of men and particularly men they know (see chapter 4). However, despite these caveats, this work alongside mainstream victimological work leaves us with an underpinning world view that constitutes the potential victim as being powerless and, in many instances, female.

To summarise, in one sense this review has led us to the view that criminology on the one hand presumes the criminal to be male and yet fails to reflect upon the impact that this presumption has on how the discipline theorises crime and the criminal. On the other hand, much victimological work implicitly leaves us with the view that victims are likely not to be male. Of course, if we examine these presumptions a little more carefully we might want to argue that both the variables of class and ethnicity impact differentially upon these core presumptions. Such an observation does not change the nature of those core presumptions, however. Feminists have argued that such presumptions of maleness within both these disciplines, whilst surfacing in views on sex differences, have their origin in the influence of positivism. It is argued that this view of science and the scientific process is in itself gender-blind. In order to understand and appreciate the potential for a feminist response to both criminology and victimology, it will be useful to review the impact that positivism, so central to the formation of each of these disciplines, has in the perpetuation of a male world view.

Science constructs the male and the female

Eagle Russett's (1989) study commented on earlier provides us with some insight into the ways in which nineteenth-century science constructed both the male and the female and the influence that this had on criminology in particular. She also comments that it is important to locate the emergence of these 'scientific' ideas in the broader context of the political processes occurring at that time. As those political processes, campaigns for the rights of black people and the women in particular, made their presence felt, she argues that ideas about black people and women became more rigid. Thus, the political context of this science, and the threat that that context posed to the existing social order, played a significant part in informing the scientific response to it. This provides us with a glimpse of the political processes deeply embedded in the production of scientific knowledge. It also illustrates how highly problematic it is to presume that such a knowledge production process is objective. It is in relation to this issue in particular that feminists have challenged traditional conceptions of positivism.

The belief that science could transform and control nature has its origins in the seventeenth century. Bacon, for example, believed that the 'man of science' could 'make nature a "slave" to man's needs and desires' (Sydie, 1989: 205). In seeking this control Bacon characterised nature as female. This association of women with nature, or being closer to nature as was observed with the nineteenth-century work on sex differences, pervades philosophical thinking, especially with respect to scientific knowledge. As Kellner Fox states:

> Having divided the world into two parts the knower (mind) and the knowable (nature) scientific ideology goes on to prescribe a very specific relation between the two. It prescribes the interactions which can consummate this union, that is which can lead to knowledge. Not only are mind and nature assigned gender, but in characterising scientific and objective thought as masculine, the very activity by which the knower can acquire knowledge is also genderised.
>
> (quoted in Sydie, 1989: 205)

Such a process of genderising science assigns women not only as a dangerous Other (the nature to be controlled) but also assigns women a particular status as knowers in relation to men. As Smith (1987: 74) remarks, 'the knower turns out after all not to be an "abstract knower" perching on an Archimedean point but a member of a definite social category occupying definite positions in the society'. Recognising that the construction of knowledge is a product of a definite social relationship in this way involves recognising that the rules which underpin such knowledge construction render some forms of knowledge legitimate and acceptable and other forms not.

Thus the 'scientifically validated' ideas of the nineteenth century, and their cultural legacy, need to be understood as part of a process and the rules that underpin it. The surface features of those rules with respect to the formation of knowledge within criminology and victimology have been commented on above (pathology, differentiation, evolutionism, scientism). However, those surface features are supported by a set of presumptions in terms of what it is to be 'scientific'. What kind of knowledge counts as scientific knowledge?

As has been suggested above, it is usual to associate 'scientific' knowledge with that knowledge which is seen to be dispassionate, disinterested, impartial and abstract. These are values which are considered to be transcendental; that is, uncontaminated by the context of time and space. These are also the characteristics associated with that kind of knowledge that is considered to be rational knowledge. The idea of rationality connects this conception of science with the foundational knowledge of both criminology and victimology. For example, in the context of nineteenth-century science, male knowledge is equated with rational knowledge consigning women's knowledge (almost a contradiction in terms) to that of 'emotional work'. Thus the presumption that underpins such dichotomous thinking, as Sydie (1989) has illustrated, is of the 'natural woman' and the 'cultured man'.

Early criminology, and later victimology, reflect these deeply embedded views of males and females and the process of knowledge acquisition; of the male of the species being the norm, the healthy, the searcher for knowledge, and the female of the species being closer to nature, the abnormal, the provider of nurture. As disciplines, they also reflect certain presumptions as to what counts as scientific knowledge and rationality.

Consequently all kinds of questions are raised concerning what is to be understood as being scientific. As Harding (1987) has pointed out, questions are raised concerning who can be a knower, what kind of things can be known, what do we mean by objectivity, etc. – questions which pose fundamental problems for both of the discipline areas under discussion here. Moreover, there are different feminist responses to each of these questions: liberal feminism, radical feminism, marxist/socialist feminism, and postmodern feminism. We shall consider the key elements of each of these positions in turn before considering their impact, or potential impact, on criminology and victimology.

Liberal feminism

Liberal feminism is a useful place to start in examining feminist responses to the questions we have raised about science, since some of the ideas informing this position are associated with writers whose work co-existed with the nineteenth-century scientific ideas discussed above; for example the work of Harriet Taylor and John Stuart Mill. However, liberal feminist ideas have their roots in a much longer history, arguably beginning with the work of Mary Wollstonecraft.

Interestingly, given our discussion here, Wollstonecraft valued rationality. In response to Rousseau, she wanted Rousseau's Sophie to have the same educational opportunities as his Emile. It was irrational, she argued, to deny women's autonomy. Tong (1989: 16) states:

> Wollstonecraft insisted that if rationality is the capacity that distinguishes brute animals from human persons, then unless girls are brute animals (a description that most men will probably resist when it comes to their own mothers, wives, and daughters), women as well as men have this capacity. Thus society owes girls the same education as boys simply because all persons deserve an equal chance to develop their rational and moral capacities so that they can achieve personhood.

This commitment to reason, and consequently to equal opportunities, characterises two key features of the liberal feminist tradition: characteristics that assume that under the right legal and political conditions heterosexual relations would be equal. Consequently, much liberal feminist political work has been associated with the pursuit of legal rights.

Liberal feminism is also associated with a particular methodological position; that which Harding (1987) has identified as feminist empiricism. This approach to engaging in scientific work presumes that it is 'bad' science which produces the sexist bias in empirical work. In other words, the rules of science and scientific enquiry are in themselves sound, what is amiss is how they are applied. To alleviate this problem feminist empiricists would argue for the presence of more women researchers in general, and more feminist researchers, both male and female, in particular. Moreover, feminist empiricists would take as given the need to include women in any empirical data-gathering process.

The appeal of feminist empiricism is obvious: it leaves the conventional standards of what counts as 'good' research untouched, thereby remaining committed to the traditional principles of science and scientific knowledge. Adherence to these principles, however, constitutes a fundamental dilemma for the liberal feminist. Such principles take as given that the yardstick by which we judge any knowledge that is produced is a male one. In other words, this position, whilst promoting equal treatment studies and the empirical examination of theories with respect to men and women, leaves intact the assumption that male values are equivalent to human values.

This assumption has led some critics to argue that liberal feminism reflects a 'normative dualism' (Jaggar, 1983). Normative dualism, according to Jaggar (1983), prioritises mental activities over bodily activities. In other words, it implicitly accepts the nineteenth-century view that women are closer to nature. Being closer to nature, being the Other, implicitly accepts the view that women's experiences, and the knowledge derived from them, are of less value than that knowledge gained through mental development. Thus, acceptance of this normative dualism maintains the emphasis on valorising rational (male) knowledge and devaluing knowledge acquired in other ways.

Whilst this might be considered to be a fundamental flaw in liberal feminism, it does not mean that either as a methodological or a political strategy it is without strengths. Indeed, there is still much to be gained from pursuing the equal opportunity stance associated with this position for women and other disadvantaged groups. As a political strategy, although appealing to the white, heterosexual, middle-class female, it may yet have the radical future predicted for it by Eisenstein (1986). Conceptually speaking, however, the liberal feminist for the most part conflates the questions associated with sex differential with those questions posed by gender. As a consequence this position cannot capture the full impact of patriarchal social relations; until, of course, a liberal feminist hits the 'glass ceiling'. This is more than aptly illustrated by Harding's (1991) point when she argues that in some ways it is impossible to add women to any agenda, but particularly a research agenda, without changing the foundation on which that agenda has been built.

Radical feminism

In contrast to liberal feminism, radical feminism focuses more clearly on the issue of men's oppression of women rather than on other social conditions that might result in women's subordination. Crucial to the radical feminist analysis is the question of sexuality. This is seen as the locus of male power (MacKinnon, 1989). Radical feminist analysis has had much to say about reproduction and mothering as well as women's experiences of male violence, though the emphasis on understanding the expression of female sexuality through the lens of patriarchal social relationships is central to all these analyses. As Tong (1989) points out, the radical feminist only needs to ask such questions as: Who rapes whom? Who batters whom? For whom does pornography exist? For whom does prostitution exist?, for the ultimate answer to the question, For whom does female sexuality exist?, to be men.

So for the radical feminist, women will always be subordinate to men until sexuality is reconstituted. This has led some radical feminists to argue that the model for female sexuality is lesbian sexuality. Indeed others would add that, in order to achieve such a reconstruction of sexuality, it is necessary to replace male culture with female culture: a position sometimes referred to as cultural feminism. In this respect this form of feminism constitutes a real challenge to men and the expression of their masculinity.

Radical feminism, whilst centring the importance of male power over other forms of domination, is sometimes presented as stemming from a key assumption: that to be female is intrinsically good and to be male is intrinsically bad. This lays radical feminism open to the charges of essentialism and reductionism. In other words, it is a position that reflects the view that there are immutable differences between males and females and that we explain male and female behaviour by reference to these differences. There are several questions which are raised by this assumption: whether such differences are biological, emotional, or indeed whether, in fact, women's goodness exists at all. All of these are necessarily open to considerable debate, but the impact of such a fundamental assumption is far reaching. It has the effect of leaving women, and women's experiences, undifferentiated and undifferentiatable. The category 'woman' is left untouched. Yet at the same time it is a position which strives to allow women to speak for themselves: a difficult contradiction to unravel. The same assumption conveys similar messages about men and men's experiences. This latter comment encapsulates a range of issues for men, often categorised as typical men by radical feminism, and is worth pursuing a little more fully.

Jaggar (1983) argued that radical feminism presumes that all men have the same power and control over their own lives as they have over women. Moreover, others have commented on how the view that 'all men are potential rapists' presumes that all men have the same relationship to violence and to the expression of their masculinity in violence towards women. Accused of simplistic thinking about men in this respect, radical feminism has nevertheless made a significant contribution towards placing men and their behaviour at the centre of academic and political concerns. Without this campaigning work and the fundamental challenge posed by it to malestream thought, current agendas would look significantly different.

Despite these difficulties the key strength within radical feminism over liberal feminism lies in the fact that as a position it does not conflate the issue of male power and domination with other social processes, or conditions. In this respect it is a position which bears some comparison with our next feminist perspective, socialist feminism, especially in relation to the methodological imperatives which flow from it.

Socialist feminism

Socialist feminism is an outgrowth of Marxist feminist dissatisfaction with the gender-blind concept of class. Marxist analysis subsumed women's oppression as being less important than the oppression experienced as a result of social class and failed to recognise the domestic nature of much of women's work. Socialist feminism identifies a concern not to reduce gender inequality to the assertion of patriarchal social relations, as in radical feminism, but to conceptualise the particular conditions under which women were both oppressed by capitalism and dominated by men. They therefore focus attention on the interplay between capitalism and patriarchy. Whilst there is much debate within socialist feminism concerning which of these systems – capitalism or patriarchy – has primacy, in empirical terms this position frequently translates into a concern with the ways in which the structural variables of gender, age, class and race have a compounding effect on one another within capitalist/patriarchal social systems. Although criticised in the past for transforming the women question into the worker question, more recent socialist feminist work has attempted to incorporate both psychoanalytical and radical insights into their analyses. Arguably what binds these different strands of thought together, and provides a connecting thread with radical feminism, is the notion of a 'standpoint'.

The idea of a standpoint is derived from the work of Hegel. Hegel (followed by Marx and Engels) argued that it was through struggle that the proletariat gained knowledge. Struggle provided the proletariat with access not only to their own knowledge and experiences of being oppressed, but also to knowledge and understanding of the process of oppression. Thus the knowledge of the proletariat could be considered more complete knowledge since it was derived from both sides of the system of oppression. Feminist standpoint theorists, for the purposes of this overview deemed to encompass both radical and socialist feminists, have used this idea to understand and elevate the nature of women's knowledge and experiences.

Standpoint theorists observe that the dualistic thinking associated with nineteenth-century liberalism places women on the nature side of the nature/culture dualism. Standpoint theorists argue that women, placed as they are on this side of this dualism, therefore have access to knowledge and experience derived from both being placed closer to nature and yet being expected to participate in cultural processes. They may be placed closer to nature by societal expectations, but they are nevertheless also a part of the cultural processes that produce those expectations. So in some senses women are both a part of and simultaneously outside the social order; they straddle the nature/culture divide.

Women's routine lives consist of the ability to constantly negotiate this dualism. So, rather like the struggle experienced by the proletariat, women's struggle in constantly negotiating this divide equips them with more complete knowledge and experience of the social order; that is, more objective knowledge. As Harding (1991: 3) states: 'From the perspective of women's lives scientific rationality frequently appears irrational'. Thus feminists who adhere to this standpoint view on the nature of knowledge are not only clearly stating that knowledge is relative, thus tempering scientific claims to universality, they are also accepting its highly contentious and political nature. At an empirical level such a position has led researchers to adopt the notion of work done 'by women, with women, for women'. It is a position, however, which also has some shortcomings.

There is an implicit assumption in much standpoint feminist work that traditional scientific knowledge with its search for universality is to be equated with the masculine desire for transcendence, man's search for control of his environment. Whilst there are certainly parallels to be drawn here, more recent debates suggest that it is mistaken to assume that there is one unitary form or expression of masculinity associated with science in this way. It perhaps makes more sense to talk of masculinities. In other words, some men may struggle in a similar, though differently structured way, with universalising claims to knowledge about them and their experiences.

The connecting thread between radical feminism and socialist feminism of a standpoint, highlights a key risk for both these feminist positions. Any theory or methodological position seeking some way of looking for commonalities or unifying factors runs the risk of eliminating or down-grading difference; a problem which applies equally to efforts concerned to unify women's experiences as well as men's. Our next feminist perspective, however, could not be accused of this: it celebrates difference.

Postmodern feminism

Originally termed French feminism, this feminist perspective has its origins in the work of Derrida, Lacan, and Foucault. Not that any of these writers had much to say, if anything, about gender *per se*. But there are two themes which draw together the most famous of the 'French feminists' (Cixous, Irigaray, and Kristeva): deconstructionism and the celebration of 'Otherness'.

The exploration of 'Otherness' stems from the work of Simone de Beauvoir. For her, to be 'other', or second, was not recommended. It was a condition that represented oppression. For postmodern feminists it is a condition that is this and much more. Otherness also represents openness, plurality, diversity and difference. This emphasis on the positive side of 'Otherness', the features of otherness which have been excluded or marginalised by phallocentric thinking, promotes a critical stance towards everything: that is, a need to deconstruct ideas and language, and the structures on which they are based.

Difference and deconstruction taken together render meaningless the search for universal truth or a unified concept of the self. Such searches are symptomatic of a phallocentric drive for an ordered, unified universe which feminist postmodernism intrinsically denies. For example, the category 'woman', used as it is to denote all women, is highly problematic since it denies the diversity and difference present in women's experiences: white, black, lesbian, etc, women.

This emphasis on diversity, difference, and the desire to deconstruct the language structures of the modern world, lead many critics to argue that postmodernism simply produces chaos. Indeed, this way of thinking about the (post)modern world is particularly problematic for those who lay claim to the universalising forces of science and scientific knowledge. For the postmodernist, such claims are a fiction. In other words, there can never be a feminist science, only the many stories that women tell. Thus at a methodological level, and in terms of setting an agenda for empirical research particularly, such a perspective is highly sceptical of the claims of a criminology (or a victimology) tied to the (modernist) project of progress and policy formation as reflected in a commitment to positivism, for example.

To summarise: all of these different feminist perspectives attempt to deal with the knowledge production process in different ways. Liberal feminism stands as a call for the implementation of 'correct' and unbiased procedures, radical and social feminism stands for the elevation of women's knowledge as constituting more complete knowledge, and postmodern feminism is sceptical of any claims for producing generalised knowledge of any kind. Of all of these positions, liberal feminism is the least threatening to conventional social scientific conceptions of science and knowledge since it accepts as valid the ability to make such claims. Radical, socialist and postmodern feminism, however, pose a much greater threat. All of these views have the potential for, or have already impacted upon, criminology and/or victimology in different ways. At this point it is worth considering how and in what ways these feminisms have

Feminism and criminology: a contradiction in terms?

In 1985 Heidensohn suggested that the feminist critique of criminology had so far focused on the fact that women are largely invisible or, at best, marginal to its studies, and that when women are studied they are done so in a limited and distorted fashion. In one sense Heidensohn is correct to pinpoint these as having been issues for feminist concern. Indeed, much of Carol Smart's early work, *Women, Crime and Criminology* (1977), was concerned to document both of these areas of neglect. Smart was also aware, however, that forging a niche called 'women and crime' might both further perpetuate the marginalisation of the issue and simultaneously draw attention to a phenomenon, especially amongst policy-makers, which might not always be in women's interests, a view developed more fully in her later work (Smart, 1989). But Smart was not the only feminist to try to redress the criminological imbalance in this way. Several other texts followed, for example: Leonard (1982), Naffine (1987) and Morris (1987). All of these writers were striving in their different ways to render the issue of women and crime more visible. What is clear, however, is that when these issues are viewed from the vantage point of the first decade of the 21st century, feminist influence in understanding the relationship of women to the phenomenon of crime has been more diverse, more subtle and, in some ways, more fundamental than 'simply' making women visible.

Gelsthorpe and Morris (1990: 2) state:

> Criminology has for many feminist writers and researchers been a constraining rather than a constructive and creative influence. Indeed, in a sense our task in this book is to fracture its boundaries.

Their choice to talk of feminist 'perspectives' emphasises the diversity of feminist work of potential importance to criminology and the challenge that this poses (see also Rafter and Heidensohn, 1995). The flavour of that diversity is reflected in the influence that the different feminist positions discussed above have had on the study of the crime problem. The following discussion will endeavour to document some of that influence. It is important to be aware that the intention here is not to locate particular writers or researchers under particular headings. It is clear, however, that more recent feminist work is more clearly associated with one version of feminism than another. The links between the feminist perspectives presented here and the kind of work done by 'feminists' within criminology is to be seen as both a heuristic device and as an issue of contention!

In some respects it is possible to argue that liberal feminism has had the longest historical impact on the study of criminology. This statement can be defended in a number of ways. Firstly, there have always been women researchers looking at the problems associated with crime. There may not have been very many of them, and the work that they produced may not have been particularly radical, but they were nevertheless present and they were examining the sex differentials associated with crime, especially delinquency (see, for example, Wootton, 1959; Glueck and Glueck, 1950; Cowie, Cowie and Slater, 1968). In other words, there is a her-story of women researching within criminology and a her-story of work addressing female offending behaviour.

It is possible to align much of that work with the liberal imperative of ensuring that females feature as a part of any empirical data set, a question of good 'scientific' practice. There is a second theme, however, to that work which we might locate as being influenced by liberal feminism: a focus on discriminatory practices. This strand reveals itself in different ways.

Arguably the work of Pollak (1950), concerned as it was with understanding the influence that chivalry might play in the under-documenting of women's criminality, is, at the same time, a study of discriminatory practice. The presumption that women are discriminated against, either favourably or unfavourably, within the criminal justice system has informed a wealth of criminological research. Research has shown that factors such as type of offence (Hindelang, 1979; Farrington and Morris, 1983), home circumstances (Datesmann and Scarpitti, 1980), personal demeanour (de Fleur, 1975) are contributory factors to the way in which women are processed by the criminal justice system.

This theme has been explored in ever more detailed and specific circumstances: in magistrate's courts (Eaton, 1986), in prison (Carlen, 1983; Dobash and Gutteridge 1986), in women's experiences as victims of crime (Chambers and Millar, 1983; Edwards, 1989). That these factors simply represent sexist practices, however, is not easy to assert. Some studies suggest that women are treated more leniently by the courts, others suggest a harsher outcome. Such contradictory conclusions point to the complex way in which factors such as age, class, race, marital status, and previous criminal record interact with each other. Moreover, Gelsthorpe (1989) found that there were organisational influences that affected the way in which females were dealt with by practitioners which were difficult to attribute to sexist or discriminatory practices alone.

Gelsthorpe (1989) goes on to discuss the key drawbacks to this anti-discriminatory theme within criminological work.

- first, it assumes that women have been neglected systematically by criminology whereas it might be more accurate to assert that criminological concerns have developed rather more erratically than this view presumes. Women were the focus of some early criminological work (see above). Moreover, women are not the only blind spot within criminology. There are others, such as, for example, race.

- secondly, the focus on sexism presumes that if criminological theory and/or practices were emptied of sexism, then the theories and the practice would in themselves prove to be sound. This presumption, of course, returns us to one of the key problematics of liberal feminism: the fact that it leaves unchallenged what the yardsticks of our under standings might be.

- thirdly, much of this work assumes that sexism only applies to women. Gelsthorpe argues that this is an 'untenable' assumption: what about men? And finally, the complexity of the findings in this area do make it difficult to assert which outcomes are a result of direct discrimination.

Some writers have argued that the pursuit of this discriminatory theme, with its underpinning assumption of equality before the law is no longer a fruitful enterprise for feminists interested in the crime problem (Smart, 1990). What is clear, however, is that the work informed by these themes has yielded a wealth of information concerning the complex way in which factors interact to produce different outcomes for different female offenders and victims of crime. Indeed, it is the sheer weight of that evidence which renders a simplistic assertion of chivalry highly problematic and points to understanding women's experiences of the criminal justice system by reference to factors outside the operation of the criminal justice system.

Some of the studies referenced above, whilst concerned with equity, do problematise the gendered experience of women in the criminal justice system and direct our attention to looking to factors outside the criminal justice system in order to understand women's experience of it (see, for example, Eaton, 1986; Worrall, 1990; Carlen, 1988). It is in the appreciation of locating women's criminality as being understandable by reference to processes outside of the criminal justice system alongside an awareness of the complexity of those interactions, that has fuelled the relevance of socialist feminist ideas for criminology. I shall draw on the writings of Messerschmidt (1986) and more recent work of both Carlen and Cain as a way of illustrating the influence and potential of these concerns. Messerschmidt (1993: 56) has this to say about his theoretical framework for understanding crime:

> My socialist feminist understanding of crime had two premises. First, to comprehend criminality (of both the powerless and the powerful) we must consider simultaneously patriarchy and capitalism and their effects on human behaviour. Second, from a social feminist perspective, power (in terms of gender and class) is central for understanding serious forms of criminality. It was theorised that the powerful (in both the gender and class spheres) do the most criminal damage to society. Further, the interaction of gender and class creates positions of power and powerlessness in the gender/class hierarchy, resulting in different types and degrees of criminality and varying opportunities for engaging in them. Just as the powerful have more legitimate opportunities, they also have more illegitimate opportunities.

Of course, as Messerschmidt himself admits, as with all theoretical constructions, this framework has its limitations. For example, it denudes the criminal actor of a sense of agency, locating the motivation for crime within the social system. It also asserts patriarchy as being unitary and uniform in its impact on both men and women. Yet despite these problems this framework does offer a starting-point which posits an understanding of criminality located within socio-structural conditions; a way of thinking about the criminal behaviour of both men and women also found in the work of Carlen.

It is important to recognise that Carlen acknowledges the importance of feminism as a politics rather than a guarantor of theoretical or empirical truth (Carlen, 1990). Moreover, Carlen is very critical of feminist efforts at explaining criminal behaviour and points to two major limitations in such efforts with respect to female law-breaking behaviour in particular. First, she argues that an exclusive focus on women's law-breaking behaviour presumes that women break the law for essentially different reasons than men do. This, for Carlen, reflects a reductionist and essentialising position similar to that adopted by the biological positivists. Second, when the historically and socially specific contexts of male and female offending behaviours are examined, the issues that emerge rapidly become issues of racism, classism and imperialism rather than gender *per se*. Carlen (1990: 110) states that:

> Nor could I conceive of any theory (feminist or otherwise) focusing solely on 'women as a group' that could adequately explain three major features of women's law-breaking and imprisonment: that women's crimes are, in the main, the crimes of the powerless; that women in prison are disproportionately from ethnic minority groups; and that a majority of women in prison have been in poverty for the greater part of their lives.

She goes on to comment that women in prison represent those whose criminalisation has been over-determined by the threefold effects of racism, sexism and classism, none of which are reducible to the other and all of which, for Carlen, point to connecting the debate around women and crime to the broader issue of social justice.

The links between Carlen's empirically based concerns and the more theoretical concerns of Messerschmidt, though, are perhaps self-evident. Whilst the work of Carlen cited here does not explicitly concern itself with the crimes of the powerful, the clear implication is that the effects of capitalism and patriarchy focus attention much more effectively on the crimes of the powerless rather than the crimes of the powerful. This does not mean, of course, that such criminal activity does not occur. What is particularly striking about both the theoretical work of Messerschmidt (1986) and the range of work conducted by Carlen on female offenders and women in prison, is the way in which both of these writers have drawn on conceptual formulations which take us outside mainstream criminological debates in order to understand the nature of criminality. This process of moving to debates outside criminology in order to understand women's and men's experiences of the criminal justice system is one of the features of what Cain has called 'transgressive criminology'.

Transgressive criminology, as Cain calls it, is concerned to identify the similarities between women's and girl's experiences both as offenders and as non-offenders, a parallel highlighted in some respects by Heidensohn's (1985) focus on social control. Cain (1989: 3) states that:

> Crimes, criminals, victims, courts, police officers, lawyers, social workers may be objects of investigation, but our explanations must reach beyond and encompass all of them, as life histories and the victim studies, the continuity studies and the ideology studies already strain to do. I am arguing that, in a sense, feminist criminology is impossible; that feminist *criminology* disrupts the categories of criminology itself. (*emphasis in the original*)

The strategies which Cain (1990) identifies as constituting a transgressive criminology are three-fold: reflexivity, deconstruction and reconstruction. *Reflexivity* demands that the concerns of women and girls are taken seriously as they understand them. Such concerns are not to be downgraded but recognised as a legitimate way of making sense of social reality. Working-class girls may have a very realistic assessment of their life chances and the relationship that this has with perceptions of their sexuality (the importance of avoiding being labelled a 'slag', for example (Lees, 1989). Researchers need not only to recognise these but also to be able to *deconstruct* their internal logic: to get beyond their mere appearances towards an understanding of the ways, and sites in which such logic is deployed. That is, to situate them within an understanding of social reality which takes seriously what the actors themselves take seriously but renders visible that which they cannot see.

The third strategy requires that we move beyond the 'binding web of co-man sense' (Cain, 1990: 8). This third element is political. It reflects a recognition that many women 'know' about the painful disjunction between how they feel and how they live. It is within this gap that the promise of political possibility and social change is constituted. The items on the 'criminological' agenda for Cain are, therefore, women-only studies, studies which explore the totality of their lives, i.e. the questions asked would be about them as women rather than about crime *per se*, and studies of men.

There are two reasons for the inclusion of this last item. First, gender is a relational concept. Women and femininity exist in the spaces left by men and masculinity; and men as males exist in relation to women as females. Second, men as men have never been the object of the criminological gaze yet the most consistent criminological finding has been that most crime is committed by men (see earlier and Introduction). However for Cain, if we are to avoid the charge of essentialism, then a transgressive criminology must place men on the research agenda. As Cain (1990: 12) suggests, such a criminology must take on board the question of 'what in the social construction of maleness is so profoundly criminogenic: why do males so disproportionately turn out to be criminals?'

Cain (1990b) has gone on to delineate the epistemological position from which these strategies are derived. This is clearly located within the framework of standpoint feminism as discussed above. That position foregrounds the need to accept both the complexity of social reality and the relativity of knowledge which stems from this. In other words, class, ethnicity, gender, sexuality, will all impact differentially on people's experiences of their everyday life; though as individuals they will not always be aware of how that has occurred.

There are clearly, then, some parallels to be drawn between the work of Carlen and Cain in bringing to the criminological debate both the questions raised by socialism and by feminism in their theoretical and empirical work. Whilst Carlen would not concur with any particular claims to a *feminist* methodology and would eschew the term 'feminist' for all but campaigning purposes, their joint focus on locating gender issues as being just one dynamic of both women's and men's experiences of the criminal justice system and their concern to place those experiences within a broader social context outside of criminology, gives some flavour as to why each of them in different ways find the label 'feminist criminology' disturbing. Moreover, each in their different ways has also found it important to challenge any approach that endeavours to essentialise the differences between males and females.

Feminism and victimology: a contradiction in terms?

The marginalisation of feminism by victimology has been commented upon on more than one occasion. Rock (1986), for example, implies that this has occurred to a certain extent in the choices made by feminists who have regarded the concept of 'victim precipitation' as 'victim blaming' not only in its everyday usage but also in the way it has been translated as 'contributory negligence' in the courts (Jeffries and Radford, 1984). Victimology has thereby been seen as a 'weapon of ideological oppression' (Rock: *ibid*).

Some aspects of this uneasy relationship between victimology and feminism are epitomised by their respective use of the terms 'victim' and 'survivor'. Genealogically, the term 'victim' connotes the sacrificiant who was often female. Moreover, the word itself, when gendered as in French is denoted as female. Feminists recognising the power of such linguistic usage regard the term 'victim' as emphasising passivity and powerlessness, in contrast to the active resistance to oppression that women routinely engage in to sustain their survival. But of course, whilst these terms are often presented as oppositional to one another, experientially speaking they frequently are not. It is possible to think in terms of an active or passive victim, as it is to identify an active or passive survivor. Indeed an argument can be mounted which presents these concepts as capturing different elements of the same process (Walklate, 1993) and moreover, rooted in women's own experiences of their lives (Kirkwood, 1993).

However, the challenge posed by feminism to victimology lies much deeper than a conceptual debate such as this one (though that is not to say that such a debate is not meaningful). It is a challenge that raises questions concerning conceptions of what counts as knowledge. In particular it is a challenge that raises the question of how we understand the nature of objectivity or the relationship between the 'academic' and the 'activist'.

The ideas associated with objectivity and value freedom that have been embraced by the social sciences have been couched, for the most part, in male terms – terms which have been hidden by what Smith (1990) has called the 'regime of rationality', rooted in the idea of an 'abstract knower'. Victimology has been no exception to this. As the quote from Smith (1987: 74) cited earlier acknowledges, recognising the definite nature of the social relationship in the knowledge construction process renders some forms of knowledge more legitimate than others. The question remains, what actually constitutes rational knowledge? This is a further point of departure for feminists from positivism.

As was quoted earlier Harding (1991: 3) states 'From the perspective of women's lives scientific rationality frequently appears irrational.' This statement implies that what has been considered rational has all too often reflected a male, white, middle-class, heterosexual view of the legitimacy of what it is that can be known. As a consequence it is important to acknowledge that what counts as objective has an important political history embedded within it. Harding (1991) not only recognises the political significance of this, but also identifies an alternative way of understanding how the knowledge production process might work.

Harding (1991) develops this alternative from Hegel. Women, she argues, being the 'Other', are outsiders to the social order, yet they spend their lives inhabiting and negotiating one of the major dualisms which underpins social thinking and social life: nature versus culture. Women's capacity to negotiate this dualism equips them with knowledge and experiences from both sides of it. In this sense, the knowledge that women possess is more objective. Thus the feminist concern with women as occupiers of both the public and the private domain means that women's knowledge can render visible and name processes which were once invisible and unnamed. In this way, then, the objectivity of a discipline (including victimology) is enhanced; not by detachment but by recognising that the researcher and the researched occupy the same critical plane.

For feminists the question of scientific detachment from one's work constitutes a key point of departure from positivistic thinking. This has been articulated most often by the feminist maxim that women, with women, for women should conduct empirical work. Such a statement argues for not only a different conceptualisation of the research process itself, but also challenges traditional conceptions of objectivity and value freedom. Victimology, like other social science endeavours, has been characterised as positivistic (see for example, Miers, 1989; Mawby and Walklate, 1994) and has certainly been party to debate and criticism concerning the relationship between the academic and the activist (Fattah, 1991). The influence of these ideas has been illustrated here through an examination of the gendered foundational ideas of victimology and the way in which those ideas have perpetuated not only a particular image of the victim but also a particular way of engaging in victimological research.

Thus it can be seen that the feminist challenge to victimology goes beyond a critique of the discipline as a weapon of ideological oppression. It strikes at the very heart of the discipline's understanding of what it is to be scientific, and concomitantly how the central concerns of this discipline might be defined and understood. However, the feminist response to this problematic relationship, as articulated by Harding, in some respects merely flips the coin: that is, transposes one form of knowledge for another. It is a moot point as to how far this constitutes progress. Arguably, it is a position that keeps us trapped in the nineteenth-century dualisms of male/female, rational/irrational, and reason/emotion. Given that this may perpetuate the visibility of women and the invisibility of men (especially as victims) it is useful to consider if there is any way such a dualism might be transgressed. As a consequence could there be a feminist-informed victimology?

The problem of essentialism is one of the criticisms frequently levelled against radical feminism. This work, focusing as it has done in this context on the interconnections between gender and violence, has had most impact in the form of 'victimisation' studies. It is a highly contentious issue, however, whether any of this work has actually impacted upon the victimological agenda (see Mawby and Walklate, 1994, chapter 1). Radical feminists have considered victimology and its related concepts to be a form of 'ideological oppression' (Rock, 1986). It is certainly the case that the concept of victim precipitation, its use in the context of rape, and its cultural and ideological power in the criminal justice process, leave many radical feminists in little doubt as to the inadequacies of work informed by such thinking. By implication, the feminist challenge to victimology transgresses the conceptual debate of 'victim' or 'survivor'.

However, as with criminology, the campaigning voice of radical feminism has pointed in the direction of understanding men as being crucial to understanding the nature of the crime problem, an evident parallel with the agenda proffered by Cain and discussed above. The extent to which the victimological agenda has been altered as a result of these claims is, however, questionable. Before this argument is developed further, let us consider the relationship between criminology, victimology and postmodernism?

Postmodernism, criminology and victimology

Of all the perspectives under discussion here it is perhaps fair to say that as yet postmodernism has had relatively little impact on either criminology or victimology. The postmodern feminism that constitutes a direct challenge to criminology (and victimology) is most readily associated with the later work of Carol Smart (1990) and the work of Alison Young (1992). Both of these writers point to the fundamental threat posed by postmodernist ideas.

Criminology and victimology, as the earlier discussion in this chapter illustrated, are both tied to the (modernist) project of effecting social change and the control of such change through the policy process. Both of these disciplines presume that this can be achieved through central adherence to the scientific enterprise; that is, through a search for a unitary, causal explanation of crime. The phenomenon of crime and crime control, then, constitutes the central core of both of these disciplines. They cannot therefore deconstruct crime. The phenomenon of crime is not only central to the existence of the discipline, the binary oppositions embedded within the narrative of criminology constrain any attempt by feminism to break free of them. This last statement clearly requires a fuller explanation.

Postmodernism attempts to give voice to those silenced by the discourses of modernism. In order to do this within criminology, Young (1992) argues that it is necessary to appreciate the power of criminology's 'semantic rectangle'. This reveals that the structure of the discipline of criminology is imbued with assumptions around two oppositional pairs: normal/criminal, male/female. These pairs subjugate the normal to the criminal, the male criminal to the female criminal, the female criminal to the criminal, the normal to the male criminal, etc. Thus, when the category 'criminal' is paired with the category 'male criminal' they are almost indistinguishable within criminology; and when the category 'female criminal' is paired with the category 'normal', normality is subjugated. As Young (1992; 76) states: 'Woman is always criminal, always deviant, always censured. This condition is utterly normal.'

To celebrate the 'otherness' of the female, as postmodern feminism demands, is impossible within criminology. As Smart (1990) suggests, this has the effect that criminology needs feminism more than feminism needs criminology!

So postmodern feminism demands that we go beyond the transgressive requirements of Cain. It demands not that we deny racism or sexual violence, but that we deny the view that the intellectual *per se* can devise any answers to these problems. This not only shakes the conceptual foundations on which criminology is based, but also shakes its assumed relevance and ability to produce Knowledge or Truth on which to make policy claims. For many writers, not unsympathetic to postmodern criticisms of universal claims to Truth, such a disentangling from the modernist (progressive) project of social science is too threatening indeed.

The resistance to postmodernist ideas does not mean that such ideas in general have not been influential in encouraging a reconsideration of the relationship between the social scientific search for knowledge and the claims that can be attached to such knowledge. It is clear that giving voice to diversity is an explicit concern of the agendas of both Carlen and Cain, for example. Giving voice to that diversity has led not only to a reconsideration of the way in which feminism in general has presumed that the category 'woman' represents all women but it has also led to a re-examination of what is implied by the category 'man' and the way in which this has been used to delineate all men. The blossoming literature on masculinity/masculinities stands testimony to this. The question remains, however, as to where these debates leave criminology and victimology.

Feminist criminology/feminist victimology: projects in construction?

Gelthorpe and Morris (1990), in presenting their edited collection *Feminist Perspectives in Criminology*, suggest that if a feminist criminology is to be constructed at all, then at present it is clearly a project that is still in the process of such construction. Indeed the preceeding discussion has served to illustrate the problematic view that some feminists have of formulating a feminist criminology at all.

Of all the feminist perspectives discussed here, liberal feminism has had the most discernible impact to date on criminological knowledge. The reasons for this are to be found, not only in the kind of work this perspective has generated, but also in its implicit acceptance of the conventional rules of science and the knowledge production process. Such liberal feminist work reflects a tendency, however, to narrow feminist concerns to the 'women and crime' question as though this represented an area demanding specialised explanation. Carlen has more than adequately expressed the difficulties inherent in this position.

Radical – and socialist – inspired feminism has led to the construction of agendas for criminology and, in the context of victimisation studies, for victimology, drawing on theoretical concepts and concerns outside the criminological and victimological domains. This has led feminist researchers of different theoretical and political persuasions to focus on the interconnections between *gender* and the crime experience. In other words, this feminist work directs criminology to take seriously how an understanding of men and masculinity(ies) can contribute to an understanding of the phenomenon called crime.

So, from the 'woman question' of liberal feminism we are returned to the 'man question' of radical and socialist feminism and the challenge that these positions present for the underlying construction of what counts as knowledge. The same observations may be made of the impact that feminism has had upon victimology (Walklate, 1994) as well as criminology, although Walklate (forthcoming) has argued that embracing a Bhaskerian realist position might offer one avenue of transgressing the dualism of male and female in favour of considering a more appropriate understanding of central human concerns. However, one might agree with those feminist writers who in their different ways deny the tenability of a 'feminist criminology' or a 'feminist victimology'. As for the likelihood of a postmodern feminist criminology, the future looks bleak indeed!

So it is clear that feminist work has, and still does, pose some serious questions for criminology and victimology. The following chapters will endeavour to illustrate the way in which the different feminist perspectives discussed here cast a different light on the issues to be addressed in relation to crime and victimisation. At the same time, they will also explore what is meant by the crime problem and what factors might need to be addressed in order to forge a meaningful explanatory framework for the phenomenon of crime, influenced by feminist work. The question is, as Tony Jefferson (1992) so aptly expresses it, 'Is criminology [or victimology] man enough to take it'?

Suggestions for further reading

For a vision of criminology still influential and still worth reading see Taylor, I., Walton, P., and Young, J. (1973) *The New Criminology*. An updated version of this, *The New Criminology Revisited*, edited by P. Walton and J. Young (1998), would be a sound way to follow through some of the issues presented in this chapter.

For a feel for the way in which criminology would benefit from feminist work inspired by ideas outside of criminology, see Cain (ed) (1989) *Growing Up Good*.

For a selection of articles by feminists working within criminology see Gelsthorpe, L. and Morris, A. (eds) (1990) *Feminist Perspectives in Criminology*. See also N. Rafter and F. Heidensohn (eds) (1995) *International Feminist Perspectives in Criminology*.

For an introductory review of victimology, see Walklate, S. (1989)

Victimology: the victim and the criminal justice process, and for more developed theoretical and policy concerns, see Mawby, R. and Walklate, S. (1994) *Critical Victimology: the victim in international perspective.*

2 Criminology, victimology and masculinism

Introduction

> A stolen car is driven straight through the plate glass doors of an electrical goods store. Men in balaclava hoods jump out, quickly load the car with TVs, hi-fi's, etc. and reverse out and away. The goods are unloaded then the car is burned. Elsewhere another stolen car, wheels screeching, is undertaking high speed handbrake turns in front of an applauding crowd. At a third location, yet another stolen car is being driven round for the hell of it. A police patrol car spots it and gives chase. The stolen car crashes. Two men die. Scenes from Newcastle night life *circa* 1991.
>
> (Jefferson, 1992: 10)

> What is it about men, not as working-class, not as migrant, not as under privileged individual, but as men that induces them to commit crime? Here it is no longer women who are judged by the norms of masculinity and found to be 'the problem'. Now it is men and not humanity who are openly acknowledged as the objects and subjects of investigation.
>
> (Grosz, 1987: 5 quoted by Liddle, 1993: 65)

Foregrounding men as 'the problem' in relation to the question of crime became an increasingly important part of the criminological equation during the 1990s. As the previous chapter has illustrated, criminology and victimology, as academic disciplines, have operated with particular gendered assumptions in relation to women. The purpose of this chapter is to engage in a similar exploratory process in relation to men. But first it will be useful to consider some of the different ways in which it is possible to think about men and their relationship with constructions of masculinity.

Ways of thinking about masculinity

The literature on masculinity has increased markedly since the early 1980s. However, whilst an increasing number of both academic and media commentators have endeavoured to draw attention to the relationship between maleness and crime, little work, with the exception of that discussed later in this chapter, has applied these developments systematically to either criminology or victimology. This lack of application does not mean that the issue of masculinity has been absent from criminological discourse. Indeed in one form or another its presence has clearly been felt, even if in a hidden form. How that presence has marked both criminology (and victimology) has varied ranging from the way in which the subject matter of these disciplines has been defined to the way in which empirical findings have been explained. But how might we begin to understand the relationship between men and the question of masculinity in more general terms?

As long ago as 1977 Andrew Tolson wrote about *The Limits of Masculinity*. In this book Tolson explored the different types of gender identities felt to be possible. The emphasis on the possibility of a plurality of gender identities is significant in Tolson's writing. He was particularly concerned to recognise that masculinity was not simply a unidimensional phenomenon which could be understood in terms of opposition to femininity. Neither, Tolson argued, was it possible to talk of some universal form of masculinity. Its expression varied across cultures and between generations. These twin themes of the multi-dimensionality and specificity of masculinity heralded the emergence of a key debate for those concerned to understand men and their expressions of themselves as men.

The observations made by Tolson about the nature of masculinity and its expression (especially the negative, restraining impact of masculinity on men and the expression of their emotions), alerts us to one of the central features of this debate: is there one transcendent form of masculinity or many diverse masculinities? Moreover, there is a further significance associated with Tolson's work. He also implies that it is as important to develop an understanding of masculinity in terms of gender relations as it is to explore what masculinity means for individual men. These twin themes constitute the key feature of the debate around masculinity in the 1990s and its contribution to criminal behaviour of all kinds.

The way in which these issues are addressed, however, varies according to the kind of theoretical framework in which we choose to understand the concept of masculinity itself. In this latter respect we shall find that some of the theoretical considerations encountered in chapter 1 re-emerge here. This is particularly the case with respect to evaluating the relevance and value of different feminist perspectives on this issue, though as we shall see the current debate on masculinity owes a significant debt to that feminist work nevertheless. But first, following Tolson (1977), it will be useful to consider the question of how might it be possible to develop a framework in which to understand both masculinity and femininity.

Morgan (1992) offers one way of organising understandings of masculinity and femininity. His framework locates this question within the broader context of gender relations. He suggests that there are two key concepts through which gender relations can be differently defined and understood. These are the concepts of power and difference. Analytically, these ideas can be related to each other in any one of four ways.

- first, a relationship between power and difference can be denied; in other words the existence of gender as a significant feature of the organisation of our social lives can be ignored.

- second, the importance of power relationships can be stressed at the expense of understanding difference. In the context of radical feminism, for example, this relationship poses the central importance of concepts such as patriarchy, oppression, exploitation, and domination. In this relationship the question of difference is sacrificed in favour of the question of power; that is, masculinity and femininity are seen to be derived from socially constructed power relationships.

- the third option suggested by Morgan poses the converse relationship between difference and power. This option emphasises difference and minimises power. Here the exploration of the differences, not only between masculinity and femininity but also within them, is celebrated and given primacy. Such a celebration of difference can take a number of forms; for example it could be rooted in the individual difference approach associated with biology. Latterly, however, emphasis on difference has been more directly associated with, and derived from, postmodernism. In whatever form, the expression of femininity and masculinity are understood as the product of individual negotiation and expression.

- fourth, it is possible to develop an understanding of the relationship between power and difference which defines them both as interdependent. This framework endeavours to identify ways in which social systems give primacy to some versions of masculinity and femininity over others. Such primacy values some versions more highly than others and thus renders them more powerful than others. Such a process, of course, has significant consequences for the versions of masculinity and/or femininity deemed 'the other'; that is, less valued and thereby less powerful. As we shall see this kind of analysis is a characteristic of the work of Connell (1987).

Morgan's schema provides a useful starting-point from which to develop an understanding of the ways in which the understandings of masculinity have influenced criminology (and victimology). Each of these different ways of thinking about the relationship between power and difference can be found in criminological work. Given the primacy placed on gender in this text it would be highly contradictory to explore the first way of thinking about gender relations identified by Morgan, since this option denies the importance of gender as a variable. Suffice it to say that much criminological work has done just this, especially historically, although, as chapter 1 endeavoured to illustrate, such a denial was in part a product of an uncritical acceptance of deeply embedded assumptions about the nature of the scientific enterprise and what could count as knowledge. Given that the central purpose of this text is to consider the relevance of gender, we shall spend time considering the implications of the other three options in Morgan's schema, each of which have, arguably, made their presence felt in criminology and victimology in different ways. In order to do this we shall focus on the influence on criminology of sex role theory borrowed from social psychology as an illustration of option three; categorical theory as characterised by Connell (1987) as an illustration of option two; and the notion of 'doing gender', borrowed from the work of Messerschmidt (1993, 1997) as an illustration of option four. In each case we shall consider some illustrative substantive criminological material to highlight the value of each of the options under discussion.

Sex role theory

The concept of role is central to social psychology and some versions of sociology. As a concept it is used as a way of organising people's behaviour into a meaningful whole. It acts as a mechanism for understanding the ways in which social expectations, actions, and behaviour reflect stereotypical assumptions about behavioural expectations; that is, what it is that should be done, by whom, and under what circumstances. In the context of understanding gender relations this leads to the identification of male roles and female roles. Such roles are presumed to outline the appropriate behavioural sets and associated expectations for men and women (males and females). Sex role theory takes as given the biological origins of defining the differences between males and females. These biological origins constitute the canvas on which specific behavioural sets, called sex roles, are painted through the process of socialisation. As a theory then it is rooted in *biological* assumptions concerning what counts as the *defining* characteristics of being male and female.

In the criminological context the underlying influence of the work of both Sutherland (1947) and Parsons (1937) embraced sex role theory. The work of these two writers has wielded a particular influence on criminology's grasp of the maleness of the crime problem, so we shall briefly examine the ideas of each of them in turn.

Sutherland

Sutherland started from the position that criminal behaviour was learned behaviour like any other. Moreover, he argued that people learned criminal behaviour when exposed to an 'excess of definitions' favouring deviant as opposed to conventional (or rule-abiding) behaviour. This view of criminal behaviour focused on not only the importance of the socialisation process in learning crime but also on understanding the importance of the value attached to the behaviour learned. In other words it is not just a matter of who you associate with but also the kinds of meanings those associations provide for an individual with respect to engaging in criminal behaviour. So an individual may know how to act criminally, but may not do so in the absence of the values, motives, attitudes, etc., which support such behaviour. The more an individual is exposed to such support the more likely it is that an individual will share in that behaviour. For Sutherland, then, criminal behaviour was learned behaviour like any other behavioural response rather than being the product of some innate atavistic or degenerative drive.

Within this general framework Sutherland argued that boys were more likely to become delinquent that girls. This, he suggested, happened for two reasons. First, because they are less strictly controlled by the socialisation process in general than girls are. Second, because in that process they are taught to be tough, aggressive, active, risk seekers: all characteristics which Sutherland considered to be prerequisites for involvement in the criminal world, a theme which will be developed in chapter 3. These two factors taken together, he argued, means that boys are more frequently exposed to the kinds of learning situations in which criminality becomes a possibility. This happens, despite the fact that in other respects both boys and girls may be growing up together in the same economically deprived neighbourhoods. Thus Sutherland was of the view that there is something more to be understood about boy's involvement in the criminal world than can be explained by reference to socio-economic factors alone.

This general theory of criminal behaviour was labelled by Sutherland as the theory of 'differential association'. When it is applied to an understanding of criminal behaviour in general it can be seen to offer a framework substantially different in some respects to that proposed by the biological positivists. However, when applied specifically to understanding the differences between male and female involvement in delinquent behaviour there are a number of issues that this theory treats as being unproblematic.

First, as a theory, it is rooted in the presumption of sex role theory and thereby a notion of biological difference. Being rooted in this way this position consequently accepts implicitly a view that biological difference constitutes part of the explanation for any observed behavioural differences, despite the importance attributed to the socialisation process by sex role theory. It must be remembered that in sex role theory the socialisation process only provides the mechanism through which specific learning takes place. In other words, the fact that girls get pregnant and not boys, i.e. biological difference, constitutes the basis for explaining both their different experience of the socialisation process and their subsequent different rate of criminality. This is particularly evident in that work influenced by functionalism. Indeed the work of Parsons added a further dimension to this way of thinking about the relationship between sex differences, the socialisation process and the maleness of criminal behaviour.

Talcott Parsons

The functionalist sociology of Talcott Parsons placed the family at the centre of the social learning associated with the sex roles. In the family children learn that the expressive role, the role associated with nurturing, caring, and keeping the family together, is what women do; the instrumental role, that concerned with achievement, goal attainment, breadwinning, is what men do. In the work of Parsons, these roles are the basis for the stability of society from one generation to the next. Moreover, society in general and the family in particular is presumed to operate at its most effective with the family constructed in this form. This presumption is made on the basis of the fact that because women have the reproductive capacity to bear children they are thus deemed to be best suited for the expressive role – a role which is denied to men and which young men experience as being denied to them.

The process of learning these sex roles poses different problems for boys than for girls. Exposed to feminine care, girls have little difficulty in finding appropriate role models for themselves. Boys, on the other hand do not have a readily and routinely available male model to follow. Exposed to the female model as young children they quickly learn that the feminine role model is not one for which they will be accepted as men. Parsons argues, therefore, that boys engage in what he calls 'compensatory compulsory masculinity'. In other words, boys reject any behaviour seen to be feminine. So tenderness, gentleness, and the expression of emotion are rejected because they are seen to be not masculine.

In the place of these feminine qualities boys pursue that which they observe to be masculine: being powerful, tough, and rough. The pursuit of these masculine characteristics is engaged in vigorously, in order to avoid any doubt being cast on the boys' sense of themselves as men or of them being recognised by others, as men. This pursuit of masculinity, and its approved forms of expression, results in boys engaging in anti-social behaviour much more often than girls. It is this greater likelihood of engaging in anti-social behaviour that is subsequently related to their greater chance of engaging in delinquency. This view of the relationship between sex differences and the socialisation process is implicit in some of the formative work on delinquency within criminology.

Cohen

The work of Cohen (1955) draws together both the work of Sutherland and Parsons and was very influential in the development of delinquency studies during the 1950s and 1960s. As was stated in chapter 1, Cohen did attempt to address the observed sex differences associated with delinquent behaviour, and he did this by drawing on the work of Parsons in particular. Following Parsons, Cohen accepted that the process of socialisation in the home was neither a smooth nor an easy process for boys. He accepted the view that the lack of a readily available masculine role in the home, alongside the availability of a feminine role associated with nurturing, raised anxious questions for boys. Given that the nurturing role in the domestic context is so readily identified as 'being good', boys are left unsure as to how to be good yet not be seen to be feminine. The resultant anxiety generated by this for boys is, according to Cohen, resolved in the street gang. Here the assertion of power through physical prowess rather than negotiation, the taking of risks rather than keeping safe, the thrill and excitement of breaking the rules rather than accepting them: all provide not only the avenues and the motivation for delinquent behaviour but also provide for an expression of themselves as young *men*.

Cohen, however, did not really pursue his analysis of delinquency in this way. He presumed that delinquency was primarily a working-class phenomenon. So his explanation of delinquent behaviour ultimately downgrades what he has to say about masculinity in favour of upgrading an emphasis on class and class conflict. For Cohen, the delinquent subculture is to be seen as a consequence of a working-class collective response to the shared experience of being judged by middle-class values and the frustration that results from this.

This does not mean that Cohen did not recognise other possible motivations for delinquent behaviour; he did. For example, he viewed female delinquency primarily in terms of the expression of deviant sexuality; and he viewed middle-class delinquent behaviour primarily in terms of 'drag racing' or 'joy riding' (in the 1950s American sense of the term). This latter type of delinquent behaviour was also seen by Cohen as a masculine protest against female authority. Yet, despite the intriguing nature of some of the observations Cohen makes about gender in relation to delinquency, his concern with social class left these observations relatively underdeveloped, thus having a very influential effect on a whole generation of delinquency studies.

Cohen's observations are provocative but not without their problems. For example, Cohen, like Sutherland, presumed that the biological basis of sex role theory is a non-problematic starting-point for an explanation of routes into crime. This alerts us to the way in which the difficulties associated with sex role became embedded within this kind of criminological thinking. Whilst sex role theory does have its attractions as a starting-point for understanding gender relations in general as well as the gendered expression of criminal behaviour in particular, its biological orientation is problematic. So it is to a general assessment of sex role theory as a way of understanding masculinity that we shall now turn.

Connell

Connell (1987) has pointed out that there are a number of reasons why sex role theory in general constitutes an attractive starting-point for explanations concerned with gender and gender difference. He offers us three reasons why this might be the case:

1 sex role theory presumes to move us beyond biology as a way of explaining sex differences in behaviour. As an approach it replaces biology with learned social expectations.

2 role theory in general and sex role theory in particular provide a mechanism whereby an understanding of the impact of social structure can be inserted into an understanding of individual personality. The process of socialisation is obviously crucial in this and this facilitates a way of thinking about the contribution made by different kinds of institutions in mediating the effects of structure on individuals.

3 given the emphasis on the socialisation process, role theory offers a politics of change. If men and women are what they are because of the oppressive experience and impact of the socialisation process and if this process can be changed, so can men and women.

As Connell argues, these virtues are substantial. There is, however, a central difficulty embedded within them. This difficulty has been alluded to already in our discussion of the way in which sex role theory has been applied within criminology: the difficulty highlighted by the fundamental resilience of the biological category of sex. Connell (1987: 50-1) expresses this problem in this way:

> The very terms 'female role' and 'male role', hitching a biological term to a dramaturgical one, suggest what is going on.... With sex roles, the underlying biological dichotomy seems to have persuaded many theorists that there is no power relationship here at all. The 'female role' and the 'male role' are tacitly treated as equal.

Moreover there is something further hidden here. Sex role theory, given its emphasis on social expectations, has more often than not been concerned to identify that which should be the case in social relationships as opposed to that which is actually the case. In other words, it concerns itself with what is considered to be normative as opposed to that which actually occurs empirically. If we take the impact of this alongside the resilience of the biological category of sex, it has the resultant effect of disabling role theory's grasp of *gender* relations. In other words sex role theory cannot see gender in terms of negotiated power relationships. It can at best only see gender as given through fundamentally biologically determined individual adaptations to social expectations. In this respect sex role theory bears comparison in its strengths and limitations with those associated with liberal feminism, especially with respect to its political promise (see chapter 1).

This emphasis on what is normative as distinct from what actually occurs in practice, not only has the effect of drawing attention away from social reality in terms of power relationships, but simultaneously has the effect of drawing attention away from the critical question of whose interests might be best served by such concerns. In other words, emphasis on the normative aspects of social behaviour, what people should do, serves the interests of particular groups in society, the socially powerful. This is of particular importance in relation to understanding the influence of academic and policy agendas informed by sex role theory. One consequence of this is that while attention is focused on the normative dimensions to gender relations, other aspects to those relations remain under-explored. Disentangling the tension between the normative and the actually experienced is particularly important, then, in order to develop a more accurate picture of the nature and impact of gender relations. Such a disentangling will also reveal some interesting insights into the question of masculinity. But how might such a disentangling be achieved?

In the context of understanding masculinity Brittain (1989) has drawn a similar distinction to that being drawn here by identifying what he calls 'masculinism' as distinct from 'masculinity'. According to Brittain (1989), masculinism comprises the ideological roots of masculinity. Fundamentally masculinism attributes masculinity with essential transcendent qualities. These qualities point to a number of assumptions frequently made about gender relations: for example, that there is a fundamental difference between men and women, that heterosexuality is normal, that men's *nature* determines their behaviour. In other words, masculinism naturalises male-domination; it is deemed natural. Sex role theory, in its inability to transcend the temptations of biologism, buys into such masculinism. It reflects a fundamental belief that differences between the sexes as displayed in behaviour are natural in their origins.

In this way sex role theory lends further support to the interests of male-domination. Consequently, in its failure to question such ideological roots, sex role theory does a further disservice to actually experienced femininity and masculinity insofar as it can capture neither the negotiated quality of them nor their fragile or tentative character. In addition, the universalism of biological categories, sustained by the ideology of sex differences being constructed in nature, militates against an understanding of the actually experienced categories of male and female (masculinities and femininities).

So whilst sex role theory has had some influence on criminological thinking in attempts to understand the maleness of crime, that influence has been limited not only by the failure of criminology and criminologists to reflect upon its value (the downgrading of class over gender for example), but also by the limitations inherent within the sex role framework itself. Such limitations, as highlighted above, point to the need for a theoretical framework that can at least encompass an understanding of the power basis to gender relations. It is in developing an understanding of masculinity in this respect that the influence of both radical and socialist feminism can be found and has been drawn together in the work of Connell (1987) amongst others.

Categorical theory

The term categorical theory has been used by Connell (1987) as a way of drawing together a number of different feminist perspectives on gender. Its use here is not intended to imply that Connell himself accepts the principles of categorical theory; but to reiterate some of the issues raised by him about feminist work. It constitutes a valuable device for introducing the developments that have arisen from feminist-inspired work, including the theoretical work of Connell himself, in thinking about masculinity. As a way of understanding gender relations it matches the second option identified by Morgan (1992).

Categorical theory refers to a range of theoretical perspectives, emanating primarily from the feminist movement, that aim to further an understanding of gender relations by reference to two opposing categories: men and women. Understanding gender relations in these terms identifies both a theory and a politics for action (see chapter 1). The categories, men and women, constitute both the units of analysis in which to understand gender relations and the source of explanation for those relations. The key concepts of categorical theory are patriarchy, domination, oppression, exploitation. Within these concepts men are deemed the powerful and women are deemed the other.

In criminology and victimology, categorical analysis has had its most profound effect in the study of sexual violence. In chapter 4 we shall explore different ways of thinking about the nature and extent of sexual violence. In that chapter we shall consider the compelling evidence for thinking about sexual violence in terms of power relations and particularly in terms of the power which men wield over women. The notion that all men keep all women in a state of fear, as articulated by radical feminism, was revolutionary not only in its public, personal, and political implications but also in the avenue it provided for recognising a further dimension to the maleness of the crime problem. Though, as will be discussed in chapter 4, sexual violence is not exclusively a male activity and neither are all the victims of sexual violence exclusively female. Nevertheless an ungendered understanding of sexual violence would only be a partial one and a criminology that failed to acknowledge the nature and extent of sexual violence would be incomplete. However, an analysis of sexual violence couched in categorical terms is severely limited as a way both of understanding the nature and extent of that violence and as a way of understanding either the expression of masculinity or of femininity. This occurs for two reasons.

First, a concern with the category man generates statements that characterise the behaviour of typical men. In this context of sexual violence, such a typification equates the category 'man' with the potential for sexual violence. Hence the statement, 'All men are potential rapists'. Such a process does a disservice to any individual experience of being male and/or being female. As Connell states, it presents a 'false universalism' which does not resonate with lived social reality. In one sense then, it could be said that categorical analysis takes us little further, theoretically, than sex role theory with the exception, of course, that biological universalism has been replaced by social universalism.

Second, a focus on the category man equates that category with masculinity. This equation presumes that there is one universal form of masculinity (or on the other hand femininity) which is static. In one sense, of course, this tendency towards universalism and quiescence in understanding gender relations present in radical versions of feminism was designed as much to serve political purposes as it was to serve theories of gender relations. Such thinking does provide one way of constructing a policy agenda. But politics are not always predicated on adequate theorising!

These limitations taken together should not serve to undermine the profound importance that feminist work, which has been loosely identified here as categorical, has had on our understanding of the nature of gender relations in general and the expression of masculinity in particular. Without this work it would not have been possible for theorists to recognise the need to connect the emphasis on patriarchally rooted power relations with both individually and collectively negotiated identities of masculinity and femininity. But in a sense the question left unanswered by feminist work is the same as that posed by Brittain (1989) earlier in this discussion. He identified the problem of trying to understand the relationship between masculinism, the ideology which supports male-dominance, and masculinity(ies), the individually negotiated and fragile identities constructed by men. This is the gap left by feminist work in this area which both Connell (1987, 1995) and Messerschmidt (1993, 1997) have attempted to bridge, the latter in the particular context of understanding crime.

'Doing gender'

This way of thinking about gender relations matches with Morgan's fourth option. It is an attempt to explore the interdependent interconnections between power and difference. In some respects the problem of 'doing gender' is the problem of understanding how any social action is constituted; how to find the balance between the impact of social structure and the choice of social action. In general sociological theory the work of Giddens has been particularly significant in finding a way to avoid the determinism inherent in a structuralist position on the one hand and the voluntarism inherent in a position which gives primacy to freedom of choice on the other. His work encourages us to think about the ways in which structure is constituted, reconstituted and changed by human actors through their everyday activities. These processes which apply to the general construction of social action also apply to the way in which gender relations are negotiated. The theoretical question to answer then, to paraphrase Connell (1987), is how is gender organised as an ongoing concern?

Connell's (1987) analysis focuses on three specific social structures which underpin gender relations: the gender division of labour, the gender relations of power, and sexuality. None of these are constant entities. Their specific form varies through time and space but, taken together, they define the conditions under which gender identities are constructed. In other words, these structures define the conditions under which expressions of masculinity and femininity are constructed and reconstructed. The interplay between, and impact of, these different structural relations has been defined by Connell (1987) as 'hegemonic masculinity'.

Hegemony is a term borrowed from Gramsci which he used to refer to the way in which one class or group can dominate a society by consent. According to Connell (1987), in the expressions of masculinity found in late modern societies hegemonic power is possessed by those males who give expression to normative heterosexuality. This is achieved in the three domains of gender relations identified above in different but related ways. So, for example, it is found in the dominant notion of the male as breadwinner (from the gender division of labour); it is found in the definition of homosexuality but not lesbianism as a crime (from the gender relations of power); and it is found in the objectification of heterosexual women in the media (from the arena of sexuality).

Normative heterosexuality is that form of masculinity which is valued in all aspects of social life (as suggested by the examples offered above) and in being so valued it defines both the structure and the form of the struggle of any individual man to live up to the power of its expectations. At the same time it structures the lives of those who fail, or choose not to engage in such a struggle. As Messerschmidt (1993: 76) states, 'it defines masculinity through difference from, and desire for, women'. It also defines the kinds of possibilities available for variations in masculinity.

So, if this version of masculinity (normative, white, heterosexual masculinity) possesses hegemonic power then it follows that not only does this serve to provide individual men with a sense of themselves as more of a man or less of a man, it also serves to downgrade other versions of masculinity – homosexuality for example – as well as downgrading femininity. This 'hegemonic masculinity' gives credence to a hierarchical structure which underpins the sense we have of ourselves as gendered subjects whilst simultaneously permitting an array of expressed masculinities and femininities. Such variations from the norm offer templates for individual action which are differentially valued and differently expressed in relation to normative heterosexuality for both men and women. In this sense, as Messerschmidt (1993: 79) states, 'gender is an accomplishment'; something we are all required to work at, and to provide some account of, in our relationships with others. From this starting-point in understanding gender relations, Messerschmidt (1993) goes on to offer one of the most thorough-going descriptive accounts of the relationship between masculinities and crime, which we shall discuss briefly here.

Messerschmidt (1993: 119) states that: 'Research reveals that men construct masculinities in accord with their position in social structures and therefore their access to power and resources'. For Messerschmidt (1993, 1997), following Giddens and Connell, points to the importance of understanding the dynamic of not only the gendered nature of social structure but also its class and race dynamic (the complex way in which these three variables interact with one another is a key problem for those who would focus on only one of them, and is an issue to which we shall return). His view, however, leads him to analyse a variety of social contexts in which differential access to power and resources produces differently emphasised constructions of masculinity. In the context of crime this results in the consideration of three key locations: the street, the workplace, and the home. In each of these locations Messerschmidt provides a detailed account of the variety of ways in which masculinity is given expression; from the pimp on the street to the sharp business practice of the rising white-collar executive, to expressions of male proprietary in the form of various violences in the home.

All of these accounts are offered as a means of demonstrating the ways in which men display their manliness to others and to themselves. So whilst the business executive might use his position and power to sexually harass his female secretary in perhaps more subtle ways than the pimp controls his women, the effects are both the same. In this particular example, the women concerned are subjugated and the men concerned are affirmed as normatively heterosexual men.

The debate around the genesis of criminal behaviour and its connection with expressions of masculinity was reflected in a range of different kinds of commentary on the crime problem during the 1990s in the U.K. One of the central concerns of this debate has been what is presumed to be the increasingly anti-social behaviour of the young urban male; or what John Major, then the Prime Minister, referred to in September 1994 as the 'yob culture'. As a particular articulation of the debate around the relationship between masculinity and crime it will be of some value to consider some of the implications of this here.

A crisis in the gender order? 'New Lads', 'Ladettes' and the 'yob culture'

Taylor (1999) suggests that in order to understand the crime problem of late modern societies it is important to situate such understandings within an appreciation of a number of contemporary crises. One of the crises he identifies is that of the gender order. Borrowing this term from Connell (1987), Taylor goes on to suggest that the fear of angry young men has become the fear of crime for many contemporary publics. This fear, whilst arguably always present (see for example, Pearson, 1983) was given some propulsion through the civil disturbances of 1991.

Like the riots of 1981, the riots of 1991 provoked considerable public debate concerning their causes and effects. Campbell's book, *Goliath: Britain's dangerous places* (1993) offers one of the most readily available and thoroughgoing accounts and analysis of those disturbances. She had several concerns. One of them was to document the form and content of the public debate which took place after the events in 1991. That debate, in her analysis, elevated some features of those events to causal status whilst simultaneously failing to render visible or even to comment on other features of the disturbances which were also evident. One of those features, which the public debate was reluctant to acknowledge at the time, was the way in which the events that happened were dominated by young men.

Campbell's account of this debate was, of course, primarily a journalistic rather than an academic one. The observations she has to make about the nature of the involvement of these young males in criminal behaviour, however, constitute a particularly illuminating case study of the more theoretical concerns under discussion here. For that reason we shall consider her observations in some detail. To elucidate: the disturbances of

1991 occurred for the most part in areas where unemployment was high, particularly amongst young males; where public amenities were few; where housing was largely owned by and rented from the local council; and where there was a higher than average proportion of households headed by young, female, single parents. In other words areas which criminologists in particular and social scientists more generally would describe as 'high risk' and 'multiply deprived'. The statistical features associated with these areas indeed served to fuel images of them as being peopled by the (dangerous) underclass in which the young mother, being single, unmarried, and a failure to respectability, had failed to control her male offspring. The political view was widely expressed (and moreover still is) that the failure to control, alongside the presumed moral disrepute of the underclass, taken together result in criminal activity.

This view of the riots, according to Campbell, fails to acknowledge a number of other features of those disturbances. For example, it fails to see the abandonment of these communities by the state, and the caring, self-help, constructive activities that went on in the aftermath of such abandonment, largely done by women. It also fails to see the criminal activity taking place in these areas, and the response to it, in terms of an assertion of masculinity. Campbell (1993: 319) states that: 'Crime and coercion are sustained by men. Solidarity and self-help are sustained by women. It is as stark as that.'

Of course, as Campbell recognises, it is not quite as stark as that. Criminal activity and the policing response to it both rely on an hierarchically structured, militaristic organisational response rooted in the assertion of male bonding and solidarity. What the role of both men and women is in respect to their experience of their communities is perhaps not so clearly identifiable (but see Walklate and Evans, 1999). However, the point is well made. If we are to understand what is going on in many economically deprived council estates, then the interconnections between the possibilities for everyday gendered activities and the role of the state in relation to those possibilities would be one good place to start. But what about the question of masculinity?

Campbell's analysis of the expression of masculinity in this context challenges the presumption that unemployment leads to a crisis in masculinity. She argues that unemployment leads more accurately to the expression of another mode of masculinity, a mode which is recognisable as more tightly focused and circumscribed than the one adopted by the young lads' fathers or grandfathers maybe, but an expression and assertion of themselves as men nevertheless. It may be, for example, that their forefathers inhabited a world largely outside the domestic sphere; the world of work and the world of the public house. But in the young lads' world, the world of work is largely denied to them as an arena in which they can express themselves as men. Consequently the role of the breadwinner, as conventionally understood, is a space absent from their lives. The expectations of normative heterosexuality, to use Connell's term, exist, but they have no space in which to fulfil those expectations as bread-winners, though the lads clearly have no reluctance to provide in other ways for their (abandoned) offspring and girlfriends. In other words, what the lads do is create a sense of themselves in the space available to them, not between home, work, and the public house, (as was the case with their fathers or grandfathers), but between home (meaning their mother's or sometimes their girlfriend's home) and the street (where they hang out and do business). And whilst the street may have always been a male preserve for different forms of social activity, it takes on a crucial significance in the absence of work and the uncomfortable presence of the alternative: the domestic domain, for which they have no role with which they can easily identify. The subsequent involvement, then, of these young men in crime, whether burglary, joy riding, drugs, or rioting, needs to be understood as a product of their economic and spatial location and their need to express themselves as men.

Campbell's analysis of the 1991 riots also highlighted the fun and risk elements of young male involvement with crime, and especially car crime. One young male is reported as saying in response to his involvement in a stone-throwing incident with the police, 'I was throwing stones at the coppers because it was fun and everyone else was doing it' (Campbell, 1993: 188). Moreover it is in the particular context of car crime that the parallels between the behaviour of the young men, the police chasing them, and the predominantly male relationship with car driving in general becomes paramount. As Jefferson (1992) says, he defies any (car driving) male not to admit to the thrill and the excitement associated with testing how a vehicle can perform. The young male in his stolen XRi and the police officer in his Cosworth experience very similar processes and exhibit very similar behaviours to those experienced by all men; cars and car ownership symbolise a predominantly male preserve still and thereby an opportunity for the expression of maleness. Thus, deprived of other spaces in which to express themselves as male, car crime becomes a key arena in which young men in economically deprived circumstances can assert themselves as men.

Of course, as was indicated above, car crime is but one criminal avenue. Campbell (1993: 324) ends her book by reporting on this conversation with some young children from the Meadowell Estate in Newcastle-upon-Tyne.

> When asked what she wanted to be, a girl insisted, 'I want to be a mam'. Her playmates agreed, they wanted to be mams and dads. Then a boy dissented: 'I don't want to be a dad, I want to be a robber'.

For some young people, then, the options available to them are made abundantly clear early on in their lives. For some young men, the means to being successful, to asserting themselves as men, are evidently linked with the potential of criminal possibilities.

There are (at least) two observations to make about Campbell's analysis at this juncture in the context of this particular discussion. First, it is possible to read strong parallels between the mode of masculinity highlighted by Campbell as being present in the riots of 1991 and John Major's assertion of a 'yob culture'. Their focus of concern is the same: the young, unemployed, troublesome male a concern characterised by Coward (1994: 32) in the following way:

> The yob is foul-mouthed, irresponsible, probably unemployed and violent. The yob hangs around council estates where he terrorises the local inhabitants, possibly in the company of his pit bull terrier. He fathers children rather than cares for them. He is often drunk, probably uses drugs and is likely to be involved in crime, including domestic violence. He is the ultimate expression of macho values: mad, bad, and dangerous to know.

This demon of the 1990s is resonant of demons of earlier historical moments. Young working-class males have been seen to pose a threat to social order consistently throughout modern history (see, for example, Pearson, 1983). What is interesting about this particular demon, however, is the way in which his chosen expression of himself *as a man* is deemed to be the problem. The demon of the problematic young male has also been, as the preceding discussion implies, intimately connected with the crisis of the family and parenting (Taylor, 1999). Such connections were fuelled by the murder of Jamie Bulger by two ten-year-old boys in 1993. The debate which followed this event furthered the demonisation of the single parent (female) household (Tuck, 1993) and potentially also served to fuel the notion of a crisis in the gender order. The question is, what kind of crisis is this and for whom?

Whilst Campbell's analysis challenges the notion of a crisis of masculinity, the notion of crisis retained some political and journalistic (if not academic) currency during the 1990s. The media constructions of 'Men Behaving Badly' gave some legitimacy to the notion that that idea of the 'New Man' merely existed in the imaginations of some women or households whose domestic economy could sustain it. Indeed the increasing national concern with the rising incidence of suicide amongst young adult males would add some sustenance to the notion of a crisis in masculinity. Moreover, the emergence of the 'Ladettes', the female behaving badly, would appear to be the other side of the coin to these processes, though it would seem to be increasingly supported by the small, but growing, empirical evidence of increasing young female criminality. The explanation of such data will not be simple nor straightforward, but increasingly it would seem that young women want to claim the public space once the preserve of young men. The recorded increase in young female alcohol consumption would support this line of argument, thus adding sustenance to the notion of a crisis in the gender order. The question remains, for whom is this a crisis?

The problems being faced by young men and young women as they endeavour to construct their sense of identity can be interpreted both progressively and regressively. For example, Campbell's focus on the lads' expression of themselves as men through crime can also serve to fuel Conservative Party (and other constituency) attacks on such young men and their families (read mothers) who have failed to inculcate them with appropriate civilised values. Both views may agree, perhaps, on the locus of the problem, though both may not necessarily agree on its cause or its solution.

The differences between a progressive and a regressive interpretation of the problem of masculinity (and increasingly femininity) are, of course, crucial politically. It is particularly important, for example, not to lose sight of the role of the state in contributing to the options facing young people. State and state policy contributes to, and in some areas some would argue, contributes significantly to, setting the structural context in which any behaviour is expressed. Not only does the state set a policy agenda which frames the lives of those economically deprived; the practices and activities of the state's actors can set the tone for behavioural expectations of those who are economically deprived. Put simply, the question should be asked: what makes the often rude, and belligerent *behaviour* of the old boys' network of the House of Commons all that different from the lads who shout, whistle and jostle, hanging about on the street corner? The reply has to be that in behavioural terms, very little. As expressions of masculine behaviour, the reply also has to be very little. What differs, of course, is their public and political *acceptability*. The same might also be said about young women who engage in similar behaviours.

As Coward (1994) points out, this critique of masculinity is being used to attack some of the least powerful men in our society. We need to ask the question why? This kind of reflexive thinking rarely takes place in the discourse of politics, of course, but that does not mean that it cannot. Neither does it mean that such reflexivity could not be more keenly felt in academic debate. This latter observation constitutes a useful link to be made between a further aspect of Campbell's analysis and that more academic debate.

This second observation suggests strong parallels between Campbell's focused analysis on male crime and the relative powerlessness of those who engage in it, and Messerschmidt's more general analysis of male crime in differently powered contexts. Both analyses document the continuities and discontinuities between different modes of masculine expression and the structural localities in which such expressions occur. This desire to match an understanding of socio-structural location with differentially valued assertions of masculinity certainly offers a much more reflexive way of thinking about gender issues especially in relation to men. Some difficulties remain, however, in terms of its sufficiency as either an explanation of an individual man's desire to commit crime, or as a more general explanation of criminal behaviour. In addition we need to ask what it is, if anything, that this kind of analysis enables us to learn about women.

The political debate of the 1990s which highlighted the need to combat the 'yob culture' tapped some features of social behaviour which are certainly of popular concern (see for example, Taylor, Evans and Fraser, 1996). However, foregrounding the behaviour of certain groups of young men can serve to hide the continuities between their behaviour and other groups of men, and can result in the further targeting of those people already rendered significantly powerless in social and cultural terms; young, manless women with children. However, if Connell's (1995) observations are correct, men are themselves complicit in the perpetuation of 'hegemonic masculinity'; as a consequence the room for manoeuvre to institute change may be very small indeed. But are men, especially white, heterosexual men, always the beneficiaries of 'hegemonic masculinity'?

Can men be victims?

The observations made by Tolson (1977) and touched upon earlier concerning men's relationship with the emotional and the increasing rate of suicide amongst young males would both point to different aspects of the downside of 'hegemonic masculinity'. Given the powerful presence of dualistic thinking within criminology and victimology in their commitment to a (masculinist) conception of science, this has resulted in a gendered view of the victim as well as the offender (a discussion developed in the previous chapter). What is worth reiterating here is how this gendered view of the victim impacts differently upon men compared to women.

Much victimological work implicitly leaves us with the impression that victims are not likely to be male. It renders female victimisation visible and male victimisation invisible (see also Newburn and Stanko, 1994). Yet as more recent, though limited, work has suggested men can be victims and experience their victimisation as a key problem in their understandings of themselves as male (see for example, Hobdell and Stanko, 1993; Goodey, 1997). Through the lens of 'hegemonic masculinity' such experiences may be differently understood, but what we do not fully understand is the extent to which maleness mediates the experience of victimisation. Anger, for example, is one feeling more frequently reported by men than by women when criminally victimised, but equally men report feelings of vulnerability and powerlessness like those reported by women when sexually assaulted (see for example McMullan, 1990, on male rape). It may be possible that the lens of masculinity, of being in control or out of control, helps our understanding of men's experiences of victimisation, but this is a theoretical rather than an empirical assertion. How do we explain the continuities and discontinuities of experience alluded to here? It is at this juncture that it will be useful to offer a more general critique of what we have called 'doing gender'.

'Doing gender': a critical assessment

In this chapter we have moved from understanding gender as the expression of behaviour learned through the socialisation process to a view of gender, not as pre-given by sexual attributes, but given by and negotiated through socio-structural locations, a view which endeavours to endow an individual with structured choice. Of course, this view also implies that individuals can, and often do, choose to behave outside of these choices; but such strategies do not necessarily offer them public or private acceptability. Writers in this area have drawn heavily on the work of Giddens in order to develop a framework for analysing not only gender relations in general, but also the particular relationship between masculinity(ies) and crime. This latter concern, in particular, has produced some very provocative writing for criminology, as evidenced by the foregoing discussion. The question remains, however, what is left untouched by this way of thinking about the relationship between masculinity and crime?

The first question provoked by adopting a critical stance towards this kind of analysis arises out of the work of Jefferson (1993). Put simply, this question asks: what about the individual? How do men choose to become what they become? This question is only partially answered by the assertion of a multiplicity of possible masculinities, structured under the influence of different socio-locations. Templates of appropriate action in different structural settings for men are evident as the analysis offered by Messerschmidt (1993) suggests. Such templates still need to be played out, however; to be expressed or suppressed. In other words they still need to be chosen and worked upon by individual men. Raising the question of what motivates individual men to choose one course of action as opposed to another, of course, raises areas conventionally problematic for sociological analysis.

In general terms this raises the perennial question exemplified by the following: whilst all men might be potential rapists, not all men do rape. Why they choose to rape or not rape can only be understood in part by reference to the available, socially acceptable styles of masculine expression. Another part of the explanation for their choice must lie with understanding the contribution of motivations such as desire, pleasure, risk-seeking, etc. Raising concepts such as these may, of course, take us down the highly individualistic route of psychoanalysis; but they might also lead us to re-conceptualise our understandings of criminality in terms of what Katz (1988) calls 'The Seductions of Crime'. As Jefferson (1993) argues, unless we understand the pleasures of crime as well as the opportunities for crime, we shall never really have a complete picture of criminal behaviour.

This leads to a second and perhaps more fundamental question about the direction in which some of the more recent criminological debate is moving: can the picture of crime be completed at all by constructing a framework for explaining crime through an understanding of masculinity? If the danger of the first question is that this might lead us down the route of celebrating individual difference to its ultimate, this second question poses a very different problem for the debate on masculinity and crime.

As this chapter has indicated the debate around masculinity and crime proceeded apace in the 1990s. Indeed this constitutes part of the rationale for its coverage in this context. It is possible, however, to detect an uneasy tension within this debate. That tension emerges when the fundamental characteristics of criminology discussed in chapter 1 are reflected upon. There it was argued that one of the dilemmas facing criminology was its implicit linkage with modernism through its acceptance of traditional masculinist conceptions of science. This linkage has constantly resulted in the criminological search for a universal explanation of crime. This tendency is still present in the way in which the concept of masculinity has been explored so far.

In other words, whilst the concept of masculinity itself might have been tempered and modified, the actual debate which proceeds under its umbrella strains to fit all kinds of criminal behaviour occurring in all kinds of contexts within its terms. The maleness of crime from state terrorism to joyriding, though constituted differently and expressed differently, also becomes the source of its explanation. Thus not only does this reflect a failure to resolve fully the tendency towards universalism it can also be read as tautological. This may be, of course, the resultant effect, of the 'doing gender' approach not having, as yet, adequately addressed two remaining issues: the role of femininity and its relationship with masculinity, and the relationship between the state, masculinity(ies) and crime.

Femininity and its relationship with masculinity

The first of these issues is, perhaps, rather more contentious than the second. This relates to the role of femininity and its relationship with masculinity. Much of the work on masculinity has presumed, if not explicitly, the view that masculinity exists as an expression of difference from femininity. The need to express that difference, however, should not be taken to mean that the two modes of 'doing gender' are not related. Indeed, it may be that in the expression of individual acts, as well as the expression of more collectively identifiable and understood modes of masculinity; what women want is an important feature. This raises two questions. First, put simply, do women really want their men to be 'wimps'? And if 'their man' turns out to be a wimp, how do they deal with this? Raising this question is not intended to imply that women are therefore to blame for men's behaviour; though it is quite clearly possible that it can be read in this way. Second, it is important to recognise the complexity of feminine expression. Put simply, where do we locate an understanding of the 'female yob'; clearly identifiable, for example, in Campbell's (1984) work on female street gangs. These questions are raised merely to point up the complexities which exist between masculinities and femininities which cannot easily be resolved by privileging one framework over another.

The relationship between the state, masculinity(ies) and crime

The second of the two general concerns to be addressed here focuses on the relationship between the state, masculinity(ies) and crime. This again is an issue that has been left relatively untouched by recent work on masculinity and crime. This does not mean that the presence of the state, and state politics, has not been posed as a significant arena for the expression of masculinity(ies). This is evidently not the case. As MacKinnon (1989) states:

> However autonomous of class the liberal state may appear, it is not autonomous of sex. Male power is systemic. Coercive, legitimated, and epistemic, it is the regime.

Both Connell (1987), in understanding the relationship between gender and power, and Messerschmidt (1993), in analysing gender politics, posit not only the importance of the role of the state like MacKinnon but go on to develop ways of thinking about the state as a mode of masculine expression. The argument here is that perhaps much more of this kind of work needs to be done. As MacKinnon (1989) argues, the assertion by the state that it is objective, and consequently, gender neutral, has its impact on all aspects of social life, including crime and its control.

There is, however, a third issue here which arises from the implicit acceptance of, and the powerful assertion of, 'hegemonic masculinity'. This third issue returns us to the presumption of normative heterosexuality contained within the notion of hegemonic masculinity. The way in which this impacts upon the 'masculinity turn' within criminology has been fully explored by Collier (1998). In his view, not only does this turn result in the perpetuation of a false universalism, it also perpetuates the false dualism of sex/gender and, as a consequence, is rooted in heterosexism. The recent tussle over the retention or removal of Section 28 in the context of education stands as a good illustration of some of the analytical tendencies that Collier is alluding to. The importance of such tendencies lies in what is made visible and invisible by them. What is given a name, how is it named, and how is it responded to. It is simply not enough to replace one agenda with another and assume that you have, as a consequence, dealt with each of them. The implications that this line of thinking has for the masculinity project in general, and the gender project within criminology in particular, is an issue to which we shall return in the Conclusion of this book.

Conclusion

In this chapter we have been exploring different ways of thinking about masculinity and the way in which those different ways have expressed themselves within criminology and to a lesser extent victimology. We have reviewed some of the more recent work in this field and have suggested that some issues still remain unresolved by the efforts to see all criminal behaviour through the lens of masculinity. A number of implications may follow from the difficulties outlined above; but one is of significant importance to consider here.

This book began by documenting the evidence on the relationship between sex and crime. In that discussion it was stated that other variables are also of significance in exploring issues relating to crime. Which variable is taken to be the most important is most frequently decided upon *theoretically*. This is nowhere more the case that in the current literature on masculinity and crime. However, decisions made by theoretical fiat do not necessarily render them empirically accurate. How and under what circumstances masculinity is the key variable in committing crime, and how and under what circumstances social class might be the key explanatory variable, are questions which remain to be answered. Raising them clearly posits a theoretical and empirical agenda informed by a concern with the focused specificity of the relationship between particular crimes and particular contexts rather than a search for broad (and brave) assertions.

Suggestions for further reading

Messerschmidt, J. (1993), *Masculinities and Crime*, the only book to date to have attempted a thoroughgoing analysis of the interconnections between masculinity and crime. See also his later book, *Crime as Structured Action* (1997).

Connell, R.W. (1987), *Gender and Power*. The analysis of gender relations offered here has exerted a significant influence on much work on masculinity since it was published.

Katz, J. (1988) *The Seductions of Crime*. An interestingly different framework for understanding the motivations for criminal behaviour that may apply equally to males and females.

3 Crime, fear and risk

Introduction

In some respects the growth in sensitivity shown to the question of the fear of crime has paralleled the growth in the more generally expressed concern about the victim of crime. Arguably that process began in the 1950s with the campaign, led by Margery Fry, for the establishment of the Criminal Injuries Compensation Board alongside the apparent increase in recorded crime (see Mawby and Walklate, 1994). This process was given a special boost in the early 1970s through the coverage given by the media to the crime of 'mugging'. As Hall *et al* (1978) have documented, the social construction of the crime of 'mugging' left its indelible mark on the relationship between colour, crime, and criminal victimisation. That mark, in contributing to the construction of colour as the Other, that to be feared, arguably delineates the initial construction of the fear of crime debate.

In the first instance, then, it can be argued that the fear of crime was to be understood very much as a racial issue. It stood for the fear of black crime. However, whilst this aspect to the fear of crime has never disappeared, other developments which occurred during the 1970s, especially work emanating from the feminist movement, alongside victim-centred initiatives developing within the voluntary sector, saw to it that the picture of criminal victimisation evolved further. At the same time there was increasing political and policy concern about the rising rate in recorded crime. That concern led to the piloting of the criminal victimisation survey (reported in Sparks *et. al.*, 1977) and its subsequent adoption for use by the Home Office in 1982. Arguably it was at this juncture that real impetus was given to the exploration of the fear of crime.

In some ways, then, the 'fear of crime' debate took on a life of its own during the 1980s. As Sparks (1992: 119) states:

> ... the fear of crime has become more than simply a focus of empirical disagreements [it] has assumed a heavy polemical charge in theoretical and political disputes.

The 1980s, however, were marked particularly by what Miers (1978) has called in a different context the 'politicisation of the victim'; that is, a process of invoking the imagery of the crime victim as the basis on which to formulate policy. So much so that Karmen (1990) has observed that crime prevention policy became crime victimisation policy and what Garland (1996) has referred to as the requirement of citizens to be literate about crime. However, as this chapter will illustrate, the struggle over the 'fear of crime' not only took place in the political and policy arenas. It was also a struggle in which criminology and victimology were, and still are, intimately implicated.

This chapter aims to examine the debate around the fear of crime, paying particular attention to the assumptions underpinning the different views expressed within it. It will endeavour to examine those assumptions through an exploration of their implications for the question of gender; although, as has been stated before, this is not intended to imply that other structural properties associated with the expression of fear in relation to crime are not also important. It will be argued, however, that the absence of a gender-informed conceptual approach especially on this issue has rendered some questions visible, marginalised others and sustained the invisibility of yet others. As a way of making sense of the wealth of material that has been generated around the fear of crime, we shall make an initial exploration of it under two headings. First we shall explore the idea that the fear of crime is irrational; and second, that the fear of crime is rational.

The 'irrationality' of the 'fear of crime'

The notion that the 'fear of crime' expressed by some sections of the population is 'irrational' is a view that stems from what has been called the 'administrative criminology' of the Home Office (Young, 1986). This version of criminology is characterised by Young (1986: 12) as having 'abandoned the search for causal generalisations and instead [having] adopted a neo-classicist problematic centring around the principles of effective control'. Whilst administrative criminology may have abandoned the search for the cause of crime, this does not mean that as a criminological enterprise it has failed to recognise the problems inherent in trying to measure the extent of the crime problem. Indeed, recognition of this very issue constituted part of the motivation underpinning the introduction of the national criminal victimisation survey in 1982 (Mayhew and Hough, 1988). But this was only part of the story. Mayhew and Hough (1988: 157) go on to state:

> Another attraction lay in the survey's promise as an antidote to public *misperceptions* about crime. It was thought within the Home Office that

> *misconceptions* about crime levels, trends and risks were widespread among the public. A survey-based index of crime would demonstrate the possibility – if not the reality – that the index of crime based on offences recorded by the police might be subject to statistical inflation by virtue of changing reporting and recording practices.... In other words, the survey promised a more informed picture of crime that might help create a more balanced climate of opinion about law and order. (*my emphasis*)

These criminal victimisation surveys, which have been repeated more or less every two years since 1982, are intended, then, to provide a more accurate picture of the extent of crime, and the crime experience, than is provided by police statistics alone. As the statement above illustrates, the way in which the data produced by them, was foreseen to be politically valuable. Given both these factors, the way in which these surveys have been implemented, and the data produced by them analysed and used, has made a significant, though controversial, contribution to the 'fear of crime' debate. In order to understand the nature of this contribution it is useful to have some idea of how these surveys have operationalised the question of the 'fear of crime'.

Operationalising fear

In general terms criminal victimisation surveys operationalise the fear of crime in relation to perceptions of risk from crime. This process presumes that these two phenomena are connected in some way and consequently leads to particular kinds of questions being asked. For example, respondents are asked how long they have lived in their area, their levels of satisfaction with their neighbourhood, and their views of the kind of neighbourhood they live in. This constitutes a way of trying to contextualise experiences of fear. These questions are then followed by others which focus on how safe they feel walking alone at night in their area, how safe they feel when they are alone in their own home, and how much they worry about different kinds of crime happening to them. The respondent is then moved on from discussing these 'fears' to their estimation of the chance of different crimes happening to them and the extent to which they think certain crimes in their area are common or uncommon. These are subsequently followed by questions which ask the respondent to recall their actual experience of criminal victimisation during a given time period. Operationalising the exploration of the 'fear of crime' in this way raises a number of issues.

However, as Maxfield (1984) points out in his analysis of the fear of crime based on British Crime Survey data, operationalising the concept of fear is fraught with difficulties. From the summary offered above it is possible to see that in this process some effort is made to distinguish 'fears' from 'worries' though the term 'fear' itself is not used in the questions asked. The questions in fact display an interesting preference for 'how *safe* do you feel?' Individual levels of expressed safety are therefore used as indicators of levels of fear. Without entering questions of semantics here, this does appear to be a little odd. The conceptual transformation from fear to safety is neither an easy nor a straightforward one to make, as we shall see below. At a minimum it raises questions concerning what is actually being measured by this transformation in particular, and by this kind of questioning in general. A number of issues associated with this are worthy of further comment.

First, whilst making the distinction between 'fears' and 'worries' might be useful, this distinction is then pursued with the respondent in the vacuum of criminal victimisation. In other words, this data provides us with little sense of how these 'fears' and 'worries' measured in this way compare with other 'fears' and 'worries' that people might have. There is some evidence to suggest, for example, that when the fear of crime amongst the elderly is placed in the context of elderly people's worries about financial problems or health, fears about crime recede in relative importance. The same observation could be made about the use of the idea of safety in the questions themselves. Safety can conjure a range of different issues for a respondent that may be articulated through crime but may nevertheless not be connected with crime *per se*, environmental safety for example.

Secondly, the way in which these concepts have been operationalised reflects a narrow behavioural focus. So, for example, the questions focus on when the individual is alone, reflecting an assumption that this is the behavioural condition in which fear is most likely to be experienced. The questions also make a distinction between outside the home and inside the home, as though in terms of fear these constitute separate and separable experiences. This is particularly problematic when women's expressed fear of crime is considered in more detail (see below).

Finally, though by no means least in importance, these are questions that are subsequently analysed in relation to both actual and perceived risk from crime. This raises political, empirical and conceptual questions. The political issues raised by placing fear and risk together in this way have by now been well rehearsed. For example, the oft-quoted presentation of the statistical findings of the first British Crime Survey (Hough and Mayhew, 1983) clearly downplays the risk from crime. This implied that the expressed 'fear of crime' from particular social groups, especially women and the elderly, was irrational given the actual level of risk from crime that they are exposed to. Data from the 1984 British Crime Survey was presented in a similar fashion. Those findings report that 'four out of ten women under 30 said they were "very worried" [about rape]. Aside from the alarming nature of the offence, *exaggerated estimates* of its likelihood may underpin some of this worry' (Hough and Mayhew, 1985:

41; *my emphasis*). Such exaggeration is also attributed to 'mugging' and burglary.

Interestingly enough, later surveys present fewer findings on the fear of crime and appear to have asked fewer questions on this issue in favour of covering other topics of current interest (see Mayhew, Elliott and Dowds, 1989). However, the 1992 survey reported that 30 per cent of women were 'very worried' about rape, women were more worried about being a victim of burglary or mugging than men, and that worry about each type of crime was highest amongst the young (Mirrlees-Black and Aye Maung, 1993).

What this process of operationalisation does therefore, is link fear, risk, and behaviour together. This is problematic both theoretically (as will be developed in this chapter) and empirically. For the moment suffice it to say that the relationship between these processes at the level of the individual is neither as direct nor as linear as the Home Office approach discussed above presupposes. For example, these surveys report that some respondents, especially women and the elderly, engage in precautionary behavioural strategies in (what appears to be) their response to the fear of crime, such as only going out at night accompanied or not going out after dark at all.

Formulating an equation between expressed worries and reported behavioural strategies of dealing with these worries assumes a risk management view of human behaviour. This view sees individual behaviour as being constructed as a rational response to perceived situations of worry, threat, or danger. Behavioural responses, however, can be constructed in response to a number of different processes, some known, some unknown, or can be the result of a combination of factors. In other words, this risk management view is one which, empirically, and in relation to the process of explanation, constitutes only one possibility amongst several (see, for example, Skogan, 1986). As Skogan himself argues, this risk management view is the favoured view within psychology. It is favoured, arguably, because it proffers the opportunity for both prediction and control. As we shall see it may not, however, constitute a very real or accurate understanding of how people really experience the threat of criminal victimisation. This is not only the favoured view, then, but one that is also deemed defensible. In other words, it can offer practical policy advice, reflecting the implicit modernism of criminology discussed in chapter 1. It is also a view that excludes other possible explanations and oversimplifies the relationship between fear and behaviour (see below). It also leaves unexplored what is actually meant by risk.

The way in which administrative criminology links fear, risk and danger in this way therefore raises not only empirical questions; it raises conceptual ones too. However, as these conceptual problems apply equally to those who argue that the fear of crime is rational we shall consider this view next before exploring these conceptual issues more fully.

Rationality and the fear of crime

During the 1980s (though some trace its origins to an earlier date, see for example, Lowman, 1992), and partly as a response to what was referred to as 'administrative criminology', there emerged what was to be called 'radical left realism' within criminology. This brand of criminology, largely associated with the work of Jock Young, John Lea, Richard Kinsey and Roger Matthews in the U.K., but also having its proponents in Canada and Australia, constituted an attempt to reclaim, politically, the 'law and order' debate for the left. In so doing, it was a view of criminology which argued for an 'accurate victimology' (Young, 1986). This accurate victimology was to form one corner of understanding the 'square of crime' (the other three corners being the offender, the state and society, see Matthews and Young, 1992). Attention here will be paid primarily to left realism's concern with this 'accurate victimology' as the development of this runs parallel with the work discussed in the previous section.

Radical left realists argue that the starting-point for understanding the impact of crime is to take people's experiences of crime seriously. In order to do this it is necessary to build on what is already known about the socio-structural dimensions of the crime experience. In other words, it is necessary to take account of the impact of crime in relation to age, class, race and gender. Developing local, geographically focused, criminal victimisation surveys which, through their research design, can take account of the variables of age, race, sex and class, can do this. A number of such local crime surveys have been conducted (see for example Kinsey, 1984; Jones, MacLean and Young, 1986; Anderson *et al* 1990; Crawford *et al* 1990).

The earlier versions of these surveys explored the fear of crime in a very similar way to the Home Office based surveys, asking questions about fear, worry, and perceived risk. However, the focused sample construction, sample design and data analysis enabled such statements as the following to be made:

> The picture that has emerged is one of people of the inner city – especially women – living under curfew. While, as has been seen, the actual chances of victimisation are less than many people believe, nonetheless, in Granby (a ward in inner city Liverpool) for example, three-quarters of those interviewed believe there are real risks for women who go out at night and half said they often or always avoid going out after dark.
>
> (Kinsey, 1985: 23-4)

> In either event it is clear that women generally, and particularly older black women, feel it is necessary to restrict their behaviour and avoid certain situations as a precaution against crime. In this sense, the Islington Crime Survey helps to illustrate that a 'curfew on women' appears to be implicitly operative.
>
> (Jones, MacLean and Young, 1986: 169)

Such focused analysis foregrounds the victimisation experience of particular groups of people in quite a different way from the early Home Office studies. Indeed, these analyses constituted an attempt to convey the lived experiences of those people living in communities where the threat of criminal victimisation appears to routinely inform their day-to-day activities. Moreover, it is important to note that there is no sense in which these writers were suggesting that the behaviour that has a curfew effect is to be considered irrational. Given the levels of criminal victimisation which exist in inner-city areas the argument is, indeed, to the contrary. Such behavioural responses are constructed in response to what individuals understand to be the crime experience (though not necessarily their experience) within their community. Their response is, therefore, to be considered rational.

The Second Islington Crime Survey (Crawford *et al* 1990) attempted to develop a more sophisticated understanding of the fear of crime and individual responses to it. In this survey they explored fear in a much more tightly defined fashion. In particular, efforts were made to distinguish the experience of and/or expression of the fear of crime as related to the street from that related to the use of public transport from that related to the home. The picture that emerged from this more precisely defined approach was certainly more complex than the Home Office findings. For example, this survey reported that nearly one in two women felt unsafe in their own home, and that 'for women of all ages, crime is a considerable reason as to why they do not go out after dark at night' (Crawford *et al* 1990: 49), and that, women additionally either avoid, or feel unsafe using, public transport at night. Add to this, women's experiences of what Crawford *et al* call 'public abuse' (harassment of various kinds), then what emerges is a picture of women and the fear of crime in which it is suggested that 'Maybe women are actually more in tune with reality as expressed through their fear than men' (*ibid*: 73).

In summary, the work of the 'left realists' has significantly added to our understanding of the nature and extent of criminal victimisation. This approach was certainly more successful than the Home office based surveys in providing a fuller picture of the experiences of women and black people in relation to criminal victimisation (though it must be noted that more recent Home Office surveys have paid more attention to these latter two categories of experience. For example, the 1992 British Crime Survey reported that both Asians and Afro-Caribbeans are more fearful of being alone after dark than white respondents are). However, despite the more recent work of the left realists with respect to the fear of crime, conceptual difficulties remain.

One of the key strengths of the left-realist approach lies in the more detailed empirical picture about the fear of crime that has emerged from the analysis of their data. Indeed that more detailed picture reflects the way in which this work has also been more successful at accessing some sense of the private nature of criminal victimisation, that which goes on behind closed doors. One of its key weaknesses, however, lies within the conceptual framework that informs the analysis. As Crawford *et al* (1990: 45) observe:

> From the survey's findings we discover that 49 per cent of women and 23 per cent of men said that they 'sometimes' feel unsafe. It is, of course, impossible to tell whether the threat comes from within the house (i.e. domestic violence), or from outsiders breaking in. Clearly more work needs to be done in relation to questionnaire design to elicit such information. But what it does tell us is that the home, or 'private' area of a woman's life, is not an escape from fear.... Women's fear of public abuse may increase women's dependence upon the home, but it is doubtful whether it also increases their belief that the home is a safe place.

It may be, of course, that the authors are correct in their assertion that more work does need to be done on questionnaire design in order to make the connections that they are obviously aware need to be made. Moreover, they are also aware that, given what is known about the extent of private violence against women (see chapter 4), the more reasonable question to pose might be why do women not express greater levels of fear. Or indeed, why do men not express high levels of fear at all?

Addressing these issues is not just a question of developing a more refined technical research tool nor is it an issue solely of the kinds of questions to be asked of the data, though both of these are certainly important. It is an issue of the theoretical and/or conceptual starting-point. In effect this question returns us to the issue of the relationship between rationality and expressed fears and ultimately to the question of how both of these are related, if at all, to risk.

Is the fear of crime rational or irrational?

Part of the project of 'left realism', as was stated above, was to reclaim the law and order debate for the left. This political project reasonably called into question the presumption that the criminological enterprise should focus its attention on fear reduction rather than crime reduction. So for the left realist the expression of the fear of crime for inner-city dwellers in general, and for women and people from ethnic minorities in particular, is related to their experience of crime in their locality. Criminal victimisation is a real experience, so their fear has a rational base, not an irrational one. Indeed what enables left realists to be so categorical in their acceptance of the views of their respondents is a commitment to the idea that there is no objective measure of rationality. What may be considered to be rational by a man may not be considered to be rational by a woman. So, for example, when Crawford *et al* (1990: 69) state that 'Women tend to express a greater sensitivity towards personal safety as a result of victimisation', this is to be understood from the standpoint of women. However, they go on in the next sentence to suggest that the relationship between fear and behaviour might be a little more complex.

> There is, however, no simple causal relationship between victimisation and fear. Victimisation may actually cause individuals to modify their behaviour (as we have already seen) in such a way as to limit their risk of victimisation. As well as forms of avoidance, individuals who have been victimised may neutralise their experiences in other ways, blaming themselves or protecting themselves.
>
> (*ibid.*)

The problem here, of course, is that either we take what people say seriously or we do not. Or perhaps expressed another way, how do we decide what the relationship is between victimisation and fear, and under what circumstances are the two connected? Moreover, are these two related in a different or a similar fashion when in the street or when at home? How do women and men keep themselves safe in fearful and/or dangerous situations, for example, during a violent 'domestic' incident or in the presence of a pub brawl? In other words, left realism has implicitly accepted the view that it is necessary to explain the connections between risk from crime and fear of crime in terms of rationality. And whilst they have challenged the form of this rationality (for example that there may be more than one standard of rationality), they failed to recognise that the parameters of this debate are, in and of themselves, highly problematic. Sparks (1992) explicates this argument very well.

Sparks suggests that whilst Young (1987) has himself raised the question of what a rational fear would look like, left realism has not adequately begun to explore the implications of this question, let alone suggest an answer. The desire by left realists to contextualise people's fear within their 'lived realities' (Crawford *et al* 1990) has the effect of conflating what 'fear' might mean in its day-to-day use for those people:

> ... it is such a simplification of processes of social cognition as to constitute precisely the kind of derogation of lay knowledge which the realists are concerned to avoid.
>
> (Sparks, 1992: 122)

This raises not only a theoretical inconsistency within left realism but also makes visible an assumption which appears to assert that an 'appropriate level of fear was empirically decidable, when in fact it involves moral and political choices' (*ibid*: 126).

The logic of the position adopted by Sparks suggests that calculating risk is not a necessary concomitant to deciding on the rationality or otherwise of people's fear. People's fear of crime is not based on calculating competing risks and choosing an appropriate course of action 'on the balance of probabilities'. As individuals we are likely to vary considerably in the amount of information and/or resources we have with which to engage in such a process. So any debate concerned with the rationality or otherwise of the relationship between risk and fear needs to take account of what kind of 'balance of probabilities' is likely to be available.

Moreover, it is also important to remember that as individuals we have partial information, some experiences, and some local knowledge, all embedded in our social relationships. All of these may render some situations, people, places which are commonly held to be threatening, unsafe, dangerous, not so for some people and more so for others. How individuals negotiate the familiar as well as the unfamiliar may in a very real way affect feelings of insecurity and uncertainty. Asking empirical questions around fear and risk in this way presupposes a theoretical approach to the fear of crime that challenges the conventional conceptual framework as it has been outlined here. Such a conceptual challenge has been forthcoming from feminist-informed writing.

Feminist approaches to the fear of crime

Feminist analysis of the fear of crime renders meaningless a pursuit of understanding 'fear' as being associated with either the public or the private domain, something unacknowledged by administrative criminology and struggled with by left realist criminology. Feminist work starts from the premise that women's experiences transgress such dichotomous thinking. In order to transgress this thinking, however, we must treat women's knowledge as 'expert' knowledge. Evidence from feminist research which endeavours to do this has increasingly documented that the common basis of such 'fear' for women is the endemic level of violence by men towards them. This is translated in some feminist work as a fundamental fear of sexual danger (Stanko, 1985; Warr, 1985). Not all feminists, however, would agree with the presumptions that lie behind this viewpoint.

The different feminist perspectives discussed in chapter 1 would all recognise the importance of the impact of the fear of rape and/or sexual assault on women, but they would not all concur in their analysis of such fear. A liberal feminist perspective would, for example, downplay the extent of the threat of sexual violence as constituting the basis on which such fear is generated. This perspective would adhere to a view that the issue of sexual violence was a problem associated with a few psychologically deranged men, men whom women need to learn to identify and avoid. In policy terms such a view would encourage women to take their own safety precautions: to take self-defence classes, avoid 'risky' situations, adopt the 'good sense' of staying in at night, for example. This view, rooted as it is in defining the question of gender in terms of achieving equality between the sexes, can lead to 'victim blaming' for those who fail to take advantage of the 'good' sense on offer.

On the other hand a postmodern feminist position on women's fear of crime is perhaps somewhat more difficult to delineate since this stance would eschew any tendency towards making general or universal statements about women. Moreover, a postmodernist position would be more comfortable discussing the specificity and diversity of such experiences. Thus it would be necessary to distinguish the 'fears' expressed by black women from those expressed by lesbian women, from those expressed by white women, etc. Given the terms in which the fear of crime has been debated to date, it is easy to see how such an emphasis on difference, diversity and specificity sits very uneasily with the generalised conceptual formulations of rationality, fear and risk. It generates particular problems for identifying policy initiatives. However, whilst a postmodern position on this issue is difficult to identify as such, the desire to de-construct the terms of reference of the debate has certainly been a useful and provocative influence on more recent theoretical developments relevant to this issue (see below).

The most influential feminist perspective on this debate, however, has been that of radical feminism. Radical feminists would argue that the wide-ranging empirical evidence on sexual violence lends no sustained support to the liberal feminist position. What this evidence does support is a view of the normality of sexual violence by men towards women. This translates for women into what Stanko (1993) has called an 'ordinary fear'. Indeed, it is the potential normalcy of such experiences, which is taken as a starting-point for the radical feminist on this issue.

> Suddenly there are footsteps behind her. Heavy, rapid. A man's footsteps. She knows this immediately, just as she knows she must not look round. She quickens her pace in time to the quickening of her pulse. She is afraid. He could be a rapist. He could be a soldier, an harasser, a robber, a killer. He could be none of these. He could be a man in a hurry. He could be a man walking at his normal pace. But she fears him. She fears him because he is a man. She has reason to fear.
>
> (Morgan, 1989: 23)

This quote illustrates many women's experiential response to a well-known situation. It taps what radical feminists would argue is the root of women's fear of crime: the fear of sexual danger. In this sense, the fear of crime constitutes one end of a continuum of experiences (Kelly, 1988) in which women routinely learn to manage their daily lives, structured and informed by their relationships with the men in their lives: fathers, sons, partners, lovers, colleagues, co-workers. In these relationships many women during their lifetime learn to deal with harassment, incest, violence, and rape. These learning experiences are not easily separable into a public and private domain, that is, separate feelings of being safe in the street, at home, or on public transport. But they do constitute experiences that form the backcloth against which it is possible to understand the kinds of responses that are elicited in criminal victimisation surveys.

As Stanko (1987, 1988) has argued, the criminal victimisation survey, however formulated, whether as a national survey or a local geographically focused one, informed as it is by conceptual thinking rooted in a (male-defined) rationally based, risk management view of fear, cannot fully tap the kinds of experiences which underpin women's responses to this issue. Local, geographically focused surveys appear able to tap more incidents of criminal victimisation with which to compare levels of risk and fear, but these incidents are still measured as incidents. They are countable as isolated events which people experience, can identify and can talk about. They cannot tap the routinised, daily threat to personal security which characterises many women's lives. Criminal victimisation surveys, as incident – and respondent – led measures, in their very nature cannot be a measure through which social processes can be articulated. They are thus very limited in their capacity to either measure or capture the potentially deeply embedded nature of the social relationships which feed into anyone's experience of personal safety and security, but women's in particular.

Stanko (1990) offers one way of making sense of the findings of the criminal victimisation surveys. This, she argues, needs to be done in relation to what she calls 'climates of un-safety'. In other words it is useful to consider the ways in which women routinely negotiate their lives in circumstances which render them more or less safe. Women know how to do this. They know how to negotiate the workplace, the home, and the street. All of these domains are endemically structured in such a way as to place women on the edge of them, rendering their sense of ontological security (their personal sense of being) almost permanently precarious. This does not mean that women are in a permanent state of anxiety or neurotic! It does mean that their responses to criminal victimisation survey questions need to be understood in terms of a socio-structural location which locates them as being (essentially) emotional; that, is not rational. In empirical terms this may mean, of course, that it is just as important to listen to that which is not being spoken alongside that which is.

This position moves us from considering the precautionary strategies for personal safety which inform women's day-to-day lives (the real threat from men they know) to considering the mechanisms whereby any threat to white heterosexuality becomes a marker for creating an 'other', and hence responses which are deemed abnormal, irrational, emotional. This raises fundamental questions about whose standards are used as markers of a reasonable or a rational fear; whose standards are used as a marker of connecting that reasonable or rational fear to estimations of risk. Ultimately this raises questions about what are the domain conceptual assumptions here, what messages do they convey and for whom? Indeed Stanko (1997) takes this argument further by suggesting that women's understanding of risk and risk assessment amounts to such effective mechanisms of self-regulation that they reflect the extent to which crime safety talk constructs and reconstructs the 'governing of the soul': women perpetuated as the 'other'.

Of course, there is embedded in this version of exploring the fear of crime the domain assumptions of criminology as a discipline. Such assumptions not only result in the surface manifestation of gendered empirical findings (women as fearful, men as fearless, Goodey, 1997) but also reflect the deep structures of criminology and victimology as social sciences (see chapter 1). Such deep structures assume risk to be not only a gendered concept (see below) but also a forensic one (Walklate, 1997). These assumptions, alongside the scientism of positivism (Taylor, Walton and Young, 1973), result in the assumption that fear is measurable: in other words, something we know and experience as a feeling that can be translated into measurable entities associated with location or behaviour. Whilst Garofalo (1981) pointed to some of the difficulties associated with this, criminology has nevertheless proceeded to ignore the view that fear is something experienced in the immediate threat of physical danger and consequently (potentially) unmeasurable, and continued to pursue the social scientific imperative of valuing reason over emotion, that is, measuring the fear of crime. More recent work has, however, endeavoured to explore in different ways the idea of fear as a feeling. Before we consider this work, however, it will be useful to examine further the gendered presumptions associated with risk which are to be gleaned from this debate.

To summarise: so far we have identified what on the surface appear to be competing viewpoints on the relationship between rationality, risk and fear. On the one hand we have an argument which measures the disparity between levels of risk and levels of fear, and assigns irrationality to those for whom this disparity exists empirically. This view locates the expression of fear and the experience of risk as being largely a feature of the public domain, focusing on the street as a dangerous place. From this perspective it is young men who are most at risk from crime and who are a danger to each other; yet they express lower levels of fear than women (or the elderly).

On the other hand, a second view argues that levels of fear and levels of risk are commensurate with each other. In other words, once we acknowledge people's real levels of victimisation we can understand that their fears are not irrational but rational: they are a consequence of what they know might happen. This view recognises that fear has both its public and its private dimensions and usefully challenges what may or may not be considered to be rational. At the same time, however, it fails to treat women's knowledge as expert knowledge and remains locked into a conventional conceptual framework of rationality for understanding the potential connections between fear, risk and danger.

A third view transgresses the public private dichotomy by emphasising the familiar and the familial as dangerous. From this perspective women are most at risk from men that they know. This view questions the validity of the concept of fear, preferring instead to talk of safety and un-safety, and raises fundamental questions concerning the presumptions around what is meant by rationality and/or irrationality, and in whose terms, as yardsticks of behaviour. It also raises fundamental questions about connecting fear with risk without exploring their potential gendered nature.

Gendering risk

The emphasis on the threat of sexual danger which permeates radical feminism has resulted, arguably, in an uneasy equation between women and the fear of crime question. This is an uneasy equation for two reasons. First, it illustrates the tendency within radical feminism towards biological essentialism commented on in chapter 1. In this context this has two effects. It reflects a tendency to leave the relationship between men, masculinity and fear relatively untouched, and simultaneously places a uniformity on women's experiences that can also be problematic. Second, it is a view which, whilst having problematised the concept of 'fear' and its relationship with 'rationality', leaves relatively unchallenged what is understood by risk. Yet it is clear, as this chapter has suggested, that particular understandings of risk have wielded enormous influence on criminological thought in this area. It will be useful to explore both of these questions more fully.

If we take as our starting-point, then, the view that women's 'fear' of crime needs to be connected to their experience and knowledge of what might happen to them (that is, if we take account not only of the expressed fear of crime as measured by victimisation surveys but also the nature and extent of 'domestic' violence, including 'wife' rape, 'date' rape, and murder – see chapter 4), it is clear that women are exposed to much greater levels of risk of criminal victimisation than men. If we add to this women's experiences of what Crawford *et al* (1990) call 'public' abuse, i.e. sexual harassment in the street and at the workplace, it is clear that the main offenders under all these circumstances are men. From this broad empirical position the feminist challenge to criminology's focus on the public domain is more than justified. Women's fear of crime is undoubtedly connected to both their public and their private experience of men. This, of course, does not mean that women are only afraid of men they know or only afraid of strangers. The point is that these variously constituted threats of sexual danger permeate their public as well as their private life. If these threats are the backcloth against which to understand women's expressed 'fear' of crime, the question is raised as to how to theorise this empirical reality meaningfully.

One way of embarking upon such a theorisation is to locate women's experiences of criminal victimisation in relation to what Brittain (1989) has called 'masculinism' the ideological beliefs which naturalise the differences between men and women. In other words it is necessary to understand the lived experiences of both men and women by reference to deeply held beliefs and social expectations which legitimate the difference between men and women as being natural differences. One of the areas in which such differences are naturalised pertains to both male and female responses to danger. If it is acceptable to presume that such differences are ideological as opposed to biological constructs, then this takes its toll on both men and women. It is necessary, therefore, to consider not only women's experiences of men within this ideological framework but also the relationship for men between being male, the expression of masculinity and the potential for their relationship between fear and danger.

Two related questions therefore need to be considered. First, do women fear all men equally, or do they work with knowledge which renders some situations, some people, some places as being more uncertain than others as suggested earlier in this chapter? If the latter is the case, what does this imply for our view of the relationship between fear, risk and danger for women? Second, if masculinity is the lens through which we might begin to understand more effectively women's experiences of fear, risk, and danger, what does that lens also reveal to us about men and their relationship with these processes? We shall address this question first.

Men, fear and risk

Conventional criminal victimisation survey work, emanating from the Home Office and elsewhere, clearly identifies young men as being at a greater risk from street crime than any other category of people. Moreover, Crawford *et al* (1990) and Stanko (1990) have both pointed to men's greater unwillingness to admit to or talk about their fears relating to criminal victimisation in general. As Stanko and Hobdell state:

> Criminology's failure to explore men's experience of violence is often attributed to men's reluctance to report 'weakness'. This silence is, we are led to believe, a product of men's hesitation to disclose vulnerability.
> (Stanko and Hobdell, 1993: 400)

Indeed, on the face of the evidence frequently discussed in the fear of crime debate, it could be argued that it is (young) men who behave irrationally given their greater exposure to risk from crime and their lower reported levels of fear of crime. But this view accepts unquestioningly the notion that men, by virtue of being male, do not experience fear.

How men experience, understand, and then articulate their relationship with risk, fear and danger is relatively under-explored in the context of criminology and victimology. However, in a more general context Lyng (1990: 872-3) suggests that:

> Males are more likely to have an illusory sense of control over fateful endeavours because of the socialisation pressures on males to develop a skill orientation towards their environment. In so far as males are encouraged to use their skills to affect the outcome of all situations, even those that are almost entirely chance determined, they are likely to develop a distorted sense of their ability to control fateful circumstances.

This process leads Lyng to conclude that this is the reason why more males are involved in 'edgework' (behaviour on the edge, between order and chaos, living and dying, consciousness and unconsciousness).

Lyng's observations stem from ethnographic work carried out with a group of skydivers. However, what Lyng has identified here, perhaps, is something much more deeply rooted than experience of a different socialisation process. His insight also taps readily available ideological and cultural images that deem males and females capable of different things/images that emphasise a positive relationship between men and such risk-taking behaviours. On the other hand, the interviews with men, who were victims of different kinds of violence, reported in Stanko and Hobdell's (1993) work provide a somewhat different emphasis. The men in this study clearly proffered a range of responses to, relationship with, and experience of, violence which challenges any simplistic assumptions made in respect of men's relationship with, for example, danger in the form of personal violence.

It is important to note that the responses of these men – Lyng's skydivers and Stanko and Hobdell's victims of violence – need to be understood as being not just a part of, but also fundamentally connected with, a more general understanding of masculinity. A masculinity that values excitement, adventure, power and control as being what men do. These threads capture a version of masculinity to which all men relate but which some embrace to a greater or lesser degree: an aspect of what Connell (1987) has called 'hegemonic masculinity' (discussed in chapter 3). So whilst it is possible that Lyng's skydivers might have been asserting control over the uncontrollable in a very positive and ego-enhancing way, Stanko and Hobdell's work might be viewed as being much more about how men lost control in an ego-damaging way. The question of the motivation for, and experience of, each of these different types of behaviour and responses to it is, of course, a highly individual one. The central concern here, however, is to draw attention to the way in which each of these responses captures some sense of what it is that is culturally expected of a man, and how the variable responses to those cultural expectations may be rendered silent in the discourses which claim to be speaking about them.

One implication of this argument, then, is that it is necessary to locate men's relationship to fear and anxiety within a broader cultural context of the values associated with masculinity: a cultural context which promotes certain expressions of masculinity in preference to others and can provide a framework in which to understand both the inhibition of, and the expression of fear and of risk-taking behaviour in (young) men. That cultural context might not, however, provide the complete picture. Whilst it is important to recognise that thrill and excitement frequently go alongside risk, fear, and danger, and that all of these are frequently talked about in male terms, 'talking' frequently not only silences women's experiences but silences the experiences of some men too. There is a downside to the cultural expectations associated with maleness perhaps evidenced by the increasing number of suicides committed by young males recorded during the 1990s.

However, recognition of the interconnections between these threads of masculinity – risk, fear, danger, excitement and control – raises further problematic questions. First, given that it has been argued that these interconnections are mediated by what has been identified as masculinity, is it the case that the effects of a set of cultural norms and values can only be experienced by men, and are they experienced by all men in the same way? Second, are such values, risk, thrill, excitement, thereby denied to women?

Women, fear and risk

In the light of the kind of evidence mentioned above, it would be difficult to mount a convincing argument that women's 'fear' of crime is not connected to both their public and private experience of men (Warr, 1985, Stanko, 1985). This, of course, does not mean that all women are always afraid, or that women are always or only afraid of men that they know. The point is that these variously constituted threats of sexual danger permeate their public as well as their private life. If these threats are the backcloth against which to understand women's expressed 'fear' of crime, the question is raised of how to theorise this experiential reality in a meaningful way.

Locating women's fear of crime within such ideological imperatives of masculinism raises at least two related questions that need to be considered in more detail. First, do women fear all men? Intuitively the answer to this question must be 'no'. What women have access to is their own experiences and knowledge, some of which will be shared (probably with other women) and some of which will be unique to them. This knowledge will be partial and incomplete and is likely to reflect a range of different experiences with different men they have known. Whilst women may not fear all men, the evidence suggests that their sense of security will be informed by the sex of the person(s) they are with at any one point in time, the place they are in, their structural location, etc. Thus whilst women may not fear all men, they do have considerable knowledge about men that they know, places they deem dangerous, and the potential for sexual danger from men that they know and do not know. They might also be afraid of some women (as evidenced by work on bullying in schools, for example), though this does not mean necessarily that there is a symmetrical relationship between 'women's' fears of 'men' and their fears of other women (see Dobash and Dobash, 1992). The same, of course, might also be said of men in relation to men and women that they know.

A second question raised by this discussion is the issue of whether or not women only experience their day-to-day lives in relation to the perceived threat of sexual danger, or is there a sense in which they too, rather like the young men exemplified earlier, engage in 'risk seeking' behaviour? In other words, how and under what circumstances do women seek pleasure, excitement, and thrills; take risks, make choices? How might these processes manifest themselves?

A major area of excitement – and danger – seeking for women is around sex (usually with men) (Hollway, 1984). The way in which those excitements might be expressed are highly circumscribed (Holland *et al* 1994), given the powerful influence of 'passive femininity', the norms of heterosexual behaviour, and the ways in which (young) women's sexuality is policed; but this is nevertheless an area in which the 'Russian roulette' of sexuality and pregnancy is certainly played. It is not the only area in which women might seek thrills and excitement. It is used here merely to illustrate that the answer to the general question must be, of course, yes, women do seek pleasure, excitement and thrills; they do take risks. How and under what circumstances this occurs, however, has been explored relatively infrequently and when it has it has often been pathologised. Women are after all the 'Other', defined as being outside the discourse of risk and risk seeking, but does that really mean they are outside the experience? The work of Carlen *et al* (1985) in the context of female law-breaking behaviour is perhaps the exception that proves the rule here.

So locating women as the 'Other' casts them outside the discourse, though not necessarily outside the experience of risk seeking and, at the same time it arguably fails to capture the lived reality for some men. That discourse, reflecting as it does the cultural imperatives of what counts as legitimate for men and women, explains why women who choose to engage in risk-taking activities whether that be mountaineering, motorcycling or crime, receive such a bad press. It also demonstrates how the social sciences in general and criminology in particular have consistently failed to explore the gendered nature of some of their disciplinary domain assumptions. All of which returns us to the issue of whether there is another way of thinking about the questions of risk and fear and, by implication, ultimately returns us to the question of what counts as knowledge? Or put another way, how accurate is it to think of science, whether natural or social, as a social practice that is rooted in reason at the expense of emotion? But first, is there another way of thinking about risk, fear and danger?

Risk and danger: alternative viewpoints

Douglas (1992: 41) states that:

> In spite of evidence to the contrary, avoiding loss is written into the psychology textbooks as the normal, rational, human motive. But all this means is that the commercial, risk-averse culture has locally vanquished the risk-seeking culture, and writes off the latter as pathological or abnormal. To ignore such a large segment of the human psychology tells us more about assumptions upholding the modern industrial way of life than about human nature's risk-taking propensities.

This statement crystallises a key dilemma for the way in which criminology has employed the concepts of fear, risk and danger, some of which has already been articulated by Sparks (1992).

As was stated earlier, Sparks rails against criminology's simplified use of the concepts of fear, risk and danger. He points out that these concepts, in their everyday usage, connote far more complex and subtle an understanding of, and relationship with, day-to-day experiences, than any survey technique is capable of detecting. Moreover, Sparks goes on to suggest that it is important not to presume the significance that feelings of risk and danger have for people and in what context. He states that:

> Crime presents people with certain dangers of which they must take account as best they may. In taking account of these dangers each of us engages in some version of risk analysis. But the resources available to us in making the necessary judgements are both enormously extensive, varied, complex and inherently incomplete.
>
> (1992: 132)

Sparks' analysis, then, fundamentally questions criminology's presumption of a straightforward connection between fear and risk, mediated by rationality and/or irrationality, in the fear of crime debate (as discussed above). He is absolutely correct to challenge that debate in these terms. Such a challenge follows logically from the position espoused by Douglas (1992). This challenge, however, needs to be taken further. As Douglas observes, and some of the work cited earlier illustrates, it is misleading to address the concept of risk as though it only refers to risk avoidance. Douglas's (and others') work raises the question of what do we do about risk-seeking behaviour?

Understanding and accommodating the phenomenon of 'risk-seeking' behaviour equips us with a view of human beings which, as Douglas has pointed out, appears to be less tenable in the modern world. Risk avoidance as a key social and psychological strategy appears to have become increasingly predominant as the technological world has advanced. Despite the control of the environment and the consequent reduction of risk that is presumed to proceed alongside improved technology, it is clear that we accept almost implicitly that being human is about taking risks. More particularly we accept that it is a concomitant requirement almost for (young) men to seek out pleasure and excitement, i.e. to take risks. Indeed, it is a deeply embedded cultural expectation that they do so. It is, of course, not a prerequisite that such (young) men also be criminal. The phenomenon of (young) policemen engaged in a high-speed car chase of other (young) men is shot through for all parties with the desire for excitement, pleasure, fear and risk. The behaviour and the motivation may be the same, though the legitimacy attached to it is obviously different. Yet when we examine the fear of crime debate, risk appears to have been equated only with danger, that is with risk avoidance. The question is, how has this happened? This process is connected with the ideas addressed in chapter 1. In other words, it is necessary to explore the domain assumptions of criminology (and victimology) that appear to have structured this process.

Domain assumptions of risk

The inability of social sciences to construct a debate around risk in terms of risk-seeking behaviour as opposed to risk-avoiding behaviour reflects what Gouldner once called the 'domain assumptions' of social science (see chapter 1). In many respects the social sciences have accepted implicitly the use of risk as a forensic concept. Risk and risk analysis are features of the modern era in which the calculation of probabilities in determining outcomes has been a feature of what is culturally expected from the scientific enterprise (Douglas, 1992). That such an enterprise is also implicitly connected with the desire to control the environment concomitant with the valorisation of masculine knowledge (Harding, 1991) constitutes the backcloth against which criminology has drawn the parameters to its debate on the relationship between fear, risk and danger. What this comprises needs to be spelt out a little more clearly.

In a different context Dake (1992) has argued that 'perceived probabilities of harm are not merely subjective but may best be viewed as inter-subjective – a matter of shared cognition'. If this is the case, as Dake (1992: 33) argues, 'Such world views provide powerful cultural lenses, magnifying one danger, obscuring another threat, selecting others for minimal attention or even disregard.' If this view is correct, by analogy it is possible to argue that it is cultural processes which underpin the risks and dangers we see as opposed to the ones we do not see. These cultural processes lay claims and expectations to control those risks we see at the feet of science, technology, and policy in general, including criminology. Recognising the inter-subjective aspects to the way in which risk has been understood provides a possible insight into how risk has become equated with danger within criminology. Understanding this, however, requires that we understand and accept that the discipline of criminology (and victimology) has a particular character informed, structured by, and implicitly accepting of a 'malestream' view of being scientific. In the context of this discussion this is revealed in the following way.

The transcendent qualities associated with both science and masculinity takes us down a route in which the search is on for a situation of zero risk. This would constitute the ultimate control by man of his environment. In one sense, then, emphasis on risk avoidance reflects a version of (masculine) knowledge that prefers to assert control via reasonable and rational argument rather than by brute force. Because this version of knowledge values reason, and risk avoidance is presumed to be reasonable, risk-seeking behaviour is downgraded, obscured, hidden from the debate though not from social reality or experience. It is no coincidence that these values concur with those which support a conventional view of science and what counts as scientific knowledge, a view of science that chapter 1 argued was clearly commensurate with much mainstream criminological and victimological work; a view which separates reason from emotion and, hence the drive to measure the fear of crime.

The pervasiveness of this search for zero risk facilitates an understanding of a range of questions including the persistence of such questions, as 'Why doesn't she leave?' in the context of 'domestic' violence, for example, a question often asked by both men and women, reflecting what would be considered to be a rational course of action: the avoidance of risk. But this search for zero risk is reflected within criminology in other ways too. The search for the cause of crime has never been that separate from the search for control of crime: crime prevention. An emphasis on risk avoidance fits so much more neatly for a discipline implicated in the policy-making process in this way. However, the effects of this are far reaching in terms of adequately understanding both the cause and the effect of criminal behaviour alongside the distorting effect that this has with respect to the fear of crime debate.

To summarise: criminology's implicit acceptance of a conventional scientific agenda and its associated modernist stance (its policy orientation) has resulted in that discipline's failure to work more critically with the concept of risk. Consequently this failure has impoverished criminology's understanding of the experience of the fear of crime by tying that issue to a presumption of risk avoidance; that is, a rational view of the risk management of behaviour. This has resulted in, for the most part, a masculinist interpretation and debate of what counts as risky behaviour; and simultaneously the converse, what counts as dangerous behaviour. This particular way of understanding risk, tied as it is to particular views of what counts as rational knowledge and who can possess such knowledge, is a fundamental reflection of criminology's and victimology's inability to see how their own conceptual schema are gendered (Cain, 1989; Smart, 1990 and chapter 1).

This is one way in which it is possible to see that criminology's failure to engage critically with these issues also reflects its inability to address the pervasive effects of masculinity, not only in terms of understanding and explaining crime but also reflexively as a way of understanding the nature of the discipline itself. In the context of the fear of crime debate criminology's (and victimology's) failure to engage critically in this way has resulted in the valorisation by these disciplines of a particular masculine world view, that of rational risk-assessed decision-making, a world view that downgrades alternatives, including that of risk-seeking behaviour. In so doing, it not only impacts upon the way in which much criminological work hides men's fears and their thrills but simultaneously consigns women to possessing 'legitimate fears'. This also has the effect of denying women their potential for risk and excitement. Thus these deeply embedded assumptions within criminology, though challenged by radical feminism, fail to understand risk and danger as gendered experiences.

The consequences of this are not only to be found in partially understood conceptualisations. They are also to be found in policy terms. Thus it can be argued that 'blame the victim' is the key message which emanates from work which attempts to explain the disparity between risk and fear by reference to irrationality. On the other hand, 'understand the victim' emanates from an agenda which is concerned to establish the rationality of the victim. Understanding the victim, however, points to a broader system that creates victims and victimisation in the first instance. That broader framework, from the radical feminist position, needs to be understood and articulated as patriarchal. Hence 'all men are potential rapists'. However, once the structuring processes articulated by the radical feminist are made more visible, structuring the victim through the lens of masculinity renders the impact of that patriarchal structure simultaneously both more pervasive and more complex. This is the point at which understanding the gendered nature of the very concepts in which the fear of crime has been debated, leads to a much more subtle understanding of what such fear might be about. This has led some analysts to discuss anxieties about crime rather than fear.

Fear as feeling: anxiety?

As suggested above, Garofalo (1981) observed that fear was best understood as a feeling in reaction to an immediate threat. However, more recent contributions to the fear of crime debate have taken the notion of fear as feeling in three rather different directions. Bannister *et al* (1997) and Ditton *et al* (1999) have certainly concerned themselves with the ways in which criminal victimisation surveys can be utilised to extract differential feeling responses to crime. Their work has particularly exposed anger as a feeling response to crime that seems to be differently mediated by sex. In other words men report feeling angry more frequently than women do, a response that may be connected to the uncomfortable impact that feeling vulnerable has, especially to a man's sense of his masculinity. The work of Hollway and Jefferson (1997) on the one hand, and Taylor (1995, 1997) on the other, reflect interesting different uses of the concept of anxiety with which to explore expressed concerns (feelings) about crime and criminal victimisation. Each of these approaches will be addressed in turn.

Hollway and Jefferson (1997) adopt an explicit psychoanalytic use of the term anxiety. Their work reflects the presumption that anxiety is a universal feature of the human condition and their concern is to map, through the use of individual biographies, the extent to which people's expressed fear of crime (dis)connects with the mobilisation of defence mechanisms against anxiety. In exploring fear in this way one of their main concerns is to expose the paradoxes evident in the interconnections between risk and rationality present in the earlier discussion. Their analysis reveals many and varied responses to the external threat of crime mediated by the state and status of individuals' internal threats to their sense of security.

Taylor *et al* (1996) and Taylor (1996, 1997) adopt a different interpretation of anxiety. Taylor *et al* (1996) use anxiety not in its psychoanalytical sense but as rooted in an exploration of locally constructed and locally understood 'structures of feeling'. Taylor (1996) develops this thesis by arguing for the need to understand the 'elective affinity' between the growth and impact of locally constructed coalition movements (neighbourhood watch schemes, for example) and the populations of the residential suburbs (especially in the United Kingdom). In this understanding, perceptions about crime and the fear of crime become linked to people's perceptions and experience of other kinds of 'urban fortunes'. Such perceptions are fuelled by myths and folklore rooted in what is locally known about crime in their area and simultaneously informs the management of such community safety coalitions. In this sense such 'structures of feeling' about crime act in a metaphorical capacity for (other) related concerns about the locality.

Both these uses of anxiety display a concern with Giddens' (1991) notion of 'ontological security' and the wider context of the impact of late modern societies on individual lives. For Hollway and Jefferson (1997):

> In an age of uncertainty, discourses that appear to promise a resolution to ambivalence by producing identifiable victims and blameable villains are likely to figure prominently in the States' attempts to impose social order.

Whilst their view also presumes that the impact of those discourses may be (infinitely) individually variable, that individual variability has to be situated in the context of a late modern, risk-managed society. Taylor (1997) too wishes to situate his understanding of people's expressed concerns and practices in relation to crime, in the context of the 'risk positions' in which people find themselves, though is sceptical of the ability of the risk theorists to 'recommend any public engagement (or indeed a personal praxis) with these global changes' (*ibid*: 60). So, to borrow a phrase from Hollway and Jefferson, though used in a rather different context, what do each of these positions say in respect of what is knowable and actionable in the context of the fear of crime?

For Hollway and Jefferson the answer to this question is a matter of individual biography, albeit constructed within a particular context; for Taylor it is a matter of finding a way to re-institute a conversation about the public interest, albeit a locally nuanced public interest. Expressed in a different way each of these views adopts a different emphasis to the question of feeling. Hollway and Jefferson are more about feeling than structure with the consequent problem of under-generalisability. Taylor is more about structure than feeling with the consequent problem of over-generalisability. So whilst each differently explores the paradox evidenced in the fear-risk conundrum, both face the problem of establishing the validity of their particular interpretation of that evidence, although interestingly enough each draws upon the importance of situating an understanding of individual or collective responses to the 'fear of crime' within the wider context of the 'risk society'.

Many social scientists, social commentators, and indeed politicians, draw on the notion of (late) modern society as a risk society. Giddens (1991) and Beck (1992) have differently interpreted this idea. However, in their analyses both are keen to separate the notion of risk from the notion of hazard or danger. A risk society is not one that has become more hazardous or dangerous. As Giddens (1998: 27) states: 'Rather, it is a society increasingly preoccupied with the future (and also with safety) which generates the notion of risk'.

Thus we are reminded that in traditional societies the concept of risk was quite differently constructed. Everyday dangers were simply that which people learned to take for granted or they came from God. As Giddens (*ibid*) states, 'The idea of risk is bound up with the aspiration to control and particularly the idea of controlling the future'. So in this sense, risk is not danger (despite the elision between these notions in the discussion of the dangerous offender, for example). Risk is a product of two related processes: the end of tradition and the end of nature.

Giddens and Beck agree that the increasing salience of a notion of risk is embedded in the transition from a pre-modern (or traditional) society to a modern society (the end of tradition). It is also embedded in the emergence of science as the rational foundation of knowledge and the knowledge production process. This second feature of societal change, the end of nature, does not mean that nature no longer matters but is intended to imply that we are now not so much concerned with what nature can do to us but what we have done, and can do, to nature. In highlighting the importance of the end of nature what both of these analysts are alluding to is the extent to which science has not only provided a means by which risks might be controlled but has also contributed to those risks (see also Adams 1995). Moreover science has also become deeply embedded in the risks that we see as opposed to the ones that we do not see (Wildavsky, 1988). What has become an apparent product of these processes appears to be the cultural drive for risk avoidance: the search for zero risk, returning us to an earlier theme of this chapter. However these theorists of risk society also talk about the concept of trust. Is this a more meaningful way to begin to understand people's relationship to the fear of crime?

Fear and trust

Arguably work emanating from the feminist movement, especially radical feminism, has been both implicitly and explicitly concerned to problematise the question of trust in relation to women's experiences of criminal victimisation. That work has rendered clearly problematic the notion of the safe haven of the home. Put another way, it has challenged the view that women need not fear men that they know: work colleagues, boyfriends, and relatives. These were 'trustworthy' men. The view that

'All men are potential rapists' offers a definite challenge to such a presumption. The recognition that the familiar and the familial are not necessarily any more trustworthy than the stranger, puts a very different picture on the screen of who is and who is not trustworthy. A picture which feminist research has demonstrated routinely informs women's sense of 'ontological security' (see Stanko, 1997). The question of trust, however, has largely remained absent or hidden in social scientific work in general and has been even more rarely applied to the issue of crime.

The concept of trust has been relatively under-explored in the social sciences. In discussing the question of 'ontological security' Giddens (1991) has argued that trust is most clearly evidenced in traditional societies through kinship relations, local communities or religious commitment. However, he goes on to argue that the absence of these mechanisms in late modern societies renders trust no more than a matter for individual contractual negotiation. Luhmann (1989) presents a similar argument. Gellner (1989) too suggests that urban life is incompatible with trust and social cohesion suggesting that such processes are rooted in rural, tribal traditions. Yet as Fukuyama (1996) implies, trust is also an essential part of modern life. Without it economic relations cannot flourish, and these are relations that cannot either be completely controlled. Trust is therefore essential. The kinds of trust that exist, however, may not always be necessarily about creating 'regular honest behaviour' as Fukuyama states. It may just as likely be about creating regular dishonest behaviour. Arguably, it is the regularity and reliability of behaviour that sustains or threatens social relationships.

Giddens (1991) and Beck (1992) both argue that the increasing awareness of the importance of trust is the concomitant effect of a greater awareness of the possible future damage of risk-taking activity alongside the challenge to universalism posed by postmodernism. As Misztal (1996: 239) states:

> By destroying the grounds for believing in a universal truth, postmodernity does not make our lives more easy but only less constrained by rules and more contingent. It demands new solutions based on the tolerant co-existence of a diversity of cultures. Yet although post modernism encourages us to live without an enemy, it stops short of offering constructive bases for mutual understanding and trust.

In order to 'live without an enemy', however, one requires trust. But how does trust manifest itself? Nelken (1994) raises the value of exploring the question of trust in the context of the importance to criminology of engaging in comparative research. In his review of what might be learned by engaging in a comparative analysis of white-collar and/or corporate crime, Nelken (1994) suggests that a number of questions become pertinent for criminology. These questions are: whom can you trust, how do you trust, how much can you trust, and when can you trust?

Such questions are pertinent not only for the crimes of the powerful. The argument presented by Walklate and Evans (1999) also supports the usefulness of exploring the mechanisms of trust that underpin people's sense of ontological security in high crime areas. They suggest the value of conceptualising the fear of crime through a notion of a 'square of trust' (See also Evans, Fraser and Walklate 1996; Walklate, 1997). The actual manifestation of this square of trust may be differently mediated by the nature of community relationships, age, gender, ethnicity, etc. all of which are discussed elsewhere (*ibid*).

Conclusion

This chapter has sought to argue that not only is 'fear' a gendered phenomenon (not a new observation) but that the concepts of 'risk' and 'danger' are also gendered (a relatively new observation). It has also endeavoured to demonstrate the extent to which the domain assumptions of criminology and victimology with respect to the question of risk has rendered its understanding of the fear of crime debate somewhat partial and limited. In this discussion it has not been the intention to downgrade the importance of women's likely chances of being murdered, or of being raped in marriage, or of finding themselves in a violent relationship (see chapter 4). Indeed, the intention has been the opposite. By drawing on these issues we can see that the common feature between them is not only women's fear and the threat to their personal security, but the way in which all of these processes are mediated by versions of masculinity expressed by the men in their lives. Thus whilst the fear of crime debate has certainly rendered the fear of crime as an issue to which politicians and policy-makers must attend, however inappropriately (Stanko, 1990), the debate in the policy field frequently marginalises the 'reality' of women's fears and renders invisible those fears experienced by men. The knowledge produced by criminology and the conceptual basis of much of that knowledge has been intimately connected in the processes that have had this effect.

It is quite clear, then, that the relationship between women, crime and criminology and men, crime and criminology has been done a disservice in criminology's unthinking acceptance and assertion of a simplistic understanding of the concepts of fear, risk and danger. In Scully's (1990) terms it is time that we named some of these issues as men's problems including, perhaps, the inability of criminology (and victimology) to deal with them and moved the conceptual debate further on in a way which better captures people's (men's and women's) experiences of their day-to-day lives in which other conceptual schema may be more meaningful.

Such an approach might ultimately demand that we transcend the dualism that separates reason from emotion, an issue to which we shall return in the Conclusion. The next chapter will explore the ways in which scrutinising criminological and victimological work through the lens of masculinity might enhance our understanding of the nature and extent of sexual violence.

Suggestions for further reading

Stanko, E. (1990) *Everyday Violence*. An accessible record of the ways in which women's experiences of both the public and the private domain permeate their sense of security.

Bell, N.J. and Bell, R.W. (1993) *Adolescent Risk Taking*. An interesting edited collection in which the concept of risk is explored in a number of different ways; illustrating perhaps, how much criminology and victimology have yet to come to terms with in relation to this issue.

Matthews, R. and Young, J. (Eds.)(1992) *Issues in Realist Criminology*. Offers a feel for the strengths and weaknesses of left realist criminology from a number of different dimensions.

4 Gendering sexual violence

Introduction

Chapter 3 illustrated the different ways in which the fear of crime debate has been addressed. It brought to our attention the extent to which women's expressed fear of crime as recorded by criminal victimisation survey work may more accurately be described as a fear of sexual danger. The purpose of this chapter is to explore more fully what that fear of sexual danger comprises, how we might begin to understand it, and what issues have yet to be rendered more visible in the work focusing on this area. In order to achieve this we shall focus primarily on three issues: rape, child abuse and 'domestic' violence.

These issues have been chosen because they highlight a number of problems for both the criminological and victimological gaze. As substantive issues they challenge conventional definitions of what constitutes the criminal. As empirical issues they render visible the gendered nature of criminal activity as suggested in the Introduction. At a theoretical level they put to the test the domain assumptions of much criminological and victimological thought. In policy terms they pose fundamental questions for policing, housing, the law, etc. These are also issues that strike at the heart of much political rhetoric surrounding notions of the family and family harmony. As such they represent contested terrain in which perspectives on policy are differently informed by the different theoretical and ideological perspectives on these issues. For these reasons, then, they constitute useful substantive areas in which to detail some of the more general limitations associated with criminological approaches to crime and gender. We shall discuss some of the issues surrounding the question of rape first of all.

Understanding rape

Rape has been studied primarily as something that men do to women. Estimates vary as to the likelihood of women experiencing rape or sexual assault. Some of that variation depends on how rape has been measured and defined. Significantly, estimates vary according to whether it is the incidence or the prevalence of such experiences which are under scrutiny. *Incidence rates* refer to the number of incidents occurring during a specified time period. *Prevalence rates* refer to the number of incidents occurring over a lifetime. For example, the 1988 British Crime Survey offers an incidence estimate of 60,000 sexual offences against women for 1987 of which about 13,000 were reported. Hall's (1985) prevalence study reported that one in six women have experienced rape and one in three sexual assault in their lifetime. Both Russell (1990) and Painter (1991) report a prevalence figure of one in seven for women who have experienced rape in marriage; and a study conducted amongst Cambridge undergraduate students reported a prevalence figure of 1 in 10 for 'date rape' (reported by *Public Eye*, 14 February 1992).

These figures are complicated by the fact that these studies do not define rape in exactly the same way. Some studies use definitions which resemble legal definitions in order to facilitate comparisons with police statistics (Russell's work [1990], for example). Other studies allow the respondents to define their own experiences (Hall [1985], for example). The former minimises the experience of rape the latter maximises it.

The British Crime Survey data, whilst latterly only offering estimated figures which combine rape and sexual assault, probably comes closest to identifying the kinds of incidents which are likely to count in relation to the workings of the criminal justice system, whereas Russell (1990) and Painter (1991) both deal with the legally (still) more contentious issue of 'rape in marriage'. Other work, which has attempted to measure the extent of 'date rape', taps yet another dimension to women's experiences in this area. In other words identifying the extent of rape, either as an incidence measure or as a prevalence measure, can be fraught with difficulties. So whilst measurement and definition pose problems, what is not so difficult to document is understanding why the issue of rape is so emotive and why it has been, and still is, such a focus of concern for many feminists.

Feminist campaigns around the issue of rape have been concerned to challenge both the legal definitions of rape and the myths associated with rape. The legal definition in England and Wales is problematic because, up until recently it focuses on one particular act of sexual access (a penis penetrating a vagina). This, feminists argue, reflects a male heterosexual obsession with one object and one opening. In addition the legal definition centres on the question of consent (or being reckless as to that consent) which places the burden of proof on the victim. Moreover, until recently it excluded married partners. Feminists contend that this kind of definition does not resonate with women's experiences. However, the Criminal Justice and Public Order Act (1994) which came into force in 1995, widened the definition of rape to include the non-consensual penetration by a penis of the anus as well as the vagina. This made consensual anal sex between heterosexuals legal for the first time and made legal the possibility of 'male rape' (the questions that this issue raises are returned to below.)

If we take seriously the evidence cited above from the Home Office figures through to the figures on 'rape in marriage' and 'date rape' they convey the view that for many women rape is an 'ordinary' experience: an experience which is rather more common than is generally supposed. And indeed, it is an experience that is not solely confined to a penis penetrating a vagina. Women experience rape, whatever opening is violated by whatever implement, as a life-threatening experience. This fundamentally challenges both the legal definition and the issue of how to understand 'consent'.

In addition to questioning the legal definition of rape, feminist campaigning is concerned to challenge the various myths associated with rape. For example, 'a woman runs faster with her knickers up than a man with his trousers down'; that stranger rape is 'real' rape; that women frequently make up allegations of rape (they 'cry rape'); that rape only occurs out of doors; that a prostitute cannot be raped; when a woman says 'no' she really means 'yes', etc. The persistence of these myths, as illustrated, for example, by the media coverage given to alleged cases of 'date rape', clearly indicates how important that campaigning still is. Such media coverage does not always aid the feminist cause, however, as two cases in 2000 demonstrated that in some circumstances particular women have been shown to 'cry rape'. Such cases notwithstanding, these myths, as well as being potentially damaging to any particular woman alleging a case of rape, also implicitly reflect a number of presumptions concerning the rapist. There are myths to be challenged here too; particularly the idea that men cannot control themselves once sexually aroused.

One way in which feminist work has posed a very serious challenge to some of the myths attached to women who allege rape has been to document the quite complex and subtle distinctions women make between 'pressurised sex', and 'coerced sex', with men they know and the difference between identifying an incident as rape with men that they know, as compared with rape by a stranger (Kelly, 1988). This evidence provides a clear challenge to those who believe (and many still do) that women 'cry rape'. On the whole, women do not easily choose the word rape to describe their experiences. They know the consequences for doing so. Understanding this is very pertinent to facilitating an understanding of the way in which the issue of 'date rape' has been received.

Kennedy (1992) expresses the problem in this way. A woman may have consented to dinner, to a 'good night' kiss, or to a cup of coffee; none of these activities, however, give blanket consent to any further activity. Persuading juries of this can be a difficult business since such activities are relatively easily transformed in the judicial process and by 'common sense' (or as Cain [1989] would say, 'co-man sense') understandings into the cultural activity of seduction. This highlights a problem not only because juries need to be persuaded, and are indeed persuadable, by the way in which barristers use these cultural preconceptions in the courtroom (see chapter 6), but also because, in an everyday sense, many men (and women) have bought into those same cultural stereotypes.

This does not mean, however, that 'date rape' or any other kind of rape does not occur. What this draws our attention to is the disjunction between the extent to which women experience sexual violence and yet simultaneously can remain complicit in the process of blaming the victim. In other words women, on a jury, or anywhere else for that matter, often believe that they would never let rape happen to them. They would never get themselves into such a situation. There is a flavour of this in the widely publicised essay by Roiphe (1994).

Of course, there may be some women for whom their gender and sexual relations are negotiated in their terms. But it is equally important to remember that this kind of specific experience does not apply to all. Blaming the victim means that we do not have to address our own uncomfortable experiences.

It would appear, however, that women's willingness to report rape is changing. Thus it may be that some women are less willing to remain complicit than was once the case, though others would argue that this is a consequence of improved police practices (see chapter 5). Such debates notwithstanding, what is of particular importance in endeavouring to construct any understanding of rape is, what about the rapist?

Much of the work of the 1950s and 1960s dealing with the issue of rape centred on the offender. That work either implied what Scully (1990) has called the 'disease model' of rape (in other words, an understanding that the offender was mentally or sexually 'disordered' in some way); or it reflected 'victim blaming' of some kind (in other words, focused on the extent to which what happened to the victim was 'precipitated' by her own behaviour). Indeed, it was this latter model of explaining rape that provoked the initial feminist response to work in this area in the 1970s (see the discussion of victimology in chapter 1). Another version of this way of thinking about rape, emanating from the work of evolutionary biologists, emerged during the late 1990s. This work claims that the (innate) male desire, or need, to propagate the species results in the rape behaviour of, especially young men, encouraged by the dress code of young women. However, Scully and Marolla's (1993) analysis of how convicted rapists feel about rape moves our understanding of rape and the rapist towards an understanding of that activity in terms of men and the relationship between men, rape and masculinity.

Scully and Marolla identify a range of motivations for rape amongst their sample of convicted men, from a desire to 'put them (women) in their place' to an exciting form of impersonal sex. As one man said, 'After rape, I always felt like I had just conquered something, like I had just ridden the bull at Gilley's' (reported in Scully and Marolla, 1993: 41).

Scully and Marolla argue that statements like these reveal the cultural roots of attitudes towards sex and aggression embedded in masculinity. Such cultural roots connect the act of rape with the transcendent search for control as expressed through conquest and penetration that Cameron and Fraser (1987) consider to be at the heart of masculinity. The men in Scully's study saw rape as a low-risk high-reward crime and whilst this might be differently expressed by different offenders, a common thread could be identified in their presumptions of normal forms of heterosexuality, a thread which can be identified in the gendered nature of murder statistics in terms of the phenomenon of 'male sexual propriety' (Wilson and Daly, 1992) and in 'domestic' violence as a product of unequal power relationships (see below). Re-casting rape in these terms helps an understanding of why it is difficult to see the 'ordinariness' of rape and sexual assault. Women say 'no'. Men fail (or refuse) to hear it. There is little in the heart of the cultural expectations associated with masculinity to encourage them to hear it. This does not mean that they cannot.

So far we have focused on rape in heterosexual terms. *Rape also occurs between men and between women*. These acts and experiences are frequently even more invisible than marital rape and/or date rape. A study compiled by McMullen (1990) on 'male rape' provides a useful insight into the similarity of the experience and impact of rape on men. It also illustrates the problematic nature of the law in relation to those experiences and the extent to which heterosexual myths perpetuate responses to them. For example, McMullen states 'The sexual identity, then, of the vast majority of male rapists is heterosexual', thus challenging the presumption that male rape equals homosexual rape. Indeed the advice given in this book to young heterosexual males on how to reduce the risks of rape significantly parallels the crime prevention advice given to women on this issue (McMullen, 1990: 132). Moreover, the consequences which he identifies of not 'breaking the silence' on male rape largely echo some of the excuses given by Scully's (1990) rapists for committing rape; they knew they could get away with it.

A more recent study completed by Lees (1997) endorses some of the comments made by McMullen. She states that:

> One of the most damaging insults to be thrown at a man is to call him a woman, a bitch, or a cunt. The act of coercive buggery can be seen as a means of taking away manhood, of emasculating other men and thereby enhancing one's own power.
>
> (Lees, 1997: 106)

This kind of analysis encourages a critical examination not only of how women experience the impact of what Connell (1987) has called 'hegemonic masculinity', but also the impact that this has on some men too (such an analysis also connects us to the whole question raised by Collier [1998] of presumed heterosexuality: about which, in terms of the nature and extent of actual sexual practices we know very little, and perpetuates all kinds of silences for those who do not consider themselves to be heterosexual). Of course, Lees may be correct to assert that male rape may be more meaningfully understood and explained as an ascendant form of masculinity that subordinates femininity and some forms of masculinity (Connell, 1987: 183). Increasing concern about 'male rape' also makes possible the opportunity, in policy and resource allocation terms, that because of its impact on men, striking at the heart of their identity, it should also be taken more seriously (see Gillespie, 1996, for an analysis of these developments).

To summarise: in 1981 Reeves Sanday identified the possibility of what she called the 'rape free' society, one in which there is no obvious hierarchical relationship between men and women, and in which the notion of sexual propriety does not exist. The changes, both structural and personal, for men and for women, which such a society demands, are considerable. They strike at the heart not only of masculinity but also at the heart of all our intimate and not so intimate relationships. It may be, of course, that some of these structural and personal changes are occurring for some people but, as the empirical evidence reveals, the experience of rape is not unique and therefore, consequently, neither is it a behaviour which is the preserve of some sex-craved monster.

The evidence discussed here stresses the 'normalcy' of the experience of rape and sexual assault. Rape is the ordinary product of ordinary (male, heterosexual) behaviour. It touches upon all our experiences both male and female. It is its ordinariness that renders it so difficult to grasp and embrace. It challenges us all to examine our relationships and ourselves very carefully. In so doing it can make us all uncomfortable. And so it should. Next we shall consider a further substantive issue which also makes us uncomfortable and poses problems for criminology: child abuse.

Understanding child abuse

Child abuse raises many of the same problems of definition and consequent empirical investigation as the issue of rape (see Walklate, 1989: chapter 3). It is also fraught with very similar emotional and political difficulties as it too challenges deeply embedded presumptions about the family and family harmony. It is included here for consideration since not only does it encourage us to consider the full range of potential violences perpetrated against women and some men as children but also because it encourages us to consider further the gender dimensions to that range of violences.

It must be remembered that childhood was not always a protected stage in the life cycle. Children were not always deemed in need of care and protection. Indeed, some would argue that the historical construction of childhood is a development concomitant to the emergence of the modern age. Moreover it is along with this historical construction of childhood as a protected stage in the life cycle that the myths associated with childhood, particularly the notion of 'childhood innocence' (Morris, 1987) emerged. It is against the backcloth of such myths that responses to child abuse need to be understood. These myths suggesting as they do that abuse is a product of childhood fantasy, that the child is a seducer, that the mother colludes with the abuse of the child, or that no harm is done because what happens only happens to a child, serve to hide the gendered nature of this kind of experience.

Child abuse can be sub-divided into child physical abuse and child sexual abuse. This dividing line, however, can be somewhat arbitrary since the injuries sustained by sexual abuse are also very physical, especially in very young children. It is also difficult to establish an accurate and complete empirical record of the extent of child abuse. But what is clear from the empirical evidence available is that about one in four girls and one in ten boys are likely to experience some form of abuse during their childhood. In addition that empirical evidence also indicates that both men and women engage in child physical abuse but child sexual abuse is an activity dominated by men. If we are to understand child abuse as a gendered activity it is necessary to formulate an understanding of the issue which encompasses what appears to be rather disparate empirical findings such as these.

Early explanations of child physical abuse focused on what Parton (1985) has called the 'disease model of parenting'. In other words, they attempted to locate abusive behaviour in the characteristics of individual parents: becoming parents too young, being physically abused themselves, personality traits, and psychopathic disorders. They were also explanations which were geared towards social work intervention. In a similar vein, early work with child sexual abusers revealed that paedophiles were shy, timid, and suffered from low self-esteem, and that fathers who sexually abused their children overvalued, that is expected too much from, family life (West, 1985). Explanations like these, of course, reflect certain presumptions concerning normal family life and do not fully explain the gender dimensions to the empirical findings commented on above. Hearn (1989), however, has attempted to develop a framework for understanding child abuse that seeks to embrace the empirical evidence more adequately, and, addresses the gendered dimensions to this phenomenon.

Hearn (1989) suggests that in order to fully understand the nature and extent of child abuse and who its perpetrators are, it is necessary to theorise more carefully about the nature of male violence. In other words, for him, it is necessary to locate the practice of child abuse within a framework of normal forms of masculinity rather than within an ideology of dangerousness; to look at the socio-cultural forms which condone such behaviour rather than to search for disordered individuals or disordered individual families. Consequently, Hearn opts for an understanding that combines an analysis of patriarchy with some of the insights of the feminist re-working of Freud, found in particular in the work of Nancy Chodorow.

Thus, for Hearn, it is necessary to recognise the radical feminist claim that all men have the potential for (sexual) violence. At the same time it is also necessary to offer an explanation as to why particular men are violent and under what circumstances. In other words, Hearn recognises that family life is patterned by dominant-submissive power relations derived from patriarchal social relationships that give men the power in those settings. But not all men use that power violently towards their children or their partners. Understanding why some men do not may be as crucial as understanding why some men do. Hearn's analysis ultimately draws upon a feminist-informed psychoanalytic framework as a way of considering how it is that some men identify more strongly with the central tenets of a masculine identity than others. What is of significance for the discussion here is that Hearn's work on this issue raises a similar theoretical question to that raised by the work of Scully (1990); that is, one way of understanding some of the complexity of the issues associated with child abuse is through an understanding of men and their relationship with masculinity. Our third substantive issue for consideration overlaps to some extent with the first two: that is, 'domestic' violence.

Ways of understanding 'domestic' violence

Before we can understand the nature of 'domestic' violence it is important to recognise that the term itself conveys important messages concerning the nature of the phenomenon to be understood. The reader will have noticed that this author has adopted the style of Edwards (1989) in placing apostrophes around the word 'domestic' in order to indicate its problematic status. The abuse of women by their male partners has not always been referred to in this way. In the early 1970s it was more usual to refer to 'wife battering' as in the pioneering work of Pizzey (1973). The use of this label was challenged, however, on the basis of its exclusivity, as it referred only to married women, thus neglecting to address the use of violence in intimate relationships between men and women who may have no contractual relationship with one other.

As different schools of thought emerged, designed to analyse and understand the nature of 'domestic' violence, other labels came into more common usage. The term 'family violence' became associated with one way of understanding 'domestic' violence with the term 'woman abuse' emerging as an alternative competitor, especially in the United States. Both of these labels also convey important messages about the nature, direction and the responsibility for violence between partners (see below). However, in the United Kingdom the term 'domestic' violence has appeared to enter common usage. And whilst that term too hides as much as it reveals – it hides the gender dimension of much violence between partners whilst emphasising its private nature – it will be adopted here. As we shall see, it is the label that has pervaded policy initiatives in this area (see chapter 5).

There are different ways in which we could begin to make sense of the issues surrounding 'domestic' violence. The framework to be adopted here is borrowed from work that examines public responses to technological risk. Freudenburg and Pastor (1992) identify three phases in these responses:

- the first stage emphasises the irrationality of the public, is short on empirical evidence but long on policy assertions, many of which involve blaming the victim.

- the second phase moves away from blaming the victim towards understanding them. This phase attempts to improve the information flow between the public, the decision-makers and the social scientists.

- the third phase (which in their area of work they suggest has yet to materialise) needs to go beyond understanding the victim towards 'understanding the broader system that creates victims (and victimisation) in the first place' (Freudenburg and Pastor. 1992: 51).

There are some remarkable parallels to be drawn from this analysis of risk perceptions in the technological field and the way in which the issue of the fear of crime has been understood as articulated in chapter 3. Those parallels are also present in the way in which 'domestic' violence has been traditionally conceptualised and debated. Drawing on this analysis, then, I shall identify three competing perspectives on this issue; blaming the victim, understanding the victim, and structuring the victim.

Blaming the victim

Although Frances Power Cobbe's book, *Wife Torture in England*, was published in 1878, the whole question of 'private' violence against women remained largely hidden from view until the 1970s. The invisibility of this issue was supported by a belief in the sanctity of marriage and the inviolate nature of the home, and was endorsed in official policy and practise. For example, a police view commonly expressed was:

> We are after all dealing with persons bound in marriage, and it is important for a host of reasons to maintain the unity of the spouses.
>
> (ACPO statement quoted by Johnson, 1985: 112)

This kind of police view found support in 1984 when Sir Kenneth Newman named domestic violence and stray dogs as 'rubbish' work for police officers (quoted by Radford and Stanko, 1991: 192). Such a view of 'domestic' violence offers a glimpse of some of the elements to a 'blaming the victim' approach, a view which in research and policy terms is largely informed by asking the question, 'Why doesn't she leave?'

Asking that question has generated a wealth of research. This research has been termed the 'family violence approach' and is primarily associated with the work of Gelles, Steinmetz, and Strauss (see, for example, Steinmetz and Strauss, 1974; Strauss, Gelles and Steinmetz, 1980; Gelles, 1987). Briefly, this approach has identified a range of factors as being associated with 'domestic' violence:

- the cycle of violence
- low socio-economic status
- social and structural stress
- social isolation
- low self-concept
- personality problems and psychopathology

(Gelles, 1987: 40)

The evidence in support of these generalised research findings is, however, fraught with difficulties. For example, they are based on small samples from therapeutic practice and lack standards of comparison. To overcome some of these difficulties, Strauss and his colleagues devised a Conflicts Tactics Scale as a way of measuring the nature and extent of family violence. This was utilised as a part of a national sample survey attempting to measure the nature and extent of violence in families. As a research strategy on an issue of this kind this is also full of methodological difficulties (see Dekeseredy and Schwartz, 1991, and Dobash and Dobash,

1992). Of more relevance to this discussion than such methodological issues, however, are the messages conveyed by this approach about 'domestic' violence.

As the title of this approach suggests, the family as a unit is seen as the locus of the violence and as the source of the explanation for that violence. The family, as a unit, is seen to be relatively unproblematic and is viewed in highly democratic terms. As a result, all family members are regarded as equally accusable of perpetrating violence and thereby equally capable of drawing such violence to a close. This leads to the provocative conclusion that women are equally as violent as men in the domestic context (see for example Lyndon, 1993). Moreover this analysis, identifying as it does socio-economic status as a contributory factor to family violence, also reflects a tendency to view such violence as only occurring in poor/deviant families. Consequently for the rest of society the locus of risk and danger is constituted in the threat from strangers in the street not the safe haven of the home (Stanko, 1988).

These assumptions offer a clear indication of the nature and form of the victim-blaming associated with this thinking. Thus, if things were so bad, she would leave. Historically understanding domestic violence in this way, as an inherent feature of problem families, has led social work practice to be informed by the notion of the 'problem family' with the resolution lying in improved housewifery (Wilson, 1983) with police responses informed by the dismissive view that 'its only a domestic'. Both strategies deny the risk and minimise the danger of private violence. Both strategies can also lend credence to a view that staying in a violent relationship is symbolic of women's irrationality (see chapter 3). Any rational person would leave. Therefore it cannot be so bad. This approach to analysing 'domestic' violence can be usefully contrasted with the second approach identified here: understanding the victim.

Understanding the victim

This approach to 'domestic' violence has been largely informed by the question of 'Why does she stay?' rather than 'Why doesn't she leave?' Led by the feminist movement, violence against women from this viewpoint is to be understood not by reference to individual family psychopathology but by reference to the gendered power relationships which structure everyday life; that is, patriarchy. This leads feminists to re-cast family life in terms of those gendered power relationships and to understand women's lives in the context of them.

From this viewpoint it is possible to say that women stay in violent relationships because:

- they are constrained economically;
- they have nowhere else to go;

- they are frequently socially isolated by their partner;
- they believe they can change him;
- they believe what their partner says about them;
- they believe what their partner says will happen to their children.

Understanding women's lives as they live them offers a very different picture of both the nature and the impact of men's violence on women's lives. For feminist researchers the home is far from a safe haven structured and controlled as it is by men.

Home is a risky and a highly dangerous place for women. Women in violent relationships, of course, know this. They devise many and diverse strategies of coping with and surviving the violence. From this viewpoint, staying in such a relationship is symbolic of women's rationality and their local expert knowledge of the risks and dangers associated with any other options available to them. It is particularly associated with their knowledge of the men in their lives.

Policy responses which emanate from this viewpoint recognise the gendered nature of this violence and are concerned to empower women not only to survive but also to offer them further options. Thus recent policy activity in this area in the U.K. in particular has been informed by a positive stance towards arresting the perpetrator and supporting the victim (see Home Office Circular 60/1990 and chapter 5). Whilst the success or otherwise of such policy interventions has yet to be firmly established (though see Hoyle, 1998), this position certainly offers a substantial challenge to the notion that the home is a safe place in which all members have access to equal power.

Not only have policy interventions emanating from this approach paid increasing attention to offering positive support to the 'victim' they have also been concerned to address the question of how to tackle the needs of violent men. From this work, perhaps, it is possible to see a third framework emerging within which to locate an understanding of 'domestic' violence. I have labelled this 'structuring the victim'.

Structuring the victim

This label is perhaps a little misleading. It is clearly possible to argue that the feminist work referred to in the previous section is concerned with structuring the victim. Such structuring is obviously present in a framework that understands the family in terms of patriarchal power. But until recently little of that feminist work has analysed the nature and expression of that power, that is, again, men and their relationship with and to masculinity.

This concern draws us into the domain of understanding perhaps a little more precisely the wider mechanisms that produce victims and victimisation. In order to address these wider mechanisms I shall draw on three sources: the statistics on homicide, the work of Russell and Painter respectively on rape in marriage, and survey work carried out by Mooney in North London on the nature and extent of 'domestic' violence. The findings from each of these empirical studies will be discussed in turn.

Statistics on homicide

There are several features of the statistics on homicide which appear to be incontrovertible: men commit murder much more frequently than women (Wilson and Daly, 1992); men murder their friends and acquaintances as frequently as they kill someone close to them (Campbell, 1992; Buck and Walklate, 1993); and the ratio of men killing women to women killing men is about 8 to 1 (Lees, 1992). There also appears to be some international consistency in relation to these features (Wilson and Daly, 1992).

One way of understanding these statistics is to place them at one end of a continuum of sexual violence as exemplified by the work of Kelly (1988), commented on earlier. Thus the home can certainly be seen as potentially a much more lethal place for women than men. This does not mean, of course, that women do not kill. However, very few women do kill and when they do it is largely, though not exclusively, as a response to the violence they themselves have received at the hands of their partners (Ewing, 1987; Jones, 1990).

The statistical regularities associated with homicide can of course be explained in a number of ways. Moreover, whilst Kelly's (1988) concept of a continuum draws our attention to women's experiences and understandings of violences towards them perpetrated by men, what it does not do is problematise men. We do not learn very much about men by drawing solely on this concept of a continuum, yet the behaviour of men in relation to homicide in general and domestic homicide in particular clearly needs to be understood. For example, one factor considered to be a common feature of why men kill their female partners or one-time partners is the phenomenon of male sexual propriety – often expressed as, 'if I can't have you, no-one can' (Wilson and Daly, 1992). The relationship between this and other features of women's experience of violence and men's perpetration of violence is something which constitutes an obvious common thread between rape, child abuse and 'domestic' violence and an issue to which we shall return.

Rape in marriage

The second area of study referenced here draws on feminist work on 'rape in marriage'. In this context we find that women are very reluctant to name their experiences in relationships with men that they know as rape.

Women prefer to differentiate between, for example, persuaded sex, forced sex and rape (Kelly, 1988 and discussion above). This does not mean, of course, that women are complicit in what happens to them, though some, as was suggested earlier, may be complicit in distancing themselves from such things happening to them. It does imply that whatever evidence we have on the question of marital rape, it is likely to constitute an under- rather than an over-recording of such incidents.

Russell's (1990) survey research, for example, reports that 'approximately one in every seven women who has ever been married in our San Francisco sample was willing to disclose an experience of sexual assault by their husbands which met our quite conservative definition of rape' (1990: 57), a finding replicated by Painter's (1992) U.K. study. Russell also explores the extent to which the experience of rape in marriage overlaps with other forms of violence experienced by these women. Here she found that by looking at the marriages in which rape occurred there was a 37 per cent overlap between 'wife rape' and 'wife beating', leaving 14 per cent of marriages in which rape occurred but no beating, and 49 per cent in which beating occurred but no rape (Russell, 1990: 90).

The nature and extent of domestic violence

The work of Mooney has added a further dimension to our understanding of the nature and extent of 'domestic' violence. Mooney's (1993) sample study of North London reports a 'composite domestic violence' rate of 30 per cent. This means that one in three women surveyed, from a general sample of the population, had experienced some form of 'domestic' violence ranging from mental cruelty, to actual violence and/or rape, in their lifetime; with one in ten reporting such an experience as having taken place within the last twelve months. What is particularly interesting about this survey is that they also interviewed men about their use of violence. In the sample of men, 37 per cent of them claimed they would never act violently towards a woman. However, 19 per cent actually admitted to having used violence against their partners within the range of incidents presented to them by the survey (Mooney, 1993: 17).

The readiness with which men in this survey admitted to having used violence against their partners points again to the necessity for an understanding of women's experiences of violence which focuses on the way in which violence is deemed a legitimate expression of masculinity, a clear link with what has been identified as an issue in the context of rape and child abuse.

Structuring the victim in the context of 'domestic' violence in this way clearly renders a number of issues explicit:

- first, it problematises what is meant by 'domestic' violence by extending the range of behaviours which might be included under such a heading.

- second, it ensures that we address the question of the responsibility for such violence appropriately.
- third, it draws our attention to a number of features of the fear, risk and danger debate, which need to be more fully explored (as indicated in chapter 3).
- fourth, it renders explicit the need to formulate an understanding of 'domestic' violence through the lens of masculinity. Thus we end in a similar place with this substantive issue as we have with the others addressed here: the question of masculinity.

To summarise: gendering sexual violence, then, requires more than simply being aware of who the victims and who the perpetrators of such violences are. It requires that we recognise the pervasive way in which presumptions concerning normal male heterosexuality underpin those violences and our understandings of them, though with the important caveat that not all men behave in this way. Before we go on to develop a more general framework which might facilitate an understanding of the way in which some men express their masculinity through these activities, however, it will be useful to review the way in which the different feminist positions discussed in chapter 1 might offer us an understanding of the relationship between gender and violence.

Feminist perspectives on gender and violence

Put simply, most feminists would agree that the phenomenon of sexual violence is something that men perpetrate against women. Where they would disagree would be in locating the extent of that violence and its cause. So for example, a liberal feminist would be likely to minimise the extent of violence and argue that the violence perpetrated by men towards women is largely a product of a few psychologically deranged men. A socialist feminist would be likely to locate such violences as being a product of a patriarchal capitalist system in which the frustrations of economic marginality and the power of sub-cultural norms render the incidence of such violence higher amongst blue-collar than white-collar workers. A radical feminist analysis would maximise the potential for male violence, seeing this as the basis of men's control over women. A postmodern feminist would wish to de-construct what the terms men, women and violence are intended to signify and would emphasise the diversity and difference subsumed by these terms.

Of all of these positions, it is radical feminism that has had the most to say about the relationship between gender and violence, as this discussion has so far intimated. Moreover, that discussion has also implied that the radical feminist position on the relationship between gender and violence is a problematic one (see also chapter 1). At this point, then, it will be useful to unpick the influence of that work in order to develop our understanding of the issues with which we are concerned here.

Gender and violence: a problematic relationship?

Morgan (1989: 27) states:

> It is undeniable that history is a record of most women acting peaceably and of most men acting belligerently to a point where the capacity for belligerence is regarded as an essential ingredient of manhood and the proclivity for conciliation is thought largely a quality of women.

The question is, then, what is the relationship between gender and violence? And perhaps more searchingly, how is violence legitimated and normalised, and for whom? For early radical feminist analysis the simple answer to this question was: for men.

Redefining rape as violence and control rather than an act of sex, as the work of Brownmiller (1975) and Griffin (1981) did, places those activities within the wider spectrum of violent acts. Yet, it is arguable that, in so doing this kind of analysis simultaneously denies the sex-specific nature of those acts. MacKinnon (1989a: 92) states:

> Battery as violence denies its sex-specific nature. I think that it is done sexually to women. Not only in where it is done – over half the incidents are in the bedroom. Or in respect of the surrounding events – the precipitating sexual jealousy.

MacKinnon here is attempting to reinstate the sexual dimension to such violence; to talk simply of violence, she argues, hides this. Yet at the same time the emphasis on sexual violence *per se* both draws on normal forms of heterosexual experience as its comparative yardstick and simultaneously fails to contextualise the violence as a part of the broader spectrum of male violences and experiences. In other words a number of issues remained untouched by this early radical feminist work.

First, to talk about sexual violence solely in terms of violence reduces male sexuality to that violence. Some radical feminist analyses in this vein leave us with the impression that men are completely divorced from their emotions and consequently do not have needs for sex, caring, and emotional commitment; but simply for power expressed through sex.

Second, to talk of the use of sexual violence as being solely a male capacity denies women's capabilities for sexual violence in particular and consequently for violence in general. Well hidden by early radical feminist work was the violence of both heterosexual women and lesbian women.

Third, a focus on the sexual nature of men's violence can have the effect of divorcing us from the context of understanding the general nature of access to the use of violence as a resource, in both personal (micro) and political (macro) situations.

Finally, a focus on sexual violence and its presumed heterosexual nature denies the possibility that men can experience sexual violence and can have difficulties in dealing with the associated expectations of heterosexual masculinity.

Of course, early radical feminist analysis certainly foregrounds the issues of power and control in understanding the nature of sexual violence. However, the limitations outlined above, reflecting the problems of essentialism and reductionism identifiable within radical feminism and commented on in chapter 1, indicate the weaknesses theoretically, though perhaps not politically, of remaining committed to such a simplistic analysis. These weaknesses encourage a recognition of the need for the development of an understanding of the relationship between gender and violence which is located in a broader social context but which also takes seriously the question of how do we understand men. Exploring the complex and subtle impact that an understanding of masculinity may provide could constitute one way of achieving one understanding of the relationship between gender and violence.

Hegemonic masculinity, gender and violence

Chapter 2 examined the relevance of different ways of thinking about masculinity and their influence on criminology. Here we shall consider the relevance of some aspects of that literature for the specific issue of the relationship between gender and violence. Connell (1987: 184) first introduced the term 'hegemonic masculinity' as a way of beginning to conceptualise the relationship between gender and power. This provides one route for understanding the relationship between gender and violence. By 'hegemonic masculinity' Connell means: 'a social ascendancy achieved in a play of social forces that extends beyond contests of brute power into the organisation of private life and cultural processes'. Thus hegemonic masculinity refers to that version of masculinity that possesses such an ascendancy; a version of masculinity which pervades all aspects of public and private life, providing a normative model against which all behaviours are judged. The hegemonic masculinity of which Connell speaks consists of white, male, heterosexuality.

The connection between patriarchal violence and this version of hegemonic masculinity is clearly present. This is to be found in cultural conceptions of the hero, through to the 'cut and thrust' of parliamentary debate. Whilst one may value physical prowess, and the other verbal prowess, the need to 'win' over one's opponent constitutes a thread of continuity between the two. However, the relationship between access to the use of violence and its actual use as a resource is not a straightforward one. Individual men may call upon such cultural resources in different ways in constructing their gendered identity on a day-to-day basis. Moreover, ascendancy ascribed to the version of masculinity identified here does not imply the obliteration of other cultural forms but merely their subordination. In other words, other versions of masculinity will exist and will be expressed though their impact but will not be as valued or as powerful. Thus hegemonic masculinity does not have to be present in all men's personalities nor does it require that all men be particularly nasty to women. It simply, but very powerfully, provides a cultural resource that informs all levels of social practice in different ways in order to secure the continued dominance of white heterosexual males as a culturally powerful group.

The implications of Connell's (1987) theorisation are clear. His viewpoint takes seriously the radical feminist and the socialist feminist concern with male power but offers us an analysis which is much more subtle yet, simultaneously, more pervasive in its view of the nature of that male power. Such power is not simply situated in access to material or cultural resources; it is also situated in and accomplished through everyday social practice. As Messerschmidt (1993: 73) states:

> At any point in space and time, gender relations of power promote and constrain the social action of both men and women, and conflict and resistance is pervasive. Notwithstanding, the social structure of gendered power is basic to understanding not only why men engage in more crime than women but also why men engage in different types and degrees of crime.

In this sense the perpetration of sexual violence is just one way in which the expression of 'doing gender' by men is accomplished in relation to women. The structurally based power of gender relations and the primacy achieved within those relations by hegemonic masculinity, by that masculinity most readily identified and associated stereotypically with the white, heterosexual male, provides the recipe from which particular men derive their particular expression of doing their gender. How the recipe is expressed depends on how the individual puts the ingredients together. Individual men may, of course, put the ingredients together differently. Some will therefore call upon the use of physical violence to assert their control; others will call upon more mental resources and capacities to assert themselves. For example, an abusive male may break his partner's arm or he may engage in emotional abuse. The motivation for both is the same, the assertion of control and the subjugation of their partner.

This kind of theorisation permits the foregrounding influence of masculinity and the associated legitimation of men's access to violence as a personal and political resource, without presuming that all men will use that resource. This theorisation contains within it, by implication, a certain dynamic, a certain capacity for understanding the way in which social change can occur. It is to this question that we shall now turn.

Gender, violence and social change

Some of the empirical evidence cited in this chapter suggests that some change is occurring both in the recognition of intimate violence as a social problem and in women's increasing unwillingness to remain silent about their experiences of male violence. Indeed, the theorisation of masculinity identified above offers the theoretical possibility for such change to occur; not only for women, but also for men. Other commentators, both political and academic, have recognised that the changing structural relationship between the sexes which occurred during the twentieth century, and which continues, appears to be taking its toll on personal relationships, and that they too may be changing.

Beck (1992: 113) had this to say on the matter:

> In any case the erupting discrepancies between women's expectations of equality and the reality of inequality in occupations and the family are shifted off to the private realm inside and outside the family. It is not difficult to predict that this will amount to an externally induced amplification of conflicts in private relationships.

And Giddens (1992: 122):

> A large amount of male sexual violence now stems from insecurity and inadequacy rather than from a seamless continuation of patriarchal dominance. Violence is a destructive reaction to the waning of female complicity.

Whilst I do not wish to support the assumption implied by both of these writers that the question of violence towards women is only explicable in terms of the processes of late modernity, their work raises at least two issues for our discussion here.

Both writers are expressing an awareness that women, whether feminist or not, appear to be less willing to tolerate violent relationships, and that includes sexual violence, than they once were. By implication they are also suggesting that these processes are not only resulting in personal change for some men but also demanding such personal change. It will be useful to develop this more fully.

Giddens (1991) identifies a range of historical processes in which he connects the emergence of the discourse around marriage as a relationship with the increasing global commitment to democracy. Through these interconnections he suggests that there is a moment of optimism for women and men in their potential for personal change. Such personal change in men, of course, may not always be of benefit to women. Misogyny has deep roots and social change can occur regressively as well as progressively. But it is a moment in which policy opportunities may present themselves. Some of these have been alluded to in this chapter.

Thus choices can be made around how we educate our young men in their relationships with women (as we can with women, too). Choices can be made concerning how we train police officers, judges, and barristers, as men dealing with women. Choices can be made around our commitment to a legal framework that still demands corroboration in cases in which 'women and young children are known to lie'. Choices can be made around whom we listen to in the defining and delivery of what are considered to be appropriate services, and for whom those services are considered appropriate (the extent to which some of these choices are being made is one the topics of the next chapter). Choices can be made around how we academics define our role in this process and how we define the nature of the problem to be explored. As Scully and Marolla (1993) state, not all men rape or commit sexual assault; it may be time to ask questions of those who do not, why they do not.

This potential for change exists for women too. The waning of female complicity, as identified by Giddens (1992) can no doubt be explained by reference to a range of different processes. The re-emergence of what has been called the second wave of feminism has been a part of this; but only a part. The increasing presence of women in positions powerful enough to impact upon the policy-making process is also crucial in setting an appropriate agenda. This has certainly been an influential factor in setting the Canadian agenda around these issues (Rock, 1986). So, for example, it is important to ensure that the question of policy responses to rape is not just left to men to deal with.

A waning of female complicity can be encouraged as both a personal and as a political strategy. Giddens (1992: 153) states:

> The phallus is only the penis: what a numbing and disconcerting discovery this is for both sexes! The claims to power of maleness depend upon a dangling piece of flesh that has now lost its distinctive connection to reproduction. This is a new castration indeed: women can now see men, at least at a cognitive level, as just as much a functionless appendage as the male sexual organ itself.

The processes to which Giddens is alluding here clearly mark important interconnections between, for example, technological developments and the personal empowerment of (some) women, alongside the consequent decentring of men for some purposes. But the broad social and cultural changes to which both Giddens and Beck refer, whilst providing moments of historical optimism, are painted on a huge historical canvass. So, what appears to be an increasing willingness on the part of women to report incidents of rape to the police and an increasing unwillingness to tolerate violent relationships, has to be set against the willingness or otherwise of the state to respond meaningfully to the demands that such personal changes make.

For example, the political debate on 'law and order' during the early 1990s specifically targeted the family, family responsibility, and absent fathers as being the source of the crime problem. Women with children, but without fathers, for whatever reason, were consequently identified as a legitimate political and moral target in this debate. The roots to misogyny are certainly deep! Thus it is important to note that personal change, whilst it might be constituted in the acting out of structural properties by individuals accomplishing their sense of themselves in their routine daily activities, does not necessarily move hand in hand with changes within the state and the state apparatus. Nowhere is this more evident than in the recent policy and political responses to crime cited above, and re-asserted in the focus on parenting present in some aspects of the implementation of the 1998 Crime and Disorder Act.

Therefore, whilst some individuals may be 'subjecting' themselves differently in the context of their personal lives the state may continue to 'subject' them otherwise. As Messerschmidt (1993) comments and as was quoted above, there may be conflict and resistance, but continuity and sameness also mark structured gender relations. The ascendancy of hegemonic masculinity will consequently continue to perpetrate 'violence' on women and children and some men in the process of subjugating their identities. And, of course, it is in the interests of some men for such practices to be perpetuated (Connell, 1995).

Conclusion

This chapter has been concerned to address a number of issues. It has been concerned not only to document some of the substantive issues around three areas which have historically posed problematic questions for criminology, but it has also been concerned to foreground the way in which gendered social relationships constitute a key part of understanding these substantive issues. Several important messages can be elicited from this process:

- first, the extent to which sexual violence can be understood as an 'ordinary' experience.
- second, the extent to which such 'ordinary' experiences are a product of men's behaviour towards women.

- third, the extent to which this behaviour can be understood, theoretically, as a product of the way in which men negotiate and construct their expression of themselves as men.

In the context of both criminology and victimology, these messages have important consequences. They certainly strengthen the case for examining questions relating to crime and the criminal victimisation experience from a gendered perspective rather than a 'women and crime' position. Moreover they also point to the need to formulate an understanding of crime, its production and its effects, by drawing on ideas which have yet to fully infiltrate the criminological and victimological domains.

The theoretical ideas drawn upon here to address the questions raised by a more subtle understanding of the relationship between gender and violence have consistently remained sensitive to a creatively structured understanding of individual action. This theoretical framework catches glimpses of the way in which gendered social relationships can both change and remain the same. It points, therefore, to the need to appreciate the ways in which individual behaviour is both constrained and facilitated by wider social processes. In the context of understanding crime and criminal victimisation, there are two areas which crucially highlight some features of the role of the state in constraining and facilitating individual behaviour: the police and the law. The next two chapters will consider the relevance of some of these issues for criminal justice professionals and the criminal justice policy process.

Suggestions for further reading

D. Scully (1990) *Understanding Rape.* This book offers a critical account of traditional perspectives on the rapist and an interesting and provocative interpretation, informed by perspectives on masculinity, of empirical work conducted with convicted rapists.

D. Russell (1990) *Rape in Marriage.* An updated edition of earlier works, still powerful in its formulation and impact.

S. Lees (1997) *Ruling Passions.* A relatively up-to-date empirical investigation of the way in which the criminal justice system responds to sexual crimes, including coverage of male rape.

5 Gender in policework and the criminal justice process

> Writing about co-operation and solidarity means writing at the same time about rejection and mistrust.
>
> (Douglas, 1987: 1)

Introduction: appreciating policework

In the context of crime and criminal victimisation, the police officer is more often than not, if not the only member of the criminal justice process with whom a member of the public comes into contact, then frequently the first one. Police officers then, and their public presentation of themselves as police officers, constitute a significant moment of many people's experience of the criminal justice system. Members of the public are equipped with many and varied images of police officers: if not based on their own experience, these are certainly informed by media coverage and interest in policing. For these reasons alone it is important to develop as informed a picture as possible of the nature of policework.

Of course, in one sense, we are all engaged in different ways and at different times in policing activities. In this general sense, we all contribute in varying ways to the processes of social control. The policing that is the focus of this chapter, blue-uniform policing, constitutes one key aspect of these general processes of social control of which we are all a part. Blue-uniform policing, however, carries with it a specific mandate, specific powers and a specific form of accountability. Taken together, these features equip police officers with the power to uphold law and order.

The powers granted to police officers to perform this function are, however, often discretionary. This results in the police performing a wide range of duties:

> In short, 'blue-uniform' policing or *state* policework implies a range of functions, namely, enforcing (and sometimes defining) the criminal law, main taining order, intelligence gathering, and securing consent, all directed towards a singular end: upholding the general framework of the *state* – by persuasion if possible, violently if necessary.
>
> (Brogden, Jefferson and Walklate, 1988: 2, *my emphasis*)

The range of duties that this discretionary role entails, then, leads Uglow (1988) to make the following observation:

> We all recognise contrasting, even contradictory, images of the police – the officer on the beat courteously directing tourists; the patrol car, blue light flashing, speeding in pursuit of a stolen vehicle; massed ranks of policemen clad in helmets, wielding truncheons, confronting demonstrators or strikers; officers talking to school children about road safety or the dangers of glue-sniffing; Special Branch officers tapping telephones or opening mail; incident rooms co-ordinating house-to-house enquiries; the village bobby push ing a bicycle and chatting to customers at the local shop.
>
> (Uglow, 1988: 1)

These contrasting images of policework are certainly present. The different roles they highlight illustrate some of the difficulties facing not only police officers in making sense of their day-to-day work but also the difficulties facing anyone on the receiving end of these different tasks in making sense of the policing role.

The range of images and expectations associated with policework are rendered more complex when, in times of prison officer disputes or ambulance service disruptions, it is frequently the police alongside other services (such as the armed forces) who are expected to fill the gaps in service provision. Thus, it is possible to argue that the range of potential activities police officers engage in, in support of the state, often results in confusion over what constitutes the central policing task for all concerned. The issues to be addressed in this chapter will confirm the need to clarify what the nature of this central task is.

The discretion associated with the policing role also equips police officers with (potentially) a good deal of personal and structural power. Police officers deal with this discretion, and the confusion it sometimes generates, through the construction of collectively understood and often taken for granted norms and values, frequently referred to in the academic literature as 'cop culture'. Co-operation and solidarity have frequently been commented upon as being key features of this 'cop culture', hence the relevance of the quote from Douglas cited at the beginning of this chapter. On occasions, that culture has also been seen as the source of all policing ills. Indeed, the solidarity engendered by it has been known to provide 'cover' for rather less than legitimate policing activities. Understanding the nature and impact of this culture on how the task of policing is performed is crucial to an understanding of how, in routine practice, the central task of policing is interpreted.

Reiner (1992) identifies the following as the key characteristics of 'cop culture': a sense of mission, suspicion, isolation/solidarity, conservatism, machismo, pragmatism, and racial prejudice. These characteristics inform specific policing actions under specific circumstances. The phenomenon of the 'high-speed car chase', for example, can be seen as a product of both the sense of mission and the machismo identified by Reiner; an activity which is imbued with the *same* excitement and thrill for the police officer as for those being chased! Thus in many ways these sub-cultural characteristics provide a framework in which to understand how the central task of policing is practically managed. Moreover, they also provide an insight into one way of constructing an understanding of the gendered nature of policework.

The impact of that gendered work can be felt in a number of ways both internally within the police organisation and externally in the practical accomplishment of the policing task. We shall address some of the issues associated with this latter issue first of all since it focuses our attention on some of the more recent developments that have occurred in the context of policing since the 1980s.

Policing during the 1980s

Policing during the 1980s was subjected to the same financial structures and requirements as other public service activities, that is the demand for 'value for money' and 'efficiency'. These twin themes of government policy, introduced in the early 1980s, were translated by the end of that decade, into an overt concern with consumer or customer satisfaction. This rising tide of consumerism was marked in several police forces by the establishment of Quality of Service Units (Bunt and Mawby, 1993). This external re-presentation of police forces as police services went alongside efforts to engage in internal organisational changes designed to re-commit police officers to the professional nature of their task (see below). It also represented a symbolic concern with re-orienting the focus of policework or what Reiner (1991: 105) has referred to as 'being driven to reflect upon their fundamental mission'.

It was within this rising tide of consumerism that police responses to women as victims of crime during the 1980s were located (Walklate, 1993b). There are two areas of policing relating to women that received particular attention during this time: rape and 'domestic' violence. It will be useful to examine policing policy responses in both of these areas before considering the extent to which this kind of movement does constituted a fundamental re-examination of the central policing task of which Reiner speaks.

Policing rape

The unwillingness of women to report rape to the police has been well documented. As Benn (1985: 136) stated:

> Women were told not to get upset, not to get things out of proportion, not to go out alone, not to go out at night, to avoid 'dangerous areas', not to put themselves at risk.

Such police advice reflected a victim-precipitation view of rape (see chapter 4). Changes have occurred in policing policy on this issue, though the impact of these changes is not clearly identifiable. For example, the increasing number of recorded incidents of rape is attributed to, on the one hand, women's greater willingness to report; and on the other hand, to changes in police practice. Both views may, of course, be accurate up to a point. Whilst there is some early evaluative evidence available concerning the impact of police policy changes in this area, it is equivocal on the question of impact on the women in receipt of such new services (see, for example, Gregory and Lees, 1999). So what did these changes comprise?

Smith's (1989) study states that the work completed by Chambers and Millar (1983) on police responsiveness to rape and the public outcry which followed the televised handling of a rape complainant by the Thames Valley Police (BBC 1, 18 January 1982) precipitated Home Office Circular 25/1983. This circular outlined how incidents of rape might be handled more effectively, and many forces, following the lead of the Metropolitan Police, proceeded to establish 'rape suites'. These suites comprise, primarily, more comfortable and sensitive surroundings, usually away from the police station, in which to medically examine and interview 'victims' of rape and sexual assault. Forces also endeavour to provide specially trained officers to handle such cases, in particular trained female police officers.

How far these policing changes have resulted in substantial changes for women who have reported an incident of rape is, however, subject to some debate. Smith's study covered the years immediately after the implementation of these recommendations and she reports that:

> Most police forces have recognised the need to reconsider their own responsiveness to rape. Nevertheless, the evidence from this study of two London boroughs suggests that it is still the classic stereotype of rape which is more likely to be officially recorded as a crime.
>
> (Smith, 1989: 26)

In a later study by Grace, Lloyd and Smith (1992: 5) of 335 incidents of reported rape, 80 were 'no-crimed' after a month; representing an initial attrition rate of about 20 per cent. Various reasons were given by the police for no-criming: the woman withdrawing the allegation, 43 per cent; false or malicious allegation, 34 per cent; insufficient evidence, 12 per cent; woman unwilling to testify or co-operate, 9 per cent; complainant and suspect married, 2 per cent. *This evidence clearly renders the police decision-making process as still being a key moment in the attrition rate of rape cases.*

The study conducted by Grace, Lloyd and Smith (1992) followed a sample of cases through the whole of the criminal justice process. Their findings indicated that 'Alleged acquaintance attacks are the least likely to result in a conviction; are the most likely to have a not guilty plea given by the defendant; are the most likely cases to result in an acquittal; are the most likely cases for women to withdraw their complaints', thus suggesting that the 'classic rape' is still the most likely to result in a conviction and illustrating the intransigence of the rape myths discussed in chapter 4. A further Home Office study of the processing of rape cases based on 1996 data reports that only 26 per cent of crimed cases reached the crown court and only 9 per cent of suspects were convicted of rape or attempted rape. So even in those circumstances in which the police have pursued a case other barriers also exist within the criminal justice process to their furtherance.

Overall, then, whilst there is little evidence available concerning the greater effectiveness or otherwise of current policing policy and practice in this area, that evidence which does exist suggests that what change has occurred appears to be marginal if the measure of change is successful convictions. Radford and Stanko (1991: 196) summarise these reforms in the following way:

> Window dressing reforms then have addressed the most glaring inadequacies in the police response to women reporting rape, public concern is apparently addressed and political debate relocated elsewhere, but the question of male sexual violence and the police response to it has only been addressed on the most superficial of levels.

Whether any of these reforms were really designed to address the question of male sexual violence is a moot point. And whilst there is limited evidence available on how women in receipt of such services feel about them, a small-scale study conducted by Gregory and Lees (1999) suggests that on the whole these changes have had a beneficial effect. However, many women in their sample still felt dissatisfied with the investigative process, especially the medical examination. What is clear, however, is that the 'cult of the customer' (Edgar, 1991) has made its mark on policing in this area. Such customer orientation is also evident in the development of policing policy on the issue of 'domestic' violence.

Policing 'domestic' violence

Radford and Stanko (1991: 192) state:

> In 1984 Sir Kenneth Newman attempted to shed police responsibility for what he considered to be 'rubbish' work, or non-police matters, namely

> domestic violence and stray dogs are two such examples. By 1990 police forces compete with each other to find the most creative policy to deal with domestic violence.

It is clearly the case that there has been a remarkable change of direction in terms of policing policy in this issue. It is now well acknowledged that the traditional view of 'domestic' violence was that this was not real policework (Faragher, 1981) and that when all the conditions were met for the police to make an arrest, this was rarely done (Edwards, 1986). Even in cases where women were keen to pursue a prosecution the police were not (Dobash and Dobash, 1980), choosing instead to believe in the 'myth of the reluctant victim' (Stanko, 1989). This cumulative unwillingness of the police to act left women very dissatisfied with them (Pahl, 1978; Binney, Harkell and Nixon, 1981; London Strategic Policy Unit, 1986). Given this background, Stanko (1992) is well justified in stating that the police have no history (and certainly no 'herstory') of responding actively to 'domestic' violence. One of the first questions that then arises is how the impetus for such a potentially radical change in policy direction was generated.

Feminist-inspired campaigns had drawn attention to the issue of violence against women and whilst some gains in civil proceedings had been won during the 1970s it was the Women's National Commission in the mid-1980s which brought the issue of violence against women to government attention (Smith, 1989). This Commission, influential as it was in contributing to the Home Office circular 69/1986 addressing the police handling of rape, also drew attention to the need for 'the overriding concern in dealing with domestic violence to ensure the safety of victims and reduce the risk of further violence' (Smith, 1989: 5). There were, of course, other processes occurring at the same time which provided the backcloth to a change of direction on this issue, not least of which was the rising influence of consumerism in public services commented on above (see also Jefferson, Sim and Walklate, 1992) as well as the need to re-secure consent for the policing task (Radford and Stanko, 1991).

Nevertheless, following this circular, in the years between 1986 and 1990, the Metropolitan Police established what came to be seen as a policy precedent in responding to 'domestic' violence. This took the form of the 'dedicated' Domestic Violence Unit (DVU, the nature of which will be discussed in greater detail below). The Home Office circular 60/1990 gave considerable impetus to other forces to follow this model.

Circular 60/1990 is considered to be the most definitive statement from the Home Office to date on the issue of 'domestic' violence. It states that

> The Home Secretary regards a violent or brutal assault and threatening behaviour over a period of time by a person to whom the victim is married

> or with whom the victim lives or has lived as seriously as violent assault by a stranger.

This statement is both telling and far-reaching in its potential consequences for an understanding of the central policing task. Not only does the circular proceed to remind Chief Constables of the range of legal strategies under which offenders for such incidents might be arrested, it also recommends that forces consider the establishment of 'dedicated' units. This twofold approach has now been adopted by many police forces in varyingly creative ways as Radford and Stanko (1991) observe. Implementing such recommendations, however, has not been, and is not, easy or straightforward.

Briefly, the use of arrest in incidents of 'domestic' violence is rooted in assumptions concerning the use of arrest in non-domestic situations. However, as Chatterton (1983), Shapland and Hobbs (1989) and Smith (1989) show, this is a highly problematic assumption: the discretionary power invested in the office of constable means that arrest is never the *automatic* outcome of any police involvement. In addition, the use of arrest presumes that arrest acts as a deterrent. This reflects an uncritical acceptance of the findings of American-based research (Berk and Sherman, 1984) which is not fully validated and to which the researchers themselves have since added significant caveats (Sherman *et al* 1991).

Whilst some feminists support the symbolic use of the law that arrest implies, research from different countries suggests that there are a number of significant barriers to its effective implementation as a policy response. One of these barriers is police officers' own attitudes and prejudices concerning violence against women (see, for example, Ferraro, 1989; Hatty, 1989; Stanko, 1989; Edwards, 1989; Ursel, 1990). Research has also shown that police officers tend to use the decision to arrest in 'domestic' incidents only in specific circumstances: when the officer was threatened (Hatty, 1989); when there was a breach of the peace or criminal damage (Edwards, 1989); on the absence or presence of public disorder; when victim/witness testimony is unnecessary to proceed with the case (Sanders, 1987); or in what appears to be quite arbitrary circumstances (Walklate, 1992). All of this research clearly suggests that the process of implementing change of actual practice needs either to be backed by an *unambiguous* force order (as in West Yorkshire, for example, who claim an increase in the use of arrest for 'domestic' incidents from 28 per cent to 50 per cent in the 12 months from 1990 to 1991) and/or by a considerable input into training (some forces – for example, Merseyside – have produced Open Learning packages for all officers).

The second strand to policing policy on this issue has been the creation of the Domestic Violence Unit (DVU). The concept of a 'dedicated' domestic violence unit seems to be a fluid one. The underlying principle of these units, however, is to monitor the police response to 'domestic' incidents, to offer support to the 'victim', to liaise with other agencies, and to appraise women of the range of options open to them. In other words, there is some scope here for a type of 'victim advocacy' stance on the part of police officers staffing such units (Edwards, 1989; Friedman and Schulman, 1990; Walklate, 1992b).

The success of such units depends in part upon the initial response made by the officers attending the incident, in part upon the quality of the information the unit receives from this initial contact, and in part on the unit's ability to liaise with other agencies. Whilst many forces have followed the metropolitan model in devising their responses to 'domestic' violence there have been some significant variations on this theme. Despite these variations, two common themes can be identified: the focus on supporting women in particular and the significant presence of female officers for the most part to do this kind of policework, a feature also to be found in the earlier policy response to rape. Whilst these common themes might at first glance appear both reasonable and appropriate they rest on particular assumptions concerning how best to empower women and reflect certain gendered assumptions concerning who might be best equipped to engage in such work. This is illustrated in two ways.

Firstly, the Home Office circular recommends the establishment of records within DVUs so that an 'at risk' register of 'domestic' violence can be compiled. This recommendation is contentious insofar as whilst it may facilitate the targeting of resources from a policing viewpoint, by definition it also targets the 'victim' as being the problem. This issue has been tempered in some units by the keeping of parallel records on the perpetrator. Men who are violent move on to repeat that violence in other relationships.

The issue of record-keeping raises the difficult question of whether this dedicated response actually empowers women. As Morley and Mullender (1991) point out (and as some serving police officers believe), the woman's right to protection may have been enhanced on the one hand but the power and control which she experienced in her relationship may have merely been transferred from the assailant to the police. This is particularly problematic for black and Asian women whose relationship with the criminal justice system is imbued with assumptions associated with race as well as gender. The potential for such transference in the guise of enhanced protection strikes at the very heart of the policing dilemma with respect to 'domestic' violence. However, before developing this further, there is a second issue here. It has been noted in the foregoing discussion that in the re-orientation and implementation of policy in this area policewomen feature as significant actors. An optimist might suggest that this is informed and influenced by the debates that have occurred within feminism, i.e. that women in general, and women in particularly vulnerable circumstances, prefer talking to other women. However, the policing response to this feminist-informed view is ambivalent. As Hanmer and Saunders (1991: 24) indicate:

> The appointment and promotion of women police officers remains an issue. Women in the West Yorkshire Police constituted 9 per cent of the Force in November 1987 when the earlier research was completed and this had risen to 13.5 per cent in 1991. However, 13.5 per cent of senior officers are not women. Inadequate numbers of women officers and their position in the Force continues to be commented upon by other agencies, but the Force response to this recommendation was to describe themselves as an equal opportunities employer. The employment of women officers is an issue both in relation to requests by women and agencies in the community for women officers and the transformation of a masculine police culture in order to provide a more satisfactory service for women.

The use of policewomen in the context of 'domestic' violence can in one sense be seen as a reasonable extension of the valuable role that the presence of policewomen are considered to play in relation to reported incidents of rape and issues associated with child abuse. Unfortunately, the extensive use of female police officers in this way glosses a number of issues not only for the officers themselves but also for the women they are endeavouring to support. It is to this latter issue that we shall turn first of all.

The argument that women would prefer to have their case dealt with by a female officer is supported by limited though not totally convincing evidence. Heidensohn's (1992) evidence from policewomen suggests that certain levels of satisfaction and support are maintained for both the women being supported and the policewomen themselves when they are involved in this kind of work. Heidensohn's interviewees, however, also pointed out that they could identify police*men* who were equally capable of offering the same kind of quality support. Of course, one of the problems here is that we have very little gendered empirical knowledge of what kind of policing the public want (Walklate, 1992b) on which to base policy practice.

Radford's (1987) survey of women's views of policing revealed that 44 per cent of her sample thought that women officers would be more understanding in relation to violence against women, though 32 per cent thought that they would not be. Many said that they would prefer to speak to women in the context of domestic violence but similarly others recognised that women officers had to be tougher than the men in order to succeed (Radford, 1987: 40-41). Even this evidence, then, displays some understandable ambivalence to the idea that female officers will automatically be more supportive than their male counterparts. Indeed Hoyle's (1998) detailed study of Thames Valley Police practices in this area would support the view that it would be mistaken to presume that policewomen were by definition most appropriately deployed to such work.

It may be, of course, that what women are asking for is a quality of support which is commonly associated with women; that is, sympathetic listening skills which indicate that the woman is being taken seriously. As Heidensohn's (1992) interviewees suggest, there is no necessary relationship between the possession of these skills and being female. However, the apparent ease with which female officers have been most readily accepted as suitable in this area of work raises both particular and general questions for them as workers within a male-dominated profession. This is the second issue that was raised above.

The particular questions which emerge relate to the kind of experiences women police officers have in making their work in this area effective within their own force. This may be manifested in a number of ways, but two examples come to mind. The first relates to how other officers, particularly male officers, view the work of their female colleagues working in 'domestic' violence units. There is a sense in which the separation of this work, staffed by female officers dealing with female 'victims' can potentially sustain the view of women officers as valuable but not doing 'real policework'. Policewomen deployed in this way are faced with a daily round of definition and re-definition of their work and their role in the face of what is taken to be the well-documented norms of 'cop culture' (see above).

The dilemma this presents can be experienced at a personal level in the tension between policewomen's own commitment to that culture (wanting to arrest the perpetrator) and the demands of their specific role in a DVU (to support the woman in her chosen course of action). It can also be experienced collectively. At one training session for officers (99 per cent female and all constables) engaged in 'domestic' violence work I ended the session by asking the group what they needed as officers engaged in this work. I was met with an uncategorical and heartfelt response: that they wanted to be listened to and they wanted their views to be taken seriously within their organisation, a remarkable expression of parallel experience with the women they were endeavouring to support, clearly highlighting some of the internal organisational issues that increased involvement in work of this sort is likely to produce and marking some interconnections with their gendered work experiences.

As far as the question of whether this form of policy response does represent a way of empowering women is concerned, it can therefore be seen as quite a complex issue. Certainly the women who are supported through the work of DVUs have at their disposal a potentially better service than existed prior to their implementation, though there are obviously still difficulties in ensuring that women are responded to appropriately by all officers called to the scene. There is also considerable work still to be done in ensuring that women from ethnic minorities receive appropriate support (Patel, 1992). And whilst Davidoff and Dowds (1989) report that during the 1980s women's propensity to report incidents of 'domestic' violence increased (an increase which interestingly enough predates many of the initiatives under discussion here), there is clearly a long way to go before we can say that such policies really represent empowerment for women. There is, however, another side to this question of empowerment which the foregoing discussion has illustrated; the question of the empowerment of policewomen. Before pursuing this issue more fully, it will be useful to summarise the main themes of this discussion so far.

Understanding policing responses to women from 1980 onwards

The foregoing discussion suggests that there has been some considerable activity with respect to the policing of women as 'victims' of crime during the 1980s and early 1990s. It is interesting to note from this that it is in their capacity as victims of crime that women have received this attention. This clearly resonates with the new move from crime prevention towards victimisation prevention (Karmen, 1990) within criminal justice policy in particular and political rhetoric in general during this period. Moreover, these changes resonate particularly with the processes of consumerism put in place across a range of public services. The fact that in the arena of criminal justice the customer has been identified as the victim of crime rather than the perpetrator reflects a way of thinking about free market ideals which have developed in a relatively unchallenged fashion since the 1980s (Taylor, 1990).

These developments also need to be located in new ways of thinking about the evaluation of police performance which has clearly penetrated the thinking of police managers as they search for consumer evaluation of services, as well as that of external agencies like the Audit Commission. This social construction of the customer (Jefferson, Sim and Walklate, 1992) has occurred at different rates in different force areas, but is epitomised by the redefinition of police forces as police services. This change of emphasis encapsulated by the word service as opposed to the word force draws attention yet again to the question of what constitutes the central policing task. The connections between understanding this task and role that processes such as those highlighted above play in sustaining the state is an issue to which we shall return.

The real challenge to these processes of re-orienting policework in these specific areas lies in the ability of police forces to deliver substance (rather than rhetoric) both to the women who ask for help and to the policewomen who are most frequently deployed in this specialist work. Both issues return us to the question with which this chapter began: what constitutes the central policing task? Before exploring this more fully it will be useful for us to examine the internal consequences of both the impact of 'cop culture' on policewomen alongside the impact of the changes in policy discussed here. An examination of the role and experiences of policewomen will be a valuable vehicle through which to explore this issue.

Understanding policewomen

As extensive research from other countries has shown, the extent to which implementing positive policies on 'domestic' violence might effectively change the cop culturist view of what the central policing task is about, or indeed the management view of that task, is open to considerable debate (see, for example, the collection of papers edited by Hanmer, Radford and Stanko, 1989). The difficulties of implementing change through re-orienting policy in this way has led some writers to argue that what is required is the recruitment of more policewomen. This is a view that is certainly reflected in the quote taken from Hanmer and Saunders cited above. Such a view presumes that not only will women as 'consumers' of a police service have their needs better met, but also presumes that the more women police officers there are, the better they will survive their daily working life. Before deciding on the legitimacy or otherwise of these presumptions it will be useful to construct a picture of the working life of policewomen.

If we examine more carefully the images of policing with which this chapter began, it is easy to see that many of those images presume a male police officer. Indeed, images of female officers are few and far between. The television series *The Bill* does intermittently feature story lines around policewomen, and another television series, *The Chief*, was remarkable insofar as it featured a high-ranking female police officer. Research by Soothill (1993) suggests, surprisingly, that whilst newspaper coverage of policewomen does focus on traditionally stereotypical areas for women, like a female police officer weeping at a colleague's funeral, there is also coverage of policewomen's role in the more dangerous activities of policework. However, what we expect of our policewomen as opposed to our policemen is a controversial issue and one in which the moral behaviour of the women concerned is much more likely to be subjected to scrutiny than that of their male counterparts (Walklate, 1992). Such public perceptions and expectations constitute the backcloth against which to begin to understand the more specific experiences of policewomen themselves.

In 1998, policewomen accounted for about 16 per cent of the total force establishment in England and Wales. In that same year two of the 51 Chief Constables were women. Coffey, Brown and Savage (1992) report that policewomen were under-represented in many specialist departments and totally absent from others, observations which were supported by Holdaway and Parker (1998). Brown, Maidment and Bull (1992) (cited in Anderson *et al* below) also found that the deployment patterns of women police officers gravitated towards 'low frequency, labour intensive, specialised tasks' by, for example, supporting rape victims or victims of sexual abuse, reinforcing the comments already made above. As Anderson, Brown and Campbell (1993: 11) state:

> As a consequence women officers are limited in the amount and type of experience they are able to gain. This in turn affects their job satisfaction and may inhibit their promotion prospects. That fewer women than men achieve promotion in turn can reinforce male stereotypes about women's abilities.

The mechanisms underpinning these statistics are well documented and relate to the 'cult of masculinity' which surrounds policing and the notion of what constitutes the central policing task. The studies conducted by the Policy Studies Institute (1983), Bryant, Dunkerley and Kelland (1985) and Jones (1987) evidence this. This cult leads many policewomen with a choice of either embracing the male culture as their own or of fulfilling the more traditional expectations associated with their role, strategies which have been highlighted by Ehrlich-Martin (1980) and Jones (1987).

In the face of this evidence what impact is a concerted effort on the internal policy and practices of the police organisation likely to have? This is another area in which some commentators would argue that there was considerable activity during the 1980s. It is exemplified particularly by policy statements focusing on equal opportunities. It is to an understanding of the likely impact of such strategies that we shall now turn.

Policing and equal opportunities

This issue brings us to the second Home Office Circular that is considered to have had far-reaching consequences for the police service during the 1980s: Home Office circular 87/1989 'Equal opportunities policies in the police service'. It states that the effects of force policies 'should ensure that the best use is made of the abilities of every member of the force' and that it should show 'that all members of the service are firmly opposed to discrimination within the service and in their professional dealings with members of the public'. Whilst arguably the impetus for this circular lies in the history of inner-city disturbances during the 1980s and the recognition that police forces in England and Wales gave the significant appearance of being white (male) police forces, there were also notable charges of discrimination brought by female police officers which have ensured that equal opportunities are seen to be an issue for policewomen as well as those from ethnic minorities.

Heidensohn (1992: 101-2) usefully suggests that equal opportunities policies can impact on policing in a number of different ways; in keeping the law, in achieving a representative bureaucracy, in bringing a source of innovation and change into policy, in 'feminising' policing, in undermining police tradition and 'proper policing', in increasing opportunities for individual women and for women as a whole. Two of these headings appear to be of particular value in understanding the linkages between the policies under consideration here: 'feminising' policing, and undermining 'proper policing'.

'Feminising' policing

As Hanmer and Saunders (1991) remarked earlier, when faced with the question of guaranteeing service delivery by policewomen for other women, forces frequently fall back on the statement that they are an 'equal opportunities' employer. Such a statement, couched as it is in deploying individuals according to their merits, allows forces to advertise specialist posts, for example for a domestic violence officer, openly across the force. Individual officers put themselves forward for such postings. Hypothetically speaking, but rooted in what is already known about 'cop culture', this process allows for a number of complex mechanisms to come into play.

Firstly, fewer male officers are likely to apply for such postings than female officers. This might be as a result of their evaluation of their own skills but it would also have to be seen alongside the persistent effect of 'cop culture' definitions of what counts as 'proper policing'. Secondly, women do put themselves forward for such work; perhaps seeing specialist work as an added incentive towards promotion as well as evaluating themselves as having the appropriate skills for such work. Thirdly, selection procedures pay due attention to the kinds of qualities considered appropriate for such work: sympathetic, supportive, able to listen, able to communicate effectively, etc. The resultant effect of these processes is that more women enter this specialist work and simultaneously a police force is able to defend its equal opportunities policy. However, reliance on such processes can often result in complacency and frequently leaves the reins of change in the hands of those who perhaps have least interest in seeing change occur, i.e. senior policemen. The question remains as to whether such pessimism is justified. It is at this juncture that the second area suggested by Heidensohn (1992) becomes a valuable issue to explore: what counts as 'proper policing'?

'Proper' policing

The question of what is 'proper policing' can be interpreted in a number of different ways, from what counts as the central policing task to what counts as the central skills to be associated with police officers. It is clear that the increasing involvement of police forces in a more positive response towards 'domestic' violence, for example, raises issues on both these counts. Firstly, police offices are being asked to take the policing of the private domain seriously; secondly they are being asked to be sensitive and supportive in their subsequent response to women in violent relationships. Given the evidence and argument presented here, there are (at least) two possible outcomes to this demand for such a re-orientation.

The first scenario reproduces police forces prior to integration; in other words, Police Women's Departments are re-constituted in all but name. This scenario endorses all those who believe that general policework is too dangerous for women and that using women for women's and children's issues makes best use of the qualities they have to offer. It leaves the 'dirty work' to the men. It 'ghettoises' women's issues and leaves the rest of the force relatively untouched in style and service delivery (see also Holdaway and Parker, 1998). The second scenario is one in which both statements on Equal Opportunities and statements on 'domestic' violence are embraced by all members of a police force, both male and female, in order to create an atmosphere in which male and female officers can pursue their career aspirations. It has frequently been suggested that such processes only become possible when women make up at least 25 per cent of a total organisation's workforce (Moss Kanter, 1977). It is clear that police forces in the U.K. are a long way from achieving that goal. However, what underpins this scenario is a certain optimism that if these two areas were seriously embraced it would demand a fundamental re-examination of what counts as policing. In other words, it would challenge men's conceptions of what policing is about, why they became police officers, etc.

From the analysis presented here, then, it is clear that there are tendencies in each of these scenarios present in the 1990s, though there are perhaps clearer tendencies towards the former than the latter. Nevertheless, through the implementation of these policies, police forces are presented with an opportunity of listening to and taking seriously the views and experiences of their own policewomen. Those views and experiences will not be uniform. They will, however, convey in very real terms an agenda for the central policing task that would be very difficult to ignore. Listening to such views would certainly constitute a step towards empowering them as women as well as policewomen.

Some would argue that the empowerment of policewomen is likely to be a long and painful process. Arguably, it is the case that in the aftermath of the pursuit of an equal opportunities case on the part of Alison Halford that more policewomen have been confident to pursue such cases and cases of sexual harassment (see Gregory and Lees, 1999). However, there is a sense in which the Halford case poses much more fundamental questions than this. It touched upon our fundamental understanding of the relationship between gender and violence and hence returns us in a different way to the question of the gendered nature of policework.

Dorothy Smith (1990) comments on an old Lancashire saying: 'Whistling women and a crowing hen, let the devil out of his pen.' This saying draws our attention to the powerful effect anomalies can have. Alison Halford was an anomaly. Not only was she a powerful woman, a difficult enough combination for a male-membered organisation to contemplate; she was also a powerful policewoman. It is the anomalous combination of womanhood, power and access to the use and deployment of legitimate force (violence) which raises particular questions in Halford's case.

If we take this observation seriously and relate it to a gendered understanding of the workplace, it is clear that soldiering, policing, etc. articulate a particular cluster of gendered expectations. These expectations are not absolute or fixed but locate different jobs in different gendered places and offer differential access to the use of power as force (Morgan, 1992). Policework with its potential for entering risky situations and its use of visible direct force defines that work not only as predominantly male but also as being predominantly focused on those situations defined by males as risky, usually the street. Thus we can perhaps see more clearly why Alison Halford might have been considered threatening, not only as an individual, but also as a symbolic structural representation of an image which does not quite fit together. In some respects, then, it matters little what personal qualities or failings Alison Halford had as an individual. What she represented was a threat to a key assumption that violence and/or access to force is legitimated and normalised for men but not for women.

Thus it can be argued that whilst both the promotion of equal opportunities and re-orienting policework to the world of the private domain (behind closed doors) are both legitimate and necessary, such a re-orientation does little to tackle the fundamental anomaly articulated by the case of Alison Halford. To presume that such a re-orientation is only of concern for policewomen, or only a focus of work activity for policewomen, ensures that we remain within the liberal feminist trap of failing to render problematic the assumptions on which such a view is based. This does not mean that there are not some significant gains to be made for policewomen in using this kind of strategy. It does imply, however, that it is important to remember that such changes also have the potential for impacting upon policemen and, indeed, if effective change is required, should impact upon policemen. This is necessary both in terms of encouraging them to enter specialist work for which as individual men they might have the appropriate skills, and in terms of challenging their own conceptions of what policing is about – an issue which has run through the heart of this chapter.

In some respects, the 1990s presented a unique opportunity for this question to be debated. The Royal Commission on the Criminal Justice System, the Government White Paper concerned with the role of the Police Authorities, and the Sheehy Inquiry (1993) on policing, the Macpherson Report (1998) might have provided the backcloth against which such a debate could have occurred. However, such a debate still remains to take place. Nevertheless a closer look at the recommendations of the Sheehy Report (1993) will take us further towards understanding the importance of such a debate.

The Sheehy Report: key recommendations

Sheehy's terms of reference were to examine the rank structure, remuneration and conditions of service for the police service. The Inquiry team set themselves a number of objectives in pursuing these terms of reference (see Executive Report: 2). Whilst recognising the special nature of some aspects of policework (Executive Report: 4), the team were of the view that this claim to special status was not always justified. Within this framework of objectives and with a view to challenging the special status of policework, attention appears to have focused on three related issues:

- management structure and control;
- systems of reward, especially for front-line operational duties;
- and conditions of service.

In brief;

> The inquiry team were of the view that there is little encouragement for the police to manage their resources.... There is no financial or other incentive to buy in or adopt best practice from other forces and organisations, to make improvements of an organisational nature or to seek other efficiency savings.
>
> (Executive Report: 4)

In addition, they pointed to 'top heavy' management structures which limit the 'exercise of discretion' and 'inhibit initiative' (*ibid*: 5). The recommendations which flowed from these concerns proposed to rationalise the rank structure overall with an immediate severance exercise to facilitate this process.

Arguably, the Sheehy Inquiry team focused on a crucial issue here for the police 'service'. It was also an issue that police forces had themselves been aware of for some time. Home Office circular 114/83 provided an impetus to develop and improve management style in many forces through the adoption of 'policing by objectives' or 'planned policing' strategies (for a brief overview of these developments see Brogden, Jefferson and Walklate, 1988: chapter 2). Latterly such concerns have been translated into a focus on customer satisfaction and service delivery; the Plus Programme in the Metropolitan Police, for example (see earlier discussion; Reiner, 1992: chapter 7; Weatheritt, 1993). These initiatives, however, alongside the proposals suggested by Sheehy failed to address one of the key features of police management: the question of discipline.

In a seminar organised as a part of the Sheehy consultation process in January 1993 a number of academics offered a range of different contributions on 'Reforming British Policing: missions and structures'. As a part of that seminar, Paul Wiles offered an interesting analysis of the possibilities for policing by looking to other similarly structured organisations. He commented that:

> In reality senior officers do not manage policing. They usually lack the management skills that are necessary to create change and often do not have the kind of control over resources that would be necessary. Instead the rank structure creates the illusion of management. Senior officers believe they can manage because *they have the authority to issue orders.*
>
> (Wiles, 1993: 65; *my emphasis*)

Addressing the question of authority and its expression within the police organisation is crucial for the effective implementation of organisational change. It is clearly the case that rationalising the management structure and offering greater autonomy over resources does little to tackle the key management problem as identified by Wiles.

The Sheehy Report appeared to be particularly concerned to ensure that the 'police service is seen as a service rather than a "race apart"' (Executive Summary: 5). It takes as being of central importance the quality of the day-to-day contacts between members of the police and the public and the need to recognise the importance of this routine work. The Inquiry team seemed particularly concerned to ensure that those doing a 'good job' in this routine way should be appropriately motivated to continue to do so and to be rewarded for it but not just, or only, through promotion.

These recommendations and the debate they generated assumed that the central task of policing is concerned with 'service' delivery. This assumption reflects a failure to appreciate the nature of policing, not as a special task or job to be performed *per se*, but as a task performed in relation to the question of the legitimate use of *force*. In other words the idea of a police service was presumed to be non-problematic, thereby resonating with the issues addressed earlier in this chapter with respect to women and policing. We are therefore returned to the question of how to understand the central policing task and the question of both the internal organisational, as well as the external implications, for implementing change in that task. Such issues raise the question of management.

Management in the police

As was clearly implied by the contribution of Wiles (1993) to the Sheehy Inquiry seminar, senior police officers frequently believe that they can manage because they possess the authority to do so. Arguably, this belief is one of the crucial stumbling blocks in translating elements of 'good practice' from other organisations to policing and demands some closer scrutiny.

Historically, a militaristic model of management has underpinned policing. This is evidenced by the historical practices of marching on parade, the use of the salute, the routine reference to senior officers as 'sir', amongst other practices. However, whilst some of these more symbolic militaristic practices might be waning, the legacy of the need for discipline runs through policing in a fundamental manner. As Wiles (1993: 55) points out, it has been argued that 'since some policing jobs require obedience to command, and all policing requires a high level of accountability for individual actions, then only a disciplined service can fulfil these two requirements'. However, the extent to which the militaristic model, rooted in a notion of discipline, actually achieves these requirements has consistently been open to criticism, misuse and abuse, and only represents one interpretation of what an accountable police force might look like. The failure to grasp the pervasive influence of this militaristic model, however, inevitably acts to undermine any management initiative which does not take either its influence into account or questions its legitimacy. The question is, why is its influence so important?

Hearn (1987: 94) states that:

> Those parts of the state that are more concerned with repression and violence are more fully male-dominated and male-membered than those parts which are concerned with caring, welfare and reproduction which are usually male-dominated and female-membered.

This serves to remind us of who occupies positions of power in society. Using this, for the moment, to refer to positions that also offer the opportunity for the legitimate use of violence or force, the relationship between gender, power, violence and the state becomes a significant one. The definition of blue-uniform policing adopted at the beginning of this chapter, for example, particularly foregrounded the relationship between policing and the state. In its practical accomplishment soldiering, for example, represents a clustering of gendered expectations relating to work and the workplace, a clustering of expectations which arguably underpinned how the Halford case was managed and responded. The practical accomplishment of policework needs to be similarly located within a gendered framework.

Centring the special nature of policework – its potential for danger, for entering risky situations, for the use of visible direct action – defines some of the commonalities between soldiering and policework. The gendered assumptions underpinning both areas of work, and their relationship to the maintenance of the boundaries of the state, place central importance on the notion of discipline for the internal organisation of policework. Such assumptions have a particular legacy for policework in terms of defining what is or is not acceptable for organisational management as well as what is and what is not acceptable as practical policing work. As Lukes (1974) once pointed out, the exercise of force is only one face of power: the ability to control agendas, information flow and self-perception are also crucially important. It is also of crucial importance for understanding the external definition of the policing task.

The influence of the militaristic model is important, then, because it serves to remind us not only of the key characteristics of the policing task (to be developed below) and its access to the legitimate use of force, but also its gendered nature. Thus management in policing has not been to date concerned with developing the best expertise and skills of officers, but it has been about ensuring hierarchical adherence to authority and the solidarity which emanates from that control. Such management initiatives that have been introduced have, in their effect, been more concerned about managing relationships with the public rather than reflecting a real concern for the internal effectiveness of such developments. In other words, these initiatives have had little effect on the 'cop culture' features of solidarity and control.

It is, of course, difficult to separate the way in which these questions relating to management in the police are intrinsically related to what is understood as the central policing task. The demand for obedience in order to command is predicated on a particular view of policing that centres on the legitimate use of force and highlights the militaristic parallel. The question remains as to whether this is what policing is about.

What is policing about?

As Reiner (1992) has pointed out, there has never been a full debate as to what 'blue-uniform' policing is about. What became clear towards the end of the 1980s was that a concern with 'service delivery' emerged as one of the key features of that task, an assumption that permeates the Sheehy Report and the debate it has generated. The centrality of this service ethos is indicated in the following statement from a police HMI (Her Majesty's Inspector):

> I am sure that the real test of a police service is confidence in what would happen if your own son was arrested, confidence that he would get treated in such a manner that, while he might [bear] a sense of grievance over the event, he would be left with a grudging respect for those who worked with the system.
>
> (Woodcock, 1991: 181, quoted by Reiner, 1992: 269)

In many ways this statement epitomises a number of issues, some acknowledged, some not, reflecting how the policing task may be understood. From one viewpoint it can be regarded as an 'enlightened' statement. In other words, it reflects an acceptance of the focus on service delivery and professionalism as being the key to securing consent for policing. From another viewpoint it is also a statement that tellingly reveals how little has changed in the expression of that task. In this respect it is a highly gendered statement: that is, it leaves unchallenged the view that the mark of service delivery is the level of satisfaction and/or respect that young males have for their treatment by (predominantly) young male police officers.

As Hearn and others have stated: 'Policing has itself always been gendered, and no less so in criminal work.... In the policing of crime, one set of men work against, and sometimes with, another set of men' (Hearn, 1992: 133). In many ways, then, what is represented here is a more fundamental dilemma for policing, both in the formulation of its central task and in the delivery of a 'service' which can fulfil that task; that dilemma is, what is policing about and to whom is this service delivery addressed?

As the discussion in this chapter so far has illustrated, the move towards service-oriented policing has demanded that policing take seriously the private 'safe haven' of the home, at least as seriously as the public domain of the street. The anomalies that such policy movements present are clear. There is no reason, for example, why a positive policy stance on 'domestic' violence should necessarily equate with arresting the offender, if for no other reason than the evidence supporting the effectiveness of this policy is ambivalent, to say the least.

Moreover, an equally positive stance might be constituted in terms of listening support from the officer who appears at the door. Such a position, however, takes all officers away from policing as 'pinching collars' (catching criminals) into another route for performance evaluation. This is the kind of re-orientation of policing which does constitute a real threat to all that we know about how policing tasks are prioritised and practically achieved. If, then, the central task of policing is the policing of young (working-class white and ethnic) males, and police management is rooted in a model which foregrounds masculine/militaristic values, how might an alternative view of this task be constructed?

Towards a gendered agenda for policing

One of the purposes of this chapter has been to suggest that placing these issues in a gendered framework renders visible important issues for men and for women. Moreover, taking seriously the gendered nature of policing affords an opportunity for suggesting ways in which Sheehy-style proposals might be of some value. It also points to some of the problems in assuming that any one strategy is likely to produce any fundamental change in the nature of policework.

For the Sheehy-style proposals to work effectively it is necessary to posit a management framework rooted in *facilitation* rather than discipline. This would need to be put in place alongside an understanding of the central policing task that cultivates seriously the service rather than the force ethos. Both of these carry implications for the kinds of skills and levels of expertise required of police officers and make no necessary presumptions as to the gender, sexual orientation, ethnicity, or age of those people who might possess such skills and expertise. In other words, recruitment of more female officers, or of more female senior managers as perhaps the Halford case suggested, will not in and of themselves impact upon the deep-rooted gendered assumptions on which management in policing has been based.

In addition, if we are to take seriously the notion of a police service rather than a police force, that too requires a re-examination of the motivation, skills and expertise necessary in order to provide such a service. The fact that we have as yet never debated politically what 'blue-uniform policing' is really about serves as testimony to the bracketed, taken-for-granted, presumptions on which policy-makers, academics, politicians and police organisations have proceeded.

Raising these questions in this way demands that we stop considering policing as a special task requiring particular kinds of organisational frameworks and responses, but start to understand policing in relation to what is considered to be normal organisational behaviour in other settings. Through the forging of interconnections such as these, dissemination of good practice might occur, but only if we are prepared to downgrade the centrality of the notion that policing is about the legitimate use of force. As Weatheritt (1993: 44) states:

> The task of improving police performance, that is improving the standards of behaviour of individual police officers, can only be achieved if officers themselves come to believe that that is important and necessary. The police quality of service initiative involves imparting that sense of belief not just through obeisance to the 'customer' and what that implies for measures of police performance but also through the cultivation of a different organisational ethos and a different managerial style.

To that list we need to add a redefined conception of what policing is about, which would automatically include an awareness of alternative policing styles, alternative models of deployment, alternative conceptions of what counts as 'good' policework. In all of these areas there is no need for any necessary presumption to be made concerning the sex of the officer engaged in the work.

To summarise: this chapter has been concerned to offer an appreciation of policework through documenting some of the more recent policy developments in this area and the questions which those developments raise, for police forces as internal organisations and for the 'consumers' of those services. It has been noted that women have featured as significant players in both the implementation and receipt of such services. Our review has raised a number of fundamental questions about the underlying processes at play here. Primarily it has cast considerable doubt on the extent to which it is possible to respond to women as 'consumers' of a police 'service' in the absence of considering what the fundamental character of that service might be. It has been argued, by illustration, that an absence of a debate around policing as a gendered task inhibits both our understanding of that task and what policies are likely to succeed and for whom. Some suggestions have been made which illustrate the possibilities for an alternative policing agenda which might better address the issue of gender. This in itself is not, of course, without its difficulties.

One of the defences frequently offered for the militaristic, disciplined approach to policing is that this is the kind of structure that operates best in public order situations. It is easy to be persuaded by the logic of such a position given the frequency with which such situations seem to generate violence, regardless of whom the participants in the process are. But perhaps here we are too missing the mark. One needs to ask how often the kind of policing associated with football matches, for example, is also evident at large rock concerts? It is not the size of the crowd that matters; more importantly perhaps is the purpose of the gathering: who the crowd is made up of, what their purpose is, and to whom do they pose a threat? It is possible to view all of these questions through a gendered lens. This is not the place to engage in such an analysis, however. The observation is made here to suggest that public order situations in and of themselves do not provide a defence for militaristic policing; there are other ways of handling large crowds. The persistence of this kind of response lends weight to the view that there is a continued reluctance to engage in a differently structured debate around policing.

If more light is cast on the policing task when viewed through a gendered framework, we are perhaps in a better position to understand the impact that the practice of policing has on its recipients, both the victims of crime and those who break the law. That gendered understanding has highlighted a number of dilemmas for women, policewomen, and policemen in this chapter. These dilemmas exist regardless of the ratio of policemen to policewomen but do matter given, as was stated at the beginning of this chapter, that the police officer is often the only member of the criminal justice process with whom a member of the general public has contact. Moreover, to be fair, many police forces have put considerable effort into, and have been required to put considerable effort into, rendering their activities more publicly sensitive and accountable. The same cannot necessarily be said for the other agencies that comprise the criminal justice process.

Conclusion: gender past the policing post

As the statistics presented in the Introduction illustrate, criminal justice work is largely men's work. Although the ratio of men to women varies between policing, probation, the Crown Prosecution Service and the judiciary, it nevertheless remains the case that criminal justice work is primarily men's work. The same can be said of criminology, of course. This point takes us beyond the question of equal opportunities for women (or any other minority group) to the question of the domain assumptions that underpin criminal justice work. In some respects this question is considered in more detail in chapter 6. However it leads us to reflect upon how justice is conceptualised, for whom such conceptualisations make sense, and who are considered to be the most appropriate persons to deliver justice.

As Naffine (1987) has cogently argued elsewhere the 'man of law' is the middle-class entrepreneur. He 'wins' by intellectual stealth rather than by brute force, but his masculinity nevertheless pervades the day-to-day operation and experience of the criminal justice process for men, whose masculinity may be differently constructed and for women. Raising awareness of the pervasiveness of this version of masculinity offers us one way of thinking about not just the adversarial process of the crown court (where establishing the truth is sidelined in the interests of winning), but the success or otherwise of those practitioners who do not embrace this version of masculinity (male or female), down to the likely outcome of partnership working between, for example, a probation service committed to 'reflective practice' and a police force embedded in militarism. In other words, because we all 'do gender', albeit in differently structured ways mediated by class, age, sex and ethnicity, it is still something that we all do. A gendered lens can help us think more critically, and may be more constructively, about different ways in which, in this case, justice can be conceptualised. Some of the questions generated by such a discussion as this are considered in the next chapter.

Suggestions for further reading

Reiner, R. (1992, second edition) *The Politics of the Police* A must as an introduction to an appreciation of the nature of policework.

Heidensohn, F. (1992), *Women in Control? The role of women in law Enforcement* A useful development of Heidensohn's own distinction between 'women under control' and 'women in control' and a valuable empirical study of policewomen.

For a more policy-oriented consideration of contemporary policing problems and issues see F. Leishman, B. Loveday and M. Savage (eds), (2000), *Core Issues in Policing*.

6 Gender, the law, and criminal justice policy

> So rationality itself, whether theoretical or practical, is a concept with a history: indeed since there are a diversity of traditions of enquiry, with histories, there are, so it will turn out, rationalities rather than rationality, just as it will also turn out that there are justices rather than justice.
>
> (MacIntyre, 1988: 9)

Introduction

This book began by identifying some of the key themes which have underpinned both the disciplines of criminology and victimology as they have tried to develop an understanding of the nature of criminal behaviour and its impact. One of those themes, which feminist work has challenged, provides a thread of continuity between these disciplinary areas and other social sciences. That thread is concerned with the question of what constitutes rational knowledge for the social sciences. The feminist challenge on this issue has encouraged a critical analysis of what counts as knowledge and who can possess it. In a similar vein to the implications derivable from the quote by MacIntyre, that feminist work has led to a consideration of alternative ways of characterising that which counts as rational knowledge. In the context of the study of crime and the law this has also led to a consideration of alternative ways of characterising what counts as justice. The debate engendered by these explorations raises a more fundamental debate concerning whether, as a consequence, this means that all knowledge is relative; a position which those fully committed to positivism would find difficult to accept but one which postmodernism would accommodate more readily. These issues aside, the general purpose of this chapter is to consider the fruitfulness of alternative ways of thinking about the law and justice which have been derived from feminist work in this area, and the value of exploring such questions through the lens of masculinity.

This chapter falls into two halves. The first half concerns itself with how the process of the law works. In other words, when a male or a female defendant (or complainant) appears before the court, how are decisions made about them? What kinds of constructs does the court draw upon to make its decision and are those constructs used in the same way or differently for males and females? The second half of the chapter concerns itself more directly with the question of punishment. Again the question here is not so much, are male and females disposed of differently by the court, but what are the effects of that disposition, and do those effects impact upon males and females differently? In both instances we shall be concerned to examine what the possibilities might be for constructing either the law or the penal process differently in such a way which might benefit both sexes.

As the previous chapters have illustrated, one way of understanding the response of the criminal justice process to the phenomenon of crime is through a gendered lens. This lens illustrated, for example, the way in which understanding policework as a product of gendered social relationships constitutes a key mechanism for understanding policing itself. In this chapter we shall also be focusing on the way in which assumptions associated with gender underpin the structure and the implementation of the law. This will lead to a consideration of two substantive issues: whether or not there is a case for a 'feminist jurisprudence', and whether or not a case can be made for a 'woman-wise penology', and the implications of each of these debates for men. But first it will be useful to construct a working understanding of the law.

Understanding the law

Those outside the professional discipline of the law frequently struggle with how the law operates. In the context of crime, the criminal law obviously acts as a defining framework for understanding that behaviour which is understood to be criminal as distinct from that behaviour which is not. Whilst the law might act as a framework in this way its impact is never definitive. In other words, not all of the guilty who are brought to court are either found guilty or necessarily 'punished'. Understanding how this happens poses (at least) two problematic issues for the lay person. The first stems from the presumption that the process of enacting the law is a process concerned with establishing the truth or falsity of a case: that is, that the function of the law is to establish the guilt or innocence of the defendant, especially in criminal cases. Anyone who has been called to be a witness in a criminal trial, or who has sat in the public gallery during a trial, is soon relieved of this view! The adversarial tradition of the law embraced in the U.K. and the U.S.A., dictates that seeking the truth is a subservient concern to the process of establishing, beyond reasonable doubt, on the basis of admissible evidence, that the defendant is guilty of the offence for which they have been charged. Consequently the process of interpreting the evidence and convincing the jury of that interpretation is a crucial feature of the criminal trial. It is no wonder that many people called to give evidence as witnesses in such proceedings feel that they themselves have been on trial, and that in the execution of their public duty they have simply not been believed! In this adversarial process, then, there is considerable room for different interpretations of the same evidence to be constructed. It is within this space that gendered presumptions concerning both victims and offenders (complainants and defendants) are often displayed.

Recognition of the fact that the law is not primarily about establishing the truth leads to the second issue which sometimes concerns those outside the professional enclave of the law. This draws attention to the role that case law plays in both setting precedents for understanding particular cases and acting as a catalyst for changing those precedents. It is through the practice and implementation of the law, via case law, that ways of understanding and interpreting the intent of the law are constituted. Such bodies of knowledge mean that it is possible for changes to occur in such practices and interpretations without any necessary concomitant change in the kind of behaviour which has been defined as legal or illegal.

Taken together, these two issues frequently lead the lay person to the conclusion that the 'law is an ass'. However, other conclusions are also possible. Whilst these issues clearly make us aware of the flexibility of the law, that flexibility is not infinite. The law also operates *systematically*. One way in which it operates in this way is through structured presumptions relating to gender – leading Helena Kennedy QC to conclude that 'Eve was Framed' (1992). It is the systematic way in which these processes associated with the law operate, reflecting certain gendered assumptions about both the issues and the people who come before the court, which are of particular concern here. It will be useful, therefore, to have a general overview of how gendered assumptions permeate the workings of criminal proceedings before examining the implications of these processes in greater detail.

Gender in court

Some time ago now Heidensohn (1985) drew the useful distinction between 'women under control' and 'women in control' in understanding the impact of gender on women's experiences of the criminal justice process. Here we shall focus on three particular empirical studies that have revealed different ways in which 'women under control' are kept that way.

Experiences in magistrates' courts

Eaton's study, *Justice for Women: Family, Court and Social Control* (1986), was concerned to document the practices taking place within the magistrate's court which enables it to operate as a site for social control. This study compares and contrasts the experience of the magistrate's court for both male and female defendants. It is particularly concerned to document the way in which professionals operating within the magistrates' arena manage that site in the interests of their clients. In a detailed analysis of pleas of mitigation presented by lawyers, social inquiry reports prepared by probation officers, and interviews with magistrates, she reveals the ways in which notions of the family and/or the home, are differentially employed to depict both the character and the circumstances of male and female defendants in understanding and/or explaining their law-breaking behaviour.

So, for example, professional comment is often made concerning a man's employment record (read meeting the needs of his family) and a woman's child care and housewifely skills. These references are used to construct particular images of the defendant as in all other respects responsible and reliable members of a viable and needy family unit. Thus the normality or otherwise of the defendant's family life constitutes a key mechanism of appeal for sympathy from the court. The normal family life constructed in the magistrate's court, of course, is the presumed normal family life of wider society. It consists of a male and a female in a heterosexual relationship and it is an enduring, privileged unit of social responsibility. In Eaton's study it is within this conceptualisation of normal family life and its impact on the operation of the court that gendered assumptions become apparent.

From this Eaton concludes that, when a man and a woman appear before the court in similar circumstances charged with similar offences, they receive similar treatment. This results from the fact that the magistrate's court draws equally on their family life as a part of its decision-making process. But the impact of this is double-edged not only for those who fall outside this conceptualisation of normalcy, but also for those who are dealt with within it. As Eaton (1986: 143) says;

> By judging both male and female defendants in the context of their families, the court displays not only impartiality or equality of treatment, but its role of preserving difference based on sexual inequality.

So this study suggests that in terms of outcome, all other things being equal, the magistrate's court on the surface treats male and female defendants equally. However, the basis on which the court makes such decisions reflects a fundamental acceptance of quite different images of men and women. Such differences affect the process of decision-making in the court. Similar issues are also highlighted in the work of Allen (1987).

Psychiatry and the law

Allen's study considers the interaction between psychiatry and the law.

This study takes as its starting-point the empirical evidence that women are twice as likely as men to be dealt by the court by psychiatric means. In other words, they are much more likely to receive a sentence from the court that includes some form of medical or psychiatric treatment. Allen's concern is to understand how this empirical fact is produced – regardless, it would appear, of the actual mental state of the defendant. In order to understand this process, Allen argues, it is necessary to understand the ways in which psychiatry and the law intersect.

In order to establish criminal responsibility, the court requires evidence of a wrongful deed (*actus reus*) and a wrongful mind (*mens rea*). Allen's study indicates that the way in which these two sources of evidence are connected is conducted differently for men than for women. For example, in examining psychiatric reports written for male and female defendants this study indicates that there is more written about the mental life of females; males are written about in terms of what they do, that is, how they participate in the world, while females are written about in terms of what happens to them rather than in terms of them initiating or engaging in intentional behaviour. This latter distinction becomes particularly focused in the cases of diminished responsibility examined in the study. Reports written for male defendants in which this plea was possible indicate the readiness with which they were created as 'monsters' or 'madmen', yet simultaneously capable of intending their behaviour since men are to be understood in terms of what they do.

On the other hand female defendants under consideration in these terms were much more readily constructed as 'normal women'. The abberation in their behaviour, the law-breaking behaviour, was more often than not understood as indicative of the potential for abberation apparent in all women's behaviour. In other words, things happen to women; they do not make rational decisions or choices. Such imaging facilitates the identification of females as experiencing diminished responsibility much more readily than their male counterparts. This study, then, conveys a key message. When psychiatry and the law interact, the resultant effect is that men are, for the most part, attributed with a sense of agency and responsibility for their actions, whilst women defendants are denied this.

Female defendants

This denial of agency for female defendants is the theme of the final study to be examined here. Worrall's *Offending Women* (1990) explores the way in which the experts within the criminal justice system endeavour to make sense of women's criminality as either not really being criminal, or of the women themselves not really being women. As Worrall (1990: 35) states:

> The female law-breaker is rationally offered the opportunity to neutralise the effects of her law-breaking activity by implicitly entering into a contract

> whereby she permits her life to be represented primarily in terms of its domestic, sexual and pathological dimensions.

The process of entering into this 'gender contract' (Carlen, 1988) eliminates any uncomfortable ideological or social consequences which female criminality might present to the court. Problems only arise when female offenders refuse to enter into the contract; when they refuse to be categorised. Worrall's study documents the experiences of fifteen such women, whom she calls 'nondescript women', who refused categorisation in this way.

Worrall's work illustrates the ways in which the experts in the criminal justice system, from magistrates to social workers, struggled to render these women invisible, guilty, treatable and manageable. In other words they struggled to render their behaviour safe and non-threatening to the system.

There are a number of themes common to each of these studies which illustrate the way in which assumptions relating to gender in general and women in particular permeate the actual operational practices of the criminal justice system. In general terms it is possible to see that, of course, the criminal justice system is not immune from wider society. Stereotypical assumptions associated with male and female behaviour are, therefore, bound to be reflected in the criminal justice system. Having said this, however, the law and the criminal justice system present themselves as both a body of knowledge and a system rooted in neutrality. Yet these studies clearly indicate that, all other things being equal, female and male defendants are not processed in equal terms.

Female defendants, in particular, are frequently denied a sense of responsibility for their own actions and are placed in what Worrall (1990) calls the 'compassion trap' – a view of women which cannot separate them, as women, from the presumptions of femininity which expects them to be them caring, nurturing and domestic. In this respect, as was stated earlier, the criminal justice system presents little for women that is different from their experiences of a whole range of other institutional settings. Indeed, in a sense this muting of women's voices and experiences as offenders within the criminal justice system is a feature they share in common with female professionals working within it.

These processes, however, also distort men's lives. The studies by Eaton and Allen both illustrate, though not always explicitly, the way in which the responses to men as defendants are also bound by stereotypical assumptions concerning their manhood. For example, the presentation of evidence to the court that a male defendant is essentially a good husband (read breadwinner) can be used to impress the court in the judgement it makes with respect to appropriate sentencing. Similarly, the way in which a man on trial for murder may be constructed as a monster taps the more threatening elements of masculinity – masculinity as the embodiment of uncontrolled natural urges.

Gendered assumptions not only manifest themselves in the context of offending or law-breaking behaviour. They are also evident in the way in which the criminal justice system processes women and men who appear as complainants before the court. Such presumptions, as Collier (1998) has argued, are also sexualised; that is, they render heterosexuality visible and homosexuality invisible. The way in which such assumptions manifest themselves can be illustrated best by reviewing what is learned from rape trials in this respect.

Rape on trial

Whilst the rate at which rape is reported to the police has certainly increased in the last ten years, the chances of a defendant on a rape charge being found guilty are still relatively small(Home Office, 1996). The explanation for this disparity is in part to be found in the conduct of the rape trial itself. In rape trials the way in which corroborating evidence is used and interpreted, alongside the performance of the complainant in the face of frequently very close interrogation by the defence barrister, can prove to be crucial elements in the acquittal or conviction of the defendant. This process, then, self-evidently puts the complainant, the woman, on trial and in such a way that is possibly more emotionally problematic than that experienced by witnesses in general. This, at least, is the way in which women experience the process. Moreover a closer examination of the actual conduct of rape trials suggests that such felt experiences are both reliable and valid sources of insight into how the court treats gender.

Women's experience of rape trials is governed by what Adler (1987) has called 'the importance of being perfect'. In key ways this mechanism resonates very closely with what has been referred to elsewhere as the 'Madonna-Whore' continuum (see for example Heidensohn, 1985). Adler's empirical examination of rape trials coming before the Old Bailey in the early 1980s revealed a number of strategies adopted by defence barristers in order to discredit the woman's testimony. These strategies were effectively designed to render their evidence less than believable, on the grounds of her characteristics as a woman rather than on grounds relating to the particular incident before the court. In the cases studied by Adler, questioning by defence barristers focused very much on the woman's behaviour before, during and after the alleged incident. Such questioning has two purposes: to establish the woman's respectability (or otherwise) and to establish how worldly-wise she was (is she a nice girl?). The ultimate purpose being, of course, to cast doubt on her credibility as a witness and thereby her evidence.

In Adler's study, women identified as less than respectable were: single mothers, Greenham Common supporters, girls with punk hairstyles, mothers with children in care, women with a criminal record or anyone living in a commune. Women who fell into these categories would be presented to the court, by the implications of the defence barrister's questioning, as being unlikely genuine victims. In this way a woman's general lifestyle can be called upon to cast doubt on whether or not they should be believed about this particular event. A woman's 'niceness' is called into question by raising questions about her use of contraception, the status of her virginity, evidence of sexually transmitted disease, her drinking habits, and her willingness or otherwise to report the incident to the police. Questions like these reflect the commonly held assumption that nice girls do not get raped. Such questioning can frequently go beyond the woman's behaviour in relation to the incident under examination, and can touch upon very private aspects of a woman's body. Examine, for example, the following extract from a court case reported by Lees (1989):

> *Defence counsel*: As far as your knickers were concerned, you didn't assist him?
> *Woman*: No.
> *Defence counsel*: How could he get them off without your help?
> *Woman*: I don't know, but he did.
> *Defence counsel*: What happened to them?
> *Woman*: I threw them away and burned them.
> *Defence counsel*: Why didn't you save them to show to the police?
> *Woman*: What for?
> No answer. Defence counsel changes the subject:
> *Defence counsel*: He touched your vagina and it was lubricated.
> *Woman*: It was not lubricated.

In the same case when the defendant is on the stand, he has this to say:

> *Prosecution*: You frightened her into submitting?
> *Man*: No... women, they're really complicated, you know. I've come across women who play hard to get, but when I make a move they respond.... I'm saying she wanted it, her body wanted it, but her mind was somewhere else.

This statement by the defendant was not challenged by the prosecution. However, it reflects a remarkable parallel in thinking between the defendant and the defence counsel questioning: despite all evidence given by the woman to the contrary, at the end of the day it is implied that she does not know her own mind. A woman can want sex without her even knowing it; hence the question about 'lubrication'. Indeed, there is something more illustrated by this brief extract. Not only do women not know when they want a sexual relationship, their desires, whatever they may be, are only to be understood and interpreted in male terms; that is, in terms of penetration.

The issue of penetration, where the penis went and how far, is crucial to a rape trial given the legal definition of the act. This focus offers an insight into not only how women's bodies are viewed in law, but also provides a clue as to how men are seen to operate. Smart (1989) argues that 'phallocentrism' is celebrated in the rape trial. This means two things. Not only are women's experiences disqualified, but that this is achieved through the privileging of a male-centred view of both female and male sexuality. Women do not know what they want, they have to be persuaded. Therefore men cannot be blamed for acting on what are after all deep-seated sexual needs. In the face of temptation, these are uncontrollable!

This phallocentrism reveals something more about how the legal process thinks about men in the context of rape trials. Given that of those who are tried for rape, few are actually convicted, those few who are, must be problematic men. Those who are set free are merely helpless when confronted by their sexual desires. Those convicted are the psychologically deranged 'other men', in whose name men as a group dare not speak! In the context of the previous discussion, the study by Lees (1997) would suggest that despite some changes in the law and changes in police practices, once in court little else has changed.

There is an interesting paradox in this thinking, of course. Women are presumed not to know their own bodies. So rather like many female lawbreakers, women complainants in rape trials are denied a sense of agency for their actions. They are therefore rarely heard in their own terms or understood in relation to their own experiences. Yet simultaneously the male defendant, in rape trials especially, is also denied a sense of agency (read control) for his own actions; he succumbs to his natural sexual urges. This paradox is rendered invisible by the assertion of a phallocentric view of sexual intercourse, as Smart argues, but is simultaneously rendered invisible by the embedded structure of the law itself; the definition of rape and the way that cases in court play that definition out. The consequence of this is that we also fail to see men, perhaps, as they really are. As Naffine (1997: 119) suggests:

> It is not only women who suffer from the culture of the strong man, though it is women who are consistently dispossessed by it.... There are a range of other masculinities which are simultaneously implied, and then cast out. They are, by implication, rendered unnatural and undesirable. Thus are the men who depart from the masculine ideal rendered silent.

This line of reasoning presupposes that males and females are not treated equally by the presumptions that underpin the law. Images and understandings of the one, the former, are always privileged over the latter. This privileging of the male world view over the female is deeply embedded in the thinking which both underpins and supports the law. This has led some to argue for the law to be changed, especially in relation to those aspects of its operation which appear to have a particularly detrimental effect on women. It has led others to argue for a feminist jurisprudence, an approach which wishes to challenge the fundamental structure of legal rationale itself. We shall examine the legitimacy of each of these viewpoints in turn.

Would changing the law make a difference for women or for men?

There are two areas in which there has been considerable substantive debate concerning the effectiveness of changing the law: in cases of rape, and with respect to the use of the plea of provocation in cases of murder. We shall discuss each of these in turn.

Rape

Whilst changes in the legal interpretation of who can and cannot be raped have occurred there has been little change in what actually counts as rape. In other words, its sexual emphasis has remained. Efforts have been made in other countries to redefine the act of rape as an act of violence. This has been the case in Canada. The question remains, how effective might such a change of emphasis be?

In Canada in 1983 what was referred to as Bill C-127 came into force. This replaced the offences of rape, attempted rape and indecent assault with the offences of sexual assault, sexual assault with a weapon, and aggravated sexual assault. The intention of these changes was to emphasise the violence of the behaviour being considered before the court and to eliminate any sex-specific presumptions concerning either the victim or the offender. The actual definition of what counted as the sexual assault element of the behaviour was left for the court to decide. This new scale of offences carried with it a scale of punishments, becoming more severe with the seriousness of the offence.

Considerable evaluation work has been conducted concerning both the impact and the effectiveness of these legal changes. That work indicates four main findings:

- there was an increase in reporting behaviour subsequent to the change in the law;
- there has been no impact on the proportion of cases founded by the police;
- conviction rates have not increased;

- and the trend has been to hear cases at the lowest level of severity (Roberts, 1991).

So whilst changing the law does appear to have some impact on reporting behaviour, its impact beyond this seems to be very limited? The question is why?

First of all it is important to remember that the law is only one element in the criminal justice process. Whilst the law can, and does, set the boundary to what is legal and illegal, that boundary still has to be enforced, and enforced effectively. In practice how that effectiveness is interpreted can become crucial to the impact that any change in the law might have. In this particular example, it could be that, given the policing imperative is to secure a prosecution (McConville *et al* 1990), it was this imperative which produced the trend towards convictions at the less serious end of the scale rather than the law itself failing to fulfil its purpose. There is, however, a much more fundamental tension here between the kind of change that can be achieved through the law, and understanding what the law, in terms of legal thinking, actually represents (see discussion below).

So, it would appear from this example that where efforts have been made to define the act of rape in terms of its violence and in a non-sex specific way, such changes have not made a fundamental impact to the way in which the criminal justice process deals with such cases. It is still difficult to secure convictions. Such difficulties remain, some would argue, because of the very private nature of the activity under question. Only the complainant and the defendant really know what happened. This serves to remind us that the law deals with individual cases even though it does not always operate with an individualised understanding of individual cases. This raises a number of fundamental questions including those that relate to the premises on which the law operates. In this particular context one of questions raised by changing the law on rape in order to emphasise it as an act of violence, is how is violence recognised in law, for whom is violence deemed appropriate, and under what circumstances? These points are aptly illustrated by the use and interpretation of the defence of provocation in cases of murder. This provides an important link between these two different yet similar substantive issues.

Murder

In cases of murder, if the defendant is found guilty, there is a statutory penal response of life imprisonment. In the process of the court case it is possible for the defence to submit evidence on which such a charge may be reduced to manslaughter, for which the judge has much greater discretion in sentencing. The grounds on which this might happen can vary, but there are three main legal strategies open to the defence:

- they can present evidence that argues for diminished responsibility; a strategy which focuses on the mental health of the defendant at the time the offence was committed;
- they can present an argument rooted in a notion of self-defence; this strategy argues that the defendant's actions were justified on the grounds of them being in imminent danger;
- finally they can argue the case on the grounds of provocation. This is a strategy that admits responsibility for the act but requests that the act be excused because the behaviour of the defendant was justified: they were provoked.

What is often confusing for the lay person is that the defence can choose to follow one, two, or all three of these strategies simultaneously (not that the last of these is necessarily recommended) since their overriding purpose is to place doubt in the jury's mind as to the legitimacy of the charge of murder. The success or otherwise of any of these strategies appears to be variable.

One of the variables in the successful use of the defence of provocation appears to be the sex of the defendant. It is, however, difficult to assess how significant a variable this is since there has been no really systematic evaluation of the use of the plea of provocation that controls for the possible influence of all other extraneous variables. For example, a recent study by Hedderman and Hough (1994) suggests that for all cases of homicide between 1984 and 1992 a defence of provocation was accepted in 29 per cent of cases involving female defendants compared with 20 per cent of cases involving men. Without deeper statistical analysis alongside other variables, however, it is not possible to evaluate the significance of this finding as a general pattern. However, a number of recent celebrated cases have put to the fore the potential inequities which do exist when one examines *particular* cases.

Three cases which received particular public attention were those of Sara Thornton, Kiranjit Ahluwalia, and Amelia Rossiter. Each of these women received prison sentences for murdering their partners who, it was argued, had been persistently and systematically violent towards them. For many feminist campaigners these constituted grounds enough for a defence of provocation. Indeed in the United States, the case has been argued for a special defence plea in such circumstances of 'psychological self-defence' (Ewing, 1987) as a way of recognising the cumulative effects of living in a violent relationship.

The legal interpretation of provocation is, however, tightly circumscribed. This interpretation adopts the view that any delay between the provoking act and the act of retaliation must offer the opportunity for 'calming down'. So subsequent retaliatory action can only be seen as revenge. The notion of cumulative provocation and/or cumulative rage is, therefore, highly problematic for English law. Yet this is exactly what many women in violent relationships, who subsequently end that relationship by killing their partner, actually experience. This disjunction between the way in which women who kill their violent partners experience provocation and the sometimes blatant acceptance of the court of defences of provocation in terms of adultery or 'nagging' for male defendants, has led to a campaign to change the law to allow for a notion of 'cumulative provocation'.

Such a campaign is predicated on the view that the current interpretation of provocation is male in its orientation, delineating a traditionally male concern with finding their female partner in *flagrante delecto* and the likely response this might produce. Violence under these circumstances would be 'understood', a case of man regaining control over what was rightfully his. Violence in a woman under such circumstances would, however, be seen as a loss of control. Campbell (1993: 152) expresses this in this way:

> Reason to a man means a detached appraisal of threat and the use of appropriate violence. Reason to a woman means holding to non-violence until self-control finally snaps under too much exploitation. All reasonable women have a breaking-point and all reasonable women have a right to have that fact understood.

It is this fact that the criminal justice process has problems in dealing with. In individual terms, of course, its impact is not only problematic for women, it is also problematic for men, since their potential for and expression of rage is also circumscribed by the law's interpretation.

As with the case of rape, this discussion of the use of the defence of provocation is hampered by the extent to which individual cases can be seen to be representative of the implementation of a general practice in all similar cases. This tension between the particular and the general, whilst often used to undermine the legitimacy of the criticism levelled at the individual case, misses the more fundamental point. In some respects it matters little whether or not individual cases of rape are better served by changing the law on rape, or whether individual 'battered' women get a fairer hearing from the court if they murder their violent partner, though such changes obviously matter for those individual women. Of more fundamental concern in how these two substantive examples of the law's operation illustrate the persistence of the presumptions of abstraction, objectivity, and rationality, deeply embedded in legal thinking; presumptions which have been taken, for the most part, to mean male abstraction, male objectivity, and male rationality.

The concern with changing the law also illustrates a key problem for feminists, as Kendall (1991: 80) points out in a different context:

> The question feminists face is whether justice for women is best achieved through legal recognition of sexual difference (special treatment) or by regarding sexual difference as largely irrelevant (equal treatment).

This poses a key theoretical dilemma (as opposed perhaps to a campaigning dilemma) for feminists. The belief in and the pursuit of change in the law as a mechanism for implementing change for women as a group (as opposed to changes which might benefit individual women) implicitly accepts the law as abstract, objective and rational, and therefore as a site in which social change can be achieved. This, of course, not only buys into liberal feminism, but also the classic liberal philosophy that underpins modern legal thought. It leaves unquestioned the issue of whose interests are best served by the law as it stands.

This discussion implies that whilst changing the law may benefit individual women, as a strategy of collective gain, it is likely to be limited, unless our understanding of the law is put into a broader historical and political framework. Without that broader historical framework such changes are also likely to perpetuate the interests of the white heterosexual male. The extent to which an understanding of the profound effect of presumptions underpinning legal thought can aid our understanding of the likely effectiveness of changing the law will be examined in the next section.

Is there a case for a feminist jurisprudence?

A good deal has been written both for and against the possibility of a feminist jurisprudence. For the purposes of this overview we shall concentrate primarily on the contributions to this debate made by several key writers: Naffine (1990), Carlen (1990) and Smart (1989). The question itself presupposes that we know something of the nature of the law which justifies the construction of an alternative to it. It raises the possibility of a number of justices, as suggested by MacIntyre at the start of this chapter, and in posing this possibility demands that we examine very carefully the ways in which the notion of the 'legal man' structures both male and female, complainant and defendant, experiences of the criminal justice system.

Naffine (1990) identifies three phases of feminist response to understanding the law. The first phase, which can be equated with the liberal feminist position, accepts that the law should be, and can be, fair and impartial. Its sexist practices are a result of a failure to apply its own professional standards to women. This view of the law implicitly accepts the law as rational but in its practice fails to live up to its own aims because it constrains women. What is necessary, therefore, is for the law to be changed so that it can recognise women's rights.

This position constitutes a debate with the law in its own terms. It is a position which, whilst having made some considerable gains for women, has also backfired on them (Smart, 1989). Such a rights-based approach, as the examples above have illustrated, fails to understand the fundamental nature of the law and whose interests are served by it. Therefore it is consequently limited in the success it is likely to achieve.

The second phase of feminist response to the law Naffine (1990) labels the 'male culture of law'. This position, equated perhaps most readily with a radical feminist analysis, makes a very strong statement about the central values of the law. This implies that it is necessary to examine much more than who makes the laws, who interprets them, and who gets to practice law, all of which are predominantly male activities (see Introduction). It also means examining those values that define the law as a fundamental patriarchal institution. These are:

- detachment;
- the adversarial form;
- the commitment to rationality.

Taken together these values identify the law as an institution deeply imbued with the male perspective as to what counts as objective, rational knowledge.

The strong version of this view of the law is found in the work of MacKinnon. This view has strong parallels with the feminist standpoint theorists discussed in chapter 1. It argues that because women see the world from both the viewpoint of the oppressors and the oppressed, a body of knowledge called 'the law' rooted in a female world view would be more objective. But, of course, as both Naffine (1990) and Smart (1989) point out, this view of the law imbues it with a consistency and a uniformity that it does not possess. The law is not a simple set of coherent cultural values. It is complex and contradictory. The ways in which it lays claim to rationality, fairness and objectivity, are intimately connected with the values of the wider society of which it is a part, which adds to the complexity of understanding its operation at any particular historical moment. Recognition of these interconnections constitutes what Naffine (1990) characterises as the third phase in the feminist response to the law, which attempts to map the links between legal rhetoric and the patriarchal social order. Smart's (1989) work in particular falls into this category.

Smart (1989) develops her view of the possibilities for a feminist jurisprudence out of some concerns with the work of MacKinnon. She argues that MacKinnon's position accepts a view of men and masculinity as being beyond culture and history, a process which distorts women's experiences. Yet at the same time MacKinnon appears to want to replace one unitary and distorting view of the world, the male view, with another unitary, and presumably distorting view, the female. This desire to replace one world view with another fails to remove feminism from the traps of both essentialism (men and women are naturally and fundamentally different) and determinism (people, men nor women, have no choice). Smart (1989), influenced by postmodernist thinking, prefers to deconstruct the law. The question is, what does this mean?

Smart (1989) argues that the law articulates a 'phallogocentric discourse' – phallocentric because its character is centrally masculine and heterosexual, logocentric because the knowledge produced thereby is not neutral but is produced under patriarchal social conditions. In Smart's (1989) analysis this discourse is illustrated in the construction of the rape trial. This construction serves both to disqualify women's experiences and to celebrate phallocentrism. So it is not just a matter of establishing that consent was not given but also of showing that no pleasure was achieved by the woman (as shown by the extract quoted above). As Smart states (*ibid*: 42), 'pressing a woman until she submits is a natural pleasurable phallocentric pastime. The rape trial will not allow for any criticism of this natural activity'.

Analysing the practices of the law in this way indicates that the law itself cannot address the structured relationships of power which produce experiences like these. The rape trial, for example, acts as a site of struggle in which gendered social relationships are played out, but cannot provide an answer to those gendered relationships. Thus Smart's analysis is concerned to resist any tendencies to see the law as offering any universal claim on Truth, but argues for an understanding of the law as a gendering strategy through which men and women are brought into being, albeit not in a coherent or unitary fashion (see for example, Smart, 1992). This approach takes Smart down a route which does not neglect the importance of understanding the power and influence of the law's gendering strategies, but clearly calls for a greater critical awareness of how, and under what circumstances, those strategies are played out. This is one potential consequence of understanding the law as a part of patriarchal social relationships as opposed to being separate from them. Naffine's (1990) own concern with understanding the law in this way takes her down a different route.

Naffine (1990) suggests that these three phases of feminist response to the law lead to a critical consideration of what she calls 'the man of law'. This returns us to understanding the impact that the notion of *Gesellschaft*, 'the community of strangers', has in structuring the domain assumptions of the law. Naffine's analysis draws out the images of masculinity which underpin the liberal philosophy emergent in 'the community of strangers' and which consequently underpin legal thinking. Thus the 'man of law' is the competitive entrepreneur, the successful market individual who has the 'eye for the main chance'. This analysis is concerned, then, to do more than identify the parallels between the values of the legal profession and the values of the market place as male-dominated spheres. Naffine is concerned to identify not only who is included by this image of the legal man but also who is excluded by it.

The domain assumptions of masculinity identified above and arguably embedded in the law reflect a particular version of masculinity. It is a masculinity of the intellect, of the middle-classes, rather than a masculinity of brute force. Thus rather like Smart, Naffine's analysis challenges the radical feminist presumption that the law is unitary and uniform in its operation. Moreover Naffine's analysis in concerned to explore the ways in which some men are also marginalised by the way in which the law is constructed. So, whilst the middle-class, rational, entrepreneur articulates an image of the ideal typical male with which the law operates, its impact is felt by both men and women whose presentation of themselves does not match with this image. Thus the working-class black male is problematic for the law not just as a law-breaker but also as a man. The female offender is equally likely to be put in her place. Perhaps here lies an understanding, in part, of the ways in which professionals can work with what they know the courts will find acceptable by constructing images of their clients which tap into these domain assumptions (see earlier discussion).

This more recent feminist scholarship centring on the law directs our attention to a number of issues. First, neither the analyses of Naffine and Smart undermine campaigns to change the law, but they clearly indicate that energies focused totally in this direction will have limited effect. This does not mean that gains have not been made for women through changing the law. But it does reflect a view that placing too much emphasis on the law as being of central importance overlooks both its underlying presumptions and the complex way in which these are expressed. Whether or not recognition of this establishes the case for a feminist jurisprudence depends upon how that notion itself is understood.

The ideas and the work discussed here draw together quite a range of feminist work around the law. Whether or not the cumulative consequence of that work constitutes a feminist jurisprudence is, however, a moot point. Whether or not in fact there is a need for a feminist jurisprudence as a coherent alternative to conventional jurisprudence is perhaps a more worthwhile question to ask – a question to which different writers, not unexpectedly, have formulated different answers. For example, there is a clear scepticism in Smart's work as to whether it is either possible or even desirable to strive for a way of thinking through the law which can represent all women's (or for that matter, all men's) experiences.

In some respects this debate is tied into a more general debate concerned with sameness and difference. Given that sex, either as a biological or a cultural imperative, cannot be avoided (we are all constructed in relation to the category sex in some form or another) how do we make gender less relevant? Naffine (1997: 153) suggests that 'We need to let the exile bear witness'. In other words we need to find space to let the criminological 'Other' speak. Carlen has taken this on board in a very practical sense since, as she so aptly states, female law-breakers cannot avoid the law. They do not stand in the court voluntarily; they await punishment. In this respect Carlen argues that within the search for a feminist jurisprudence, or any other kinds of jurisprudence of which there might be several, there is also a need for the establishment of a feminist penology. It is to women's (and men's) experiences of the law in terms of punishment that we shall now turn.

Gender in the penal process

Women, on average, make up about 4 per cent of the total prison population. In 1991, 1,561 women were held in prison at any one time. The average male prison population during 1991 was 44,336. Seventy-nine per cent of women sentenced to prison in 1991 were serving sentences of less than 18 months. In that same year 41 per cent of adult women sentenced were convicted for theft or forgery compared with 22 per cent of men, and only 17 per cent of women had been convicted for offences of violence against the person as compared with 37 per cent of men. Moreover, in 1991, 29 per cent of women in prison came from an ethnic minority, compared with the fact that black people make up only 5 per cent of the population as a whole (all statistics taken from NACRO: *Women Leaving Prison*, 1993). In 1999 these figures had risen to 3,391 women in prison of a general prison population of 61,964, 350 of whom are incarcerated for crimes of violence. Whilst Hedderman and Hough (1994) point out that women receive fewer and shorter sentences than men, and women first offenders are half as likely to be given prison sentences that their male counterparts, there are only twelve women's prison's offering various levels of 'secure containment'. This means that many women are held in institutions at some travelling distance from their homes, which frequently raised difficulties with respect to the maintenance of family ties.

These are some of the facts surrounding the question of women's experience of the penal process. Other information suggests that women get sent to prison earlier in their criminal careers than men and receive prison as a punishment for less serious crimes than men. Overall, however, women make up a very small proportion of the total prison population. The question therefore arises, why focus on women's imprisonment at all? The NACRO document referenced above offers four reasons as to why we should be concerned about penal policy with reference to women:

- being a small proportion of the prison population should mean that they are well catered for. The reality is that women are expected to handle their sentences in a system designed for, and catering for, men.

- women react to imprisonment differently from men. Men are outwardly violent. Women turn their violence in on themselves that can have much more long term damaging effects.

- being sent to prison for women often means that they lose more than men. Nearly half the women in prison, for example, have dependent children.

- women face a double discrimination on release. Not only are they ex-prisoners, as ex-female prisoners they face discrimination on the grounds that they have also offended accepted standards of feminine behaviour. There is, however, a fifth reason for examining some of the issues associated with female imprisonment. From such an examination it is possible to learn valuable lessons which are also relevant to men's imprisonment.

Historically, it was not until the campaigning work of Elizabeth Fry that women were segregated from men in prison. Fry argued for a different treatment for women on the grounds that they committed different crimes, that their behaviour differed whilst in prison, and that they were different biologically and socially. More contemporarily, these differences have won women some 'concessions' in comparison with men in relation to the way in which their day-to-day life in prison is constructed. For example, women's prisons are organised in ways similar to domestic situations: first names are used; positive use is made of older female prisoners to 'stabilise' younger ones; and they are allowed to wear make-up and their own clothes (see for example, Genders and Player, 1987). Such concessions create an imagery of women's prisons being akin to a boarding-school, a parallel which is frequently though rather superficially drawn. Underpinning this kind of domestic structure is still, of course, punishment.

The rhetoric surrounding the purpose of women's imprisonment is as contradictory as the rhetoric surrounding the use of imprisonment in general, though in recent times the political rhetoric at least has not been at all hesitant in foregrounding the purpose of imprisonment as punishment. Certainly, despite the difference in internal organisation within women's prisons, women experience imprisonment as a brutalising process. It is brutalising in both structural and psychological terms: structural insofar as many women who find themselves in prison come from poor backgrounds, in which a high proportion of them have moved from care to custody (Carlen, 1988). In addition, a high proportion of them have experience of either physical and/or sexual assault. Thus many women enter prison having already had their fair share of the more brutal aspects of social existence.

The degradation ceremony (Garfinkel, 1957) of the strip search when they enter prison marks the first stage in a process in which they are also psychologically brutalised. It marks their entry into a regime in which they become non-people. For example, Eaton (1993: 54) has this to say about a suicide in prison:

> Death is a woman's ultimate act but she is not allowed to own that act. Her death is unmarked. Even after she becomes a body she becomes a nobody. And other prisoners witness that neither her existence nor her non-existence is recognised. Thus their own worth is announced.

Within this non-existence women in prison are, in Carlen's (1985) terms, disciplined, infantilised, feminised, medicalised, and domesticised. And it is certainly the case that the concessions of the female prison outlined above also become one of the mechanisms of discipline, an opportunity for inflicting pain and thereby control. Medical strategies are also used as a mechanism of control, a way of keeping problematic women quiet (see Sim, 1990).

Women can respond to the prison regime in a variety of ways: by withdrawing, by retaliating, by being incorporated into the system, and by self-mutilation (Eaton, 1993). This last strategy constitutes a key point of difference in the way in which women respond to incarceration in comparison with men, though many of the processes identified above are also apparent in men's experience of imprisonment. Understanding the nature of the prison experience, however, should not detract our attention from the central question that underpins that experience: what is prison for?

Carlen (1994) cogently argues that prison is about punishment. And perhaps what is over-ridingly brutal about the recognition of that, as far as women in prison are concerned, is that there is strong evidence to suggest that many of them find themselves there because at some point in their lives they have fallen through the gaps in welfare provision. As has already been stated, there are strong links between having been in care and ending up in custody. In the study by Genders and Player (1987), half of their sample of female prisoners had been in care. In Carlen's (1983) study of Cornton Vale in Scotland, two-thirds had histories of mental illness. Many of these women find themselves in prison because no one else knows what to do with them. This has led Carlen (1990) to argue for a cogent and coherent policy agenda for alternatives to prison for women. This constitutes her agenda for a 'woman-wise penology'.

Given that women constitute such a small proportion of the total prison population, there is a point of view which states that in policy terms it is therefore possible to experiment, to introduce new initiatives, at little cost, but which could be of great value to the prison system as a whole. Carlen's woman-wise penology is derived from this policy possibility. It has two main aims. First to ensure that the punishment of female law-breakers does not add to their oppression *as women*. Second, to ensure that the punishment of law-breaking men does not add to their brutalisation or their oppression of women in the future.

With these aims in mind, Carlen starts from the premise that it would be possible to release all women held in prison with the exception of possibly 100 offenders serving sentences for serious violent crime. This would release funds immediately to finance a range of other schemes and/or opportunities for controlling and/or rehabilitating female law-breakers. The proposals she makes range from a more imaginative use of the Community Service Order (rarely used for women because of the paucity of opportunities for women to work in the community in this way) to the development of all-female probation groups.

Indeed, many of the policy proposals suggested by Carlen can be found working already in local initiatives. They have yet to be adopted on a wide-scale basis. And, given the logic of Carlen's position, if these policies could be shown to work for women there is no logical reason why they could not be reworked or modified to meet the needs of male law-breakers. But, of course, if prisons are really about punishment, then before we can develop any alternative workable policies, we need to understand what the nature of that punishment is.
Carlen (1994: 136) states:

> I do think it matters that empirical prison research (in Britain at least) is not currently investigating and theorising prisons as deliberate and calibrated mechanisms of punishment inflicting state-legitimated pain. And pain of such magnitude that prisoners routinely suffer psychological damage, routinely suffer from prison-induced physical ill-health, and are frequently driven to suicide.

In some respects, then, prisons, in terms of inflicting punishment are quite successful at what they do. This power to punish, as Carlen (1994) argues 'grinds' both men and women, regardless of whether or not they are in a male prison or a female prison. The effects are the same. However, there is perhaps something more to be said about the nature of the process of punishment itself that might reveal one of its more hidden dimensions.

Sumner (1990: 34) points out that whilst Foucault's work has been very influential in encouraging social scientists to rethink a range of issues associated with the processes of control, Foucault himself had little to say on the way in which these processes are gendered. Understanding the ways in which gender is censured (approved of and controlled) is basic not only to understanding gender relations in general but also to understanding the nature and the operation of the criminal law. This much this chapter has so far established. However, the processes of discipline and punishment are also not immune to gender. Little work has been done to systematically analyse the gendered dimensions to punishment, though we can catch some glimpses on the way in which this works.

Eaton (1993: 16) suggests that when a close look is taken at disciplinary institutions, it reveals that 'the disciplined subject is also a gendered subject'.

> Thus through formal and informal mechanisms, through discourse and through force, the state plays a part in the construction of womanhood. Within the prison the range of acceptable models of femininity for prisoners is severely limited to those which manifest docility and subservience.

Of course, this preference for one form of femininity over another reflects the way in which the broader processes of control, sometimes referred to as 'normalisation', constrain individuals to fit with particular images of both masculinity and femininity. These images, for Eaton, reflect a hierarchically structured ranking placing the white, male, heterosexual at the top and marginalising both other versions of masculinity and femininity (Connell, 1987). It is both interesting and valuable to reflect on the experience of punishment in these terms. In so doing we are faced with the question of the connections to be made between versions of masculinity, punishment, and how they are experienced by men as well as women.

Being able to 'take it like a man' is both a demand and a constraint faced by men in all sorts of different social circumstances. Being able to 'do your time' like a man places particular demands on men in prison. In prison, 'the prisoner's masculinity is in fact besieged from every side: through loss of autonomy and independence, enforced submission to authority, lack of access to material goods, all of which are central to his status as a 'man' (Newton, 1994: 197). Of course, much prison literature has shown that men deal with this deprivation by recreating masculine hierarchies in prison. These hierarchies rest on the same kind of group solidarity and loyalty found between men in other kinds of organisations, with the ability to give and receive violence much more to the fore perhaps in the prison setting.

In addition, however, once in prison, the absence of women and the presence of enforced celibacy mean that the expression of sexuality may also need to be renegotiated. The extent of homosexual activity within prison reflects one way in which heterosexual men deal with this not as an expression of a commitment to homosexuality (seen to be passive, weak, feminine), but as an expression of power and authority over weaker prisoners. Indeed the 'true' homosexual in prison is likely to be met with aggressive homophobia. This search for an expression of themselves as masculine men whilst in prison accounts in part for the drive to be 'tougher than the rest' (Sim, 1993), and provides one way of understanding the associated condoning of violent behaviour.

There are, of course, different ways in which one might construct an explanation of the way in which men respond to imprisonment. One possibility is to look for the way in which particular structures permit, condone, offer strategies for legitimate action, and deny others. Within such structures individuals can and do choose to play out their identities in different ways. In the context of the issues here, it is important to recognise both the institutional structure of the prison and the discourse of imprisonment itself in setting the framework in which individual prisoners, male and female, manage their imprisonment.

Prisons are fundamentally authoritarian, institutional frameworks which not only deny people their freedom, but also deny them a sense of themselves as individuals with any dignity, they are brutalising institutions. In some respects, this inherent structure, with its militaristic overtones, also constitutes them implicitly as very masculine structures in which only the very masculine will survive. Disciplined, gendered and enforced in this way, they act as both a constraint and facilitator of the likely ways in which men and women manage their imprisonment. You have to be tough to survive it, whether you are a prisoner or a prison officer. Moreover there is a further dimension to this masculinisation of punishment.

Current political rhetoric on law and order presumes that being tough on law and order also means sending people to prison for punishment, as the increasing rate of imprisonment in the figures presented in this chapter demonstrate. It is interesting to reflect upon how these two conceptualisations have merged with one another. Some would argue that there are other possible ways of constructing a tough stance on law and order. The notion of 'shaming' has been suggested as one (Braithwaite, 1989).

Braithwaite and Daly (1994) provide an analysis of how the method of conferencing (rooted in the principle of shaming) might not only constitute a tougher response to 'domestic' violence but also a more effective one. The key themes in their analysis rest on a number of presumptions: that the threat of state intervention might be more powerful than the intervention itself; that shaming ceremonies shame the offender and care for the victim; that such processes provide the opportunity for those significant to both the victim and the offender to construct their own response to problematic behaviour, and that this does constitute a dialogue for changing behaviour with those who matter. At the same time the offender is not excluded but challenged to change their behaviour to secure their inclusion.

Of course, as the work by Walklate and Evans (1999) has demonstrated, in some communities the alternative structures of control which exist are also in some respects tougher and more effective than the criminal justice response, not least because they are often immediate and involve some public shaming.

Arguably both of these responses constitute a much tougher stance on law and order both in terms of political and policy implementation, and in terms of their controlling effects. This issue, of course, leads us into a consideration of the connections to be made between the masculine nature of politics and political debate – for the most part male-membered, male-dominated, and rooted in the adversarial form – and the presumptions underpinning the law. Interconnections not far, in fact, removed from the issues with which this chapter began. There may be many rationalities and many justices.

Conclusion

This chapter has been concerned to focus on the ways in which the criminal justice process, through the application of the law, deals with men and women. It has attempted to identify the circumstances in which it is useful to reflect upon the gendered dimensions to that process. In so doing it is clear that there are difficulties in presuming that the law acts in a vacuum with respect to gender (or with respect to any other structuring variable for that matter), and it is thereby important to recognise what can and cannot be achieved by addressing the law on its own. This is not intended to imply, however, that action around the law, or other policy initiatives in the context of penality, are to be abandoned as a result. The law does provide room for manoeuvre; and in that space change can occur.

The value of examining the operation of the law and images of pena-lity from a gendered perspective has hopefully been demonstrated. Hopefully, it has also been effectively demonstrated that such a gendered perspective requires that we examine these issues as much through the eyes of men as we do women.

Suggestions for further reading

Naffine, N. (1990) *Law and the Sexes*. This is a well-argued, useful critical overview of the nature of the law and how to understand its effect from a gendered perspective.

Kennedy, H. (1992) *Eve Was Framed*. A very readable first-hand account of a leading QC's encounter with the law and legal training.

Any first-hand account of the experience of imprisonment, for example: Peckham, A., *A Woman In Custody*. Boyle, J., *A Sense of Freedom*.

7 Conclusion: gender, crime and politics

> Feminist theory is likely to dismantle the long-standing dichotomy of the devilish and daring criminal man and the unappealing inert conforming woman. The threat it poses to a masculine criminology is therefore considerable.
>
> (Naffine, 1987: 133)

Introduction

This book began with a concern to document the validity or otherwise of understanding the nature of 'the crime problem' as a gendered problem, alongside an attempt to understand experiences of and within the criminal justice process as gendered experiences. In order to achieve this we have drawn both implicitly and explicitly on various aspects of feminist-informed theorising and empirical work. In so doing, this work has been particularly concerned to document the value of understanding those processes also through the lens of masculinity. This analysis has, hopefully, exposed dimensions to the understanding of criminality and the criminal justice process which have frequently remained invisible to much criminological and victimological work. The question remains, where does this kind of analysis lead the academic and policy agenda on crime?

Part of the answer to this question lies within understanding the power that the domain assumptions underpinning both criminology and victimology wield over those disciplines' respective concerns. Part of the answer also lies in understanding the discomfort caused by the questions raised as a result of deconstructing those domain assumptions, questions that challenge both feminist-informed and mainstream criminological work alike. Some of this, for example, has been revealed in the discussions on risk articulated particularly in chapter 3. The question remains as to why the criminological agenda persistently resists embracing the critical impact that the material discussed here suggests. In order to answer this question it will be necessary for us to review, briefly, some of the key characteristics of the criminological and victimological enterprises.

As chapter 1 illustrated, the emergence of the modern form of criminology occurred alongside the emergence of other social science disciplines. The common ties that exist between these disciplinary areas are to be found in the adherence to traditional conceptions of science and traditional conceptions of what counts as rational knowledge, who can possess such knowledge, and how such knowledge might be gathered. Adherence to these principles ensured that the theoretical and consequently empirical agendas that emanated from the social sciences in general, and criminology and victimology in particular, resulted in the implicit acceptance of a view of the world which equated human experience with male experience.

As Seidler (1994) has argued, this implicit acceptance of male experience as being equal to human experience has had a profound effect on social theory. It is only through the challenge of feminist work that it has been possible to identify the problematic nature of assuming that the separation of reason from emotion equates with the separation of male from female, thus calling into question the presumption that men as men have the preserve on what is considered to be reasonable behaviour and women as women have the same privilege with respect to emotion. As Seidler (1994: 202) states:

> It is for men to be the guardians of 'reason' and 'objectivity' and so to refuse to be drawn into the unbounded and the chaotic, that, like the feminine, can so easily overwhelm. Social theory and philosophy has to stay within the limits of reason, learning to stay within the province of what can be clearly said.

Challenging such dichotomous thinking, as feminist work has done in different ways, has not only a profound effect upon how we think about the categories male and female but also how we think about the various concepts which social science disciplines have used in order to understand social behaviour. As was stated earlier, the concepts of fear, risk and danger, as discussed in chapter 2 and 3 stand as evidence for the uncomfortable questions that can be raised when the logic of the feminist challenge is pursued.

However, this challenge does not necessarily imply that we replace one form of knowing with another, in other words that we flip the coin and transplant female knowing in the place of male knowing. What is necessary is to find a way of transgressing the dichotomy. To use a distinction introduced by Giddens (1984), it is necessary to search for duality rather than dualism. In some respects this might also mean that we need to re-examine our understanding of science and what science can equip us with. In everyday life people do find biographical solutions to the impact of dualistic thinking in the accomplishment of their routine lives.

For example, in discussing motorcycle repair Pirsig (1975) makes the following observations:

> a screw sticks for example, on a side cover assembly. You check the manual to see if there might be any special cause for this screw to come off so hard but all it says is 'Remove side cover plate' in that wonderful terse technical style that never tells you what you want to know.... This isn't a rare scene in science or technology. This the commonest scene of all. Just plain stuck. What you're up against is the great unknown, the void of all Western thought. You need some ideas, some hypotheses. Traditional scientific method has always been at the very best 20:20 hindsight. It's good for seeing where you've been. It's good for testing the truth of what you think you know, but it can't tell you where you ought to go, unless where you ought to go is a continuation of where you were going in the past. Creativity, originality, inventiveness, intuition, imagination – 'unstuckness' in other words – are completely outside its domain.

This example captures the clear tensions between what it is that can and cannot be delivered by the cultural adherence to science: when a specific problem emerges under specific circumstances the universal laws of science do not necessarily equip anyone (the scientist included) with either the knowledge or the ability to solve it. In these circumstances people reach for other forms of knowing, including that which might be defined as feminine knowing.

So the challenge to criminological and victimological thinking is profound indeed – and not just because, as with many academic areas, the disciplines are peopled in the majority by men, though that factor may be significant enough: since, as other chapters have illustrated, some of the questions raised by the more recent work on masculinity demands that those in power (mostly men) consider reflexively the nature of their own self-identities and their expression of themselves as men. Consider, for example, the implications of a gendered agenda for policing. Such an agenda implies that police managers, as well as 'street bobbies' reconsider their central contribution to and construction of the policing task. This also means, in part, reflecting on themselves as men. But the challenge posed by the material presented in this text is perhaps even more fundamental than this.

Recasting the criminological enterprise as well as law-breaking behaviour in terms of gender in general but in relation to the debate on masculinity(ies) in particular, challenges criminology's fundamental relationship with modernity. This is particularly the case if what is meant by that relationship is some desire to establish a general truth that can inform a general policy-making process; and which can thereby offer some form of control over the processes of social change. Here lies one way of articulating the link between the criminological enterprise, its domain assumptions concerning science, rationality, and wider political and ideological processes. This link is to be found in the gendered assumptions which both share.

Naffine (1987) articulates one part of this equation at the beginning of this chapter. Connell (1987: 126) articulates another: 'The state arms men and disarms women.' Here we have a nice play on words, since such arming and disarming can take place in the power of whoever has access to the legitimate use of force, or who controls a conversation. However, ideological and political processes which assert and sustain the authority of normative heterosexuality, as was argued in chapter 6, have powerful consequences for both men and women. They demand that men are tough, that they 'take it like a man', and are 'tougher than the rest'. And whether this is expressed in terms of physical prowess or mental prowess, it has a damaging effect on men, their emotions and the quality of the relationships they form around them. It also has a profoundly damaging effect on women (see chapter 4). Chapters 5 and 6 suggested that it was also useful to see the links between 'normative heterosexuality', what is understood by discipline and what is understood by 'tough' law and order politics. It is within this domain too that the challenge of some of the ideas articulated in this book can prove to be both privately and publicly problematic.

Once we begin to explore these links in this way we are implicitly, if not explicitly, also exploring an agenda which is concerned as much with difference as it is with sameness. To quote Seidler (1994: 197) again:

> There was an abiding tension between modernity and difference. We learned to treat differences in a particular way. We learned within a liberal moral culture to treat them as incidental to whom we are as human beings. At most they are issues of individual opinion and belief.

Yet as the argument relating to masculinity and crime suggests, difference is more that individual opinion and belief. In other words, resisting the postmodern logic of the ultimate celebration of difference yet recognising the need to incorporate an understanding of diversity, difference is more that individual opinion and belief. Difference is structured. It is articulated by individuals, yes; but within a framework which offers them templates of action which they accomplish (or fail to accomplish) on a routine daily basis. But this is not sameness. The masculinity debate generated from feminist concerns, demands, for example that we reconsider the dictum 'All men are potential rapists'. It also demands that we reconsider the genesis of criminal behaviour.

This returns us to a fundamental tension which can be identified in the debate on masculinity as it has been applied to the criminological enterprise and which runs through a text with a central project of this kind. It raises the question of how much weight we give to the issue of masculinity in setting an agenda for understanding law-breaking behaviour. Which variables do we give primacy to in formulating both our explanations of crime and the policies that might be generated by such explanations? This question, if no other, certainly identifies the problems inherent in seeking an all-embracing answer, even if that were ever possible. This is probably the real academic challenge to much of the thinking that underpins mainstream ('malestream') criminological and victimological work. It also constitutes a real political challenge. At this point it will be useful to review in a little more detail some of the themes addressed in this text which serve to identify this for us.

Women and crime or gender and crime?

This book began by articulating some of the dangers inherent in adopting an approach to criminology or victimology couched in terms of the 'women and crime' question. Hopefully, it has been demonstrated that those dangers are real at least in terms of the distraction that they can generate in terms of an intellectual agenda. This is no way implies that there have not been real gains made by that work which has been conducted under the women and crime umbrella, but merely to indicate that such an agenda in and of itself, whilst still valuable, does not provide all the answers to the sex differentials associated with understanding law-breaking behaviour. Neither does this imply that there are no dangers associated with an approach which favours looking at that behaviour as a gendered phenomenon. There are at least three worthy of further comment.

- the first exists at the level of explanation. This can be articulated in a number of different ways but it is primarily a danger of attributing gender as the explanatory concept through which to understand particular phenomenon *inappropriately*. Put another way, we may be looking for explanations in terms of gender when other conceptual frameworks might be more fruitful. This is an issue to which we shall return (see below).

- the second exists at the level of empirical investigation. Giving primacy to gender does not necessarily mean that we leave behind examining the social world through the eyes of women. Women's experiences of gendered social relationships still have much to offer us on a whole range of issues which will cast light on our understanding of men. As Cain (1990) argues, it is more about including studies on men rather than setting an agenda which explores one set of experiences in preference to another. This leads to the third danger.

- this danger is political and connects the debate here with the broader debate concerning 'women's studies' or 'gender studies'. There is a view which suggests that the movement towards the study of gender has provided a route for men to reclaim areas of empirical investigation and analysis which feminism had established as its own. In other words it is important to recognise the political nature of the knowledge production process and the power relationships between men and women which exist in that process. Women's need for 'a room of their own' (to borrow from the title of the book by Virginia Woolf) is real indeed. And some would argue that politically, women need to be in a much more powerful position than they currently are, before they concede the intellectual ground to the equivalent feminist notion that only men can study other men. There are certainly political dangers here. But perhaps the only answer to this is that we (women and men) have to continue to struggle with the process that it generates. No one ever said that there had to be easy answers!

Science, rationality, and modernity

A second theme underpinning the material presented in this text and re-asserted at the beginning of this conclusion, has been the way in which both criminology and victimology have developed with a commitment to particular views of the relationship between science, rationality and modernity. It has hopefully been demonstrated that the challenge to a conventional understanding of these ideas has arisen from feminism, though it must be said that feminism in and of itself does not have a sole preserve on such a challenge. It would be equally possible to develop a critique of rationality predicated on religious grounds as one on grounds of gender. The implications of these critique are threefold for both criminology and victimology.

1 these views argue for a relativistic stance towards knowledge and the knowledge construction process rather than a universalistic stance. And whilst many criminologists and victimologists might recognise the difficulties inherent in a universalistic position, they equally resist the move towards acknowledging the relativism in much of the work that they do. This occurs, perhaps, as a result of the sometimes latent desire to continue to seek for the cause or causes of crime. This is not to suggest that such a search is fruitless, but it is to suggest that such causes may be far more diverse and specific than some criminological work has hitherto implied.

2 these views imply that we re-examine the concepts that inform much criminological and victimological debate. This has been articulated in

this text in a number of ways. For example, the unthinking importation of risk avoidance as equating to risk itself constitutes a key example of the kind of re-examination (deconstruction) which can, and needs to, take place. The same could also be said for how we understand punishment, discipline, fear, danger, etc.

3 these views imply that we look for what is made more or less visible by and through the conceptual and research agendas we construct: not only in relation to gender-relevant studies (though some would say that it is difficult to identify a non-relevant gender study), but also in relation to how we articulate studies concerned with class, race, age, community, etc. Whose knowledge counts in these areas, how and why?

Masculinity or masculinities?

Another recurrent theme in this text has been that of masculinity. This has emerged in the context of examining the domain assumptions of science and rationality commented on above, and has woven a thread through the substantive issues addressed in the chapters that have followed. Moreover, it would be an understatement to say that this debate has the power to transform much academic and policy thinking around crime and criminal justice policy. Despite, or perhaps even as a result of this power to transform, this theme also contains within it inherent dangers for the criminological enterprise.

The main danger here articulated in chapter 6 is that the co-usage of the term masculinities becomes the catch-all term for both understanding and explaining different kinds of law-breaking behaviour occurring in different structural and material circumstances. This does not mean that masculinity as a concept is not important, or that as a concept it does not sometimes cast a new light and a different light on old criminological conundrums – although as Hearn (1996) has argued there is a significant lack of conceptual clarity around the usage of the term. However, such lack of clarity notwithstanding, the adoption of some kind of political programme like that outlined by Connell (1987) and endorsed by Messerschmidt (1993) may be a useful and worthwhile endeavour. It does reflect, however, a critical scepticism that such conceptual thinking can provide all the answers. This is the danger. There may well be ways in which it is possible to reinterpret the crimes of the powerful in terms of hegemonic masculinity. But there are other themes present too; for example, what about the processes of increasing residential segregation taking place in many large conurbations?

The way in which these processes have been conceptualised and debated may have an edge to them that can be usefully understood in terms of masculinity. But the question remains, can they be explained in these terms? This is perhaps a rather crude way of reminding us that at the beginning of this text it was argued that the primacy given to one variable over another was more often than not a theoretical decision, not necessarily an empirical one. We need at least to be both more theoretically and empirically aware of the power of masculinities but we also need to be both theoretically and empirically sensitive to exploring the circumstances when this variable matters and when other variables might matter more.

Gender, race, class

On a number occasions throughout this text and in this conclusion, we have referred to the problem of the primacy given to gender as the explanatory variable in the context of crime. The issue that such a universalising tendency poses is worthy of further comment. In responding to critical review of their seminal work *'Mean Streets'* (1997), Hagan and McCarthy had this to say:

> We also assumed gender would play a more important role than it did. Together these findings suggest that we need to give more thought to the ways that gender's relationship with crime is conditioned and mediated by background and foreground variables.
>
> (Hagan and McCarthy, 2000: 235)

Messerschmidt (1997: 113) makes the same point:

> Gender, race and class are not absolutes and are not equally significant in every social setting where crime is realised. That is, depending on the social setting, accountability to certain categories is more salient than accountability to other categories.

The work reported on by Walklate and Evans (1999) would make the same point about the mediating effect of community. The different ways in which researchers have endeavoured to conceptualise the sex/gender issue has also been well summarised by Daly (1997). The point is well made however. The complex ways in which different variables may interact with each other both in determining structural conditions for action and biographical responses of action demands critical reflection and examination. It means exploring femininities as well as masculinities. It means exploring 'whiteness' as well as 'blackness'. It means exploring class. It means exploring different sexualities and challenging normative heterosexuality (Collier, 1998). It means exploring the real world as opposed to just the discursive one. Such a process may call into question all kinds of knowledge claims, including those made by feminists and will certainly call into question any policy process which assumes that what works in one setting may work in another.

Sameness or difference?

A further theme which runs through this text is the question of the relationship between understanding the experience of men and women as standing for the experience of Men and Women. The tension between these has been identified in a number of different ways in the foregoing chapters and has been articulated in a number of different ways as well: universality versus relativity, generalisability versus specificity, modernism versus postmodernism. It may be, of course, that what is at issue here is not the tension between sameness and difference itself but the actual posing of them as dichotomous. As Giddens has argued and as is referenced elsewhere in this text, such dualisms might be better conceptualised as dualities: in other words as processes which interact with one another so that at one and the same time we are both the same and different, and we operate with both claims to universal and local (relative) knowledge. Thus, of course, whilst as Messerschmidt (1993) talks of gender as an accomplishment, at one and the same time we are also accomplishing social class, negotiating age, dealing with race and racism, living in 'high risk' or 'low risk' communities.

The role of the state?

The role of the state and its relationship to a gendered understanding of crime has been dealt with in this text more through the substantive issues it has chosen to address (policework and the law) than explicitly as a separate area of analysis. In some respects it could be argued that this is a major area of omission. It is true to say that much feminist work has asserted the importance of the patriarchal state and its operations, and indeed some brands of criminology (that labelled rather crudely as 'idealist' by Young some time ago) has concerned itself with the operational activities of the state. Certainly the work drawn upon here has placed considerable emphasis on understanding the role of the state and state politics in gender relations. As Connell (1987: 130) states:

> The patriarchal state can be seen, then, not as the manifestation of a patriarchal essence, but as the centre of a reverberating set of power relations and political processes in which patriarchy is both constructed and contested.

Moreover Connell's work has contributed significantly to thinking about the gendered nature of the state in general, not just specifically in relation to crime.

In this text the presence of the state as a gendered institution has been articulated in what is to be understood as 'proper policing', through the law's understanding of 'normal sexual relationships' as well as through the question of who has legitimate access to the use of violence. But as Connell observes above, these understandings have been presented very much as social processes; as constituted and reconstituted in the everyday actions of human actors both male and female. Changing policy responses to the policing of rape, 'domestic' violence, and the more recent emphasis on policing as a service rather than a force, are examples where the space for progressive social change and/or regressive social action can occur. They are evidence of both the fluidity and the constancy of the state and state action. Perhaps much more work needs to be done here to articulate not only how the state operates to enforce and differentially police masculinities, but how and under what circumstances the state acts as a gendered institution, or a class-based institution, or a racist institution, or any combination of these.

Conclusion

From the themes which identifiably run through this text, three issues emerge.

1 the first of these leads us to address the need for an appreciation of both diversity and specificity in both criminological and victimological theorising and empirical investigation. This is a key message derivable from this exploration of the relationship between gender and criminal justice, this is a message which is not only applicable to the study of the relationship between gender and crime. As this concluding review has argued, gender may hold some of the clues to the 'crime problem', but it would be misguided to think that it holds all of the answers. A gendered lens certainly helps us see some features of the crime problem more clearly; but how and under what circum stances is that clarity made brighter by gender or distorted by it? There is a need both theoretically and empirically to remain sensitive to this question.

2 the second of these issues illustrates how effectively both the criminological and victimological agendas could be transformed by a further embracing of ideas generated outside of these disciplinary domains. Cain (1989) was certainly correct in her assertion that feminism transgresses criminology, and Smart too (1990) in her assertion that criminology needs feminism more than feminism needs criminology. Without this pioneering work the criminological agenda would be significantly impoverished. Without developing the implications of the emergent work on masculinities and the work on diversity and difference, its agenda will continue to be impoverished.

3 the third issue addresses the question of politics. As chapter 6 contended, there is always space for politics to work progressively or regressively. This much is the case, the actual political issue under discussion notwithstanding. There are elements of both tendencies present: for example, in some quarters the current redefining of 'domestic' violence as a non-sex-specific phenomenon, or the particular articulation of masculinity as only applicable to the 'yob culture'. These examples in and of themselves stand as testimony of the need for a gendered politics and a gendered debate around criminal justice policy. Success, of course, may be a long time coming and may depend as much on criminology's willingness to meet some of the challenges posed by the material discussed in this text, as Jefferson (1992) has argued. It may also depend on the willingness of any politician to take criminology and criminologists seriously and work with a seriously informed, empirically based policy agenda as opposed to the 'sound-bite'.

Bibliography

Adams, J. (1995) *Risk*. London: UCL Press.

Adler, I. (1975) *Sisters in Crime*, New York: McGraw-Hill.

Adler, Z. (1987) *Rape on Trial*, London: Routledge and Kegan Paul.

Allen, H. (1984/1990) 'At the mercy of their hormones' in *M/F*, vol 9, pp. 19-26.

Allen, H. (1987) *Justice Unbalanced: Gender, psychiatry and judicial decisions*, Milton Keynes: Open University Press.

Amir, M. (1971) *Patterns of Forcible Rape*, Chicago: University of Chicago Press.

Anderson, R., Brown, J. and Campbell, E. (1993) *Aspects of Discrimination within the Police Service in England and Wales*, Home Office: Police Research Group.

Anderson, S., Grove-Smith, C., Kinsey, R. and Wood, J. (1990) *The Edinburgh Crime Survey: First report*, Edinburgh: Scottish Office.

Banks, O. (1981) *Faces of Feminism*, Oxford: Blackwell.

Bannister, J., Farrall, S., Ditton, J., Gilchrist, E., (1997) 'Questioning the measurement of the fear of crime', *British Journal of Criminology*, vol. 37, no. 4, pp. 658-79.

Beck, U. (1992) *The Risk Society*, London: Sage.

Benn, M. (1985) 'Policing Women' in J. Baxter and L. Koffman (eds) *Police: the constitution and the community*, Abingdon: Professional Books.

Berk, R.A. and Sherman, L.W. (1984) 'The specific deterrent effects of arrest policy for domestic assault', *American Sociological Review*, 49, pp. 261-272.

Binney, V., Harkell, G. and Nixon, J. (1981) *Leaving Violent Men: a study of refuges and housing for battered women*, London: Women's Aid Federation.

Bottomley, A.K. and Pease, K. (1986) *Crime and Punishment: Interpreting the Data.*

Braithwaite, J. (1989) *Crime, Shame and Reintegration*, Cambridge: Cambridge University Press.

Braithwaite, J. and Daly, K. (1994)'Masculinities, violence, and communitarian control', in T. Newburn and E. Stanko (eds) *Just Boys Doing Business?* London: Routledge.

Brake, M. and Hale. C. (1992) *Public Order and Private Lives*, London: Routledge.

Brittain, A. (1989) *Masculinity and Power*, Oxford: Blackwell.

Brogden, M., Jefferson, T. and Walklate, S. (1988) *Introducing Policework*, London: Unwin Hyman.

Brown, B. (1986) 'Women and crime: the dark figures of criminology', *Economy and Society*, vol. 15, no. 3.

Brown, B. (1990) 'Reassessing the critique of biologism' in L. Gelsthorpe and A.

Morris (eds) *Feminist Perspectives in Criminology*, Buckingham: Open University Press.

Brownmiller, S. (1975) *Against Our Will: Men, women and rape*, London: Secker and Warburg.

Bryant, L., Dunkerley, D. and Kelland, G. (1985) 'One of the boys?' *Policing*, vol. 1, no. 4, pp. 236-44.

Buck, W. and Walklate, S. (1993) 'The role of forensic psychiatric recommendations in cases of diminished responsibility', paper presented to the British Psychological Society Annual Conference, Criminal Justice Division, Harrogate, March.

Bunt, P. and Mawby, R.I. (1993) 'Policing the quality of service', paper presented to British Criminology Conference, Cardiff.

Cain, M. (1989) 'Feminists transgress criminology' in M. Cain (ed) *Growing Up Good*, London: Sage.

Cain, M. (1990a) 'Realist philosophy and standpoint epistemologies, or feminist criminology as a successor science' in L. Gelsthorpe and A. Morris (eds) *Feminist Perspectives in Criminology*, Buckingham: Open University Press.

Cain, M. (1990b) 'Towards transgression: new directions in feminist criminology', *International Journal of the Sociology of Law*, vol. 18, pp. 1-18.

Cameron, D. and Fraser, E. (1987) *The Lust to Kill*, Oxford: Polity.

Campbell, A. (1984) *Girls in the Gang*, Oxford: Blackwell.

Campbell, A. (1993) *Out of Control: Men, women and aggression*, London: Pandora.

Campbell, B. (1993) *Goliath: Britain's dangerous places*, London: Virago.

Campbell, J.C. (1992) 'If I can't have you no-one can: power and control in homicide of female partners' in J. Radford and D. Russell (eds) *Femicide: The Politics of Women Killing*, Buckingham: Open University Press.

Carlen, P. (1983) *Women's Imprisonment*, London: Routledge and Kegan Paul.

Carlen, P. (1988) *Women, Crime and Poverty*, Milton Keynes: Open University Press.

Carlen, P. (1990) 'Women, crime, feminism and realism', *Social Justice*, vol. 17, no. 4.

Carlen, P. (1990) *Alternatives to Women's Imprisonment*, Buckingham: Open University Press.

Carlen, P. (1994) 'Why study women's imprisonment? or anyone else's?', *British Journal of Criminology*, vol. 34, Special Issue, pp. 131-140.

Carlen, P. and Worrall, A. (1987) *Gender, Crime and Justice*, Milton Keynes: Open University Press.

Carlen, P., Hicks, J., O'Dwyer, J., Christina, D., and Tchaikovsky, C, (1985) *Criminal Women*. Oxford: Blackwell.

Chambers, G. and Millar, A. (1983) *Investigating Sexual Assault*, Edinburgh: Scottish Office.

Chatterton, M. (1983) 'Policework and assault charges' in M. Punch (ed) *Control in the Police Organisation*, Cambridge, Mass: M.I.T. Press, pp. 194-200.

Cloward, R. and Ohlin, L. (1961) *Delinquency and Opportunity: a theory of delinquent gangs*, London: Routledge and Kegan Paul.

Coffey, S., Brown, J. and Savage, S. (1992) 'Policewomen's career aspirations: some reflections on the role and capability of women in policing in Britain' in *Police Studies*, vol. 15, no. 1, pp. 13-19.

Cohen, A.K. (1955) *Delinquent Boys*, New York: Free Press.

Collier, R. (1998) *Masculinities, Crime and Criminology*, London: Sage.

Connell, R.W. (1987) *Gender and Power*, Oxford: Polity.
Connell, R.W. (1995) *Masculinities*, Oxford: Polity.
Cook, D. (1987) 'Women on welfare: in crime or injustice?', P. Carlen and A. Worrall (eds) *Gender, Crime and Justice*, Milton Keynes: Open University Press.
Cook, D. (1989) *Rich Law, Poor Law: different responses to tax and supplementary bene fit fraud*, Milton Keynes: Open University Press.
Cowie, J., Cowie, V. and Slater, E. (1968) *Delinquency in Girls*, London: Heinemann.
Coward, R. (1994) 'Whipping boys' in *The Guardian Weekend*, 3 September.
Crawford, A., Jones, T., Woodhouse, T. and Young, J. (1990) *The Second Islington Crime Survey*, Middlesex University: Centre for Criminology.
Currie, E. (1985) *Confronting Crime*, New York: Pantheon.
Dake, K. (1992) 'Myths of nature: culture and the social construction of risk', *Journal of Social Issues*, vol. 48, no. 4.
Dalton, K. (1991) *Once a Month*, London: Fontana.
Daly, K. (1997) 'Different ways of conceptualising sex/gender in feminist theory and their implications for criminology', *Theoretical Criminology*, vol. 1, no. 1, pp.25-52.
Datesmann, S. and Scarpitti, F. (eds) (1980) *Women, Crime and Justice*, New York: Oxford University Press.
Davidoff, L. and Dowds, L. (1989) 'Recent trends in crimes of violence against the person in England and Wales', *Home Office Bulletin*, no. 27, pp. 11-18.
de Fleur, L.B. (1975) 'Biasing influences and drug arrest records', *American Sociological Review*, vol. 40, pp. 88-103.
Dekeseredy, W. and Schwartz, M. (1991) 'British left realism on the abuse of women: a critical appraisal' in H. Pepinsky and R. Quinney (eds) *Criminology as Peacemaking*, Indiana: Indiana University Press.
Ditton, J., Farrall, S., Bannister, J., Gilchrist, E., and Pease, K. (1999) 'Reactions to victimisation': why has anger been ignored?' *Crime Prevention and Community Safety: An International Journal*, vol. 1, no. 3, pp.37-54.
Dobash, R. and Dobash, R.E. (1980) *Violence Against Wives*, Shepton Mallet: Open Books.
Dobash, R. and Dobash, R.E. (1992) *Women, Violence and Social Change*, London: Routledge.
Dobash, R., Dobash, R.E. and Gutteridge, S. (1986) *The Imprisonment of Women*, Oxford: Blackwell.
Douglas, M. (1987) *How Institutions Think*, London: Routledge and Kegan Paul.
Douglas, M. (1992) *Risk and Blame: Essays in cultural theory*, London: Routledge.
Downes, D.M. and Rock, P.E. (1988) *Understanding Deviance*, Oxford: Oxford University Press, 2nd edn.
Eagle Russett, C. (1989) *Sexual Science: the Victorian construction of motherhood*, Cambridge, Mass: Harvard University Press.
Eaton, M. (1986) *Justice for Women? Family, court and social control*, Milton Keynes: Open University Press.
Eaton, M. (1993) *Women After Prison*, Buckingham: Open University Press.
Edgar, D. (1991) 'Are you being served?', *Marxism Today*, May, p. 28.
Edwards, S. (1986) *The Police Response to Domestic Violence in London*, London: Polytechnic of Central London.
Edwards, S. (1989) *Policing 'Domestic' Violence*, London: Sage.
Ehrlich-Martin, S. (1980) *Breaking and Entering: Policewomen on patrol*, California:

University of California Press.
Eisenstein, Z. (1986) *The Radical Future of Liberal Feminism*, Boston: Northeastern University Press.
Evans, K., Fraser, P., and Walklate, S. (1996) 'Whom can you trust? The politics of "grassing" on an inner-city housing estate', *Sociological Review*, August pp. 361-80.
Ewing, C. (1987) *Battered Women Who Kill*, Lexington: D.C. Heath & Co.
Faragher, T. (1981) 'The police response to violence against women in the home', J. Pahl (ed) *Private Violence and Public Policy*, London: Routledge.
Farrington, D.P. and Morris, A.M. (1983) 'Sex, sentencing and reconviction', *British Journal of Criminology*, vol. 23, no. 3.
Fattah, E.A. (1991) *Understanding Criminal Victimisation*, Scarborough, Ontario: Prentice-Hall.
Feeley, M.M. and Little, D.L. (1991) 'The vanishing female: the decline of women in the criminal process', *Law and Society Review*, vol. 25, no. 4, pp. 1-35.
Ferraro, K. (1989) 'The legal response to woman battering in the United States' in J. Hanmer, J. Radford and E. Stanko (eds) *Women, Policing and Male Violence*, London: Routledge, pp. 155-84.
Freudenburg, W.R. and Pastor, S.K. (1992) 'NIMBYs and LULUs: Stalking the syndromes', *Journal of Social Issues*, vol. 48, no. 4.pp. 39-61.
Friedman, L. and Schulman, M. (1990) 'Domestic violence: the criminal justice response' in A. J. Lurigio, W. G. Skogan and R. C. Davies *Victims of Crime: Problems, policies and progress*, London: Sage, pp. 87-103.
Fukuyama, F. (1996) *Trust*, London: Penguin.
Garfinkel, H. (1957) *Studies in Ethnomethodology*, New York: Prentice-Hall.
Garland, D. (1985) *Punishment and Welfare*, Aldershot: Gower.
Garofalo, J. (1981)'The fear of crime: causes and consequences', *Journal of Criminal Law and Criminal Policy*, vol. 72, pp. 839-957.
Gelles, R. (1987) *Family Violence*, London: Sage.
Gellner. E. (1989)'Trust, cohesion and the social order', in D. Gambetta (ed.) *Trust: the making and breaking of co-operative relations*, London: Blackwell, pp. 142-57.
Gelsthorpe, L. (1989) *Sexism and the Female Offender*, Aldershot: Gower.
Gelsthorpe, L. and Morris, A. (eds) (1990) *Feminist Perspectives in Criminology*, Buckingham: Open University Press.
Genders, E. and Player, E. (1987) 'Women in prison: the treatment, the control and the experience' in P. Carlen and A. Worrall (eds) *Gender, Crime and Justice*, Milton Keynes: Open University Press.
Giddens, A. (1991) *Modernity and Self-Identity*, Oxford: Polity.
Giddens, A. (1992) *The Transformation of Intimacy*, Oxford: Polity.
Giddens, A. (1998)'Risk society: the context of British politics', in J. Franklin (ed.) *The Politics of Risk Society*, Oxford: Polity.
Gillespie, T. (1996)'Rape crisis centres and "male rape": a face of the backlash', in M. Hester, L. Kelly, and J. Radford (eds) *Women, Violence and Male Power*, Buckingham: Open University Press.
Glueck, S. and Glueck, E. (1950) *Unravelling Juvenile Delinquency*, Cambridge, Mass.: Harvard University Press.
Goodey, J. (1997)'Boys don't cry: masculinities, fear of crime, and fearlessness', *British Journal of Criminology*, vol. 37, no. 3, pp. 401-18.

Gouldner, A.W. (1973) *For Sociology: Renewal and critique in sociology today*, Harmondsworth: Penguin.
Grace, S., Lloyd, C. and Smith, L. (1992) *Rape: from recording to conviction*, Research and Planning Unit Paper, 71, London: HMSO.
Griffin, S. (1981) *Pornography and Silence*, London: The Women's Press.
Halford, A. (1993) *No Way Up The Greasy Pole*, London: Constable.
Hagan, J. and McCarthy (2000) 'The meaning of criminology', *Theoretical Criminology*, vol. 4, no. 2, pp. 232-42.
Hall, R. (1985) *Ask Any Woman*, London: Falling Wall Press.
Hall-Williams, J.E. (1982) *Criminology and Criminal Justice*, London: Butterworths.
Hanmer, J. and Saunders, S. (1991) Policing violence against women: implementing policy changes, paper presented to the British Criminology Conference, York, July.
Harding, S. (ed) (1987) *Feminism and Methodology*, Milton Keynes: Open University Press.
Harding, S. (1991) *Whose Science? Whose Knowledge?*, Buckingham: Open University Press.
Harvey, L., Burnham, R.W., Kendall, K. and Pease, K. (1992) 'Gender differences in criminal justice: an international comparison', *British Journal of Criminology*, vol. 32, no. 2, pp. 208-17.
Hatty, S. (1989) 'Policing male violence in Australia' in J. Hamner, J. Radford and R. Stanko (eds) *Women, Policing and Male Violence*, London: Routledge, pp. 70-89.
Hearn, J. (1987) *The Gender of Oppression*, Brighton: Harvester Wheatsheaf.
Hearn, J. (1989) 'Some sociological issues in researching men and masculinities', *Discussion Paper*, No. 2, Department of Social Policy: University of Manchester.
Hearn, J. (1992) *Men in the Public Eye*, London: Routledge.
Hearn, J. (1996) 'Is masculinity dead? A critique of the concept of masculinity/masculinities', in M. MacAnGhaill (ed.) *Understanding Masculinities*, Buckingham: Open University Press.
Hedderman, C. and Hough, M. (1994) *Does the Criminal Justice System Treat Men and Women Differently?* Research Findings, 8. London: HMSO.
Heidensohn, F. (1985) *Women and Crime*, London: Macmillan.
Heidensohn, F. (1989) *Women in Policing in the USA*, London: The Police Foundation.
Heidensohn, F. (1989) *Crime and Society*, Basingstoke, Macmillan.
Heidensohn, F. (1992) *Women in Control? the role of women in law enforcement*, Oxford: Oxford University Press.
Hindelang, M. (1979) 'Sex differences in criminal activity', *Social Problems*, no. 27, pp. 143-56.
Hindelang, M.J., Gottfredson, M.R. and Garofalo, J. (1978) *Victims of Personal Crime: an empirical foundation for a theory of personal victimisation*, Cambridge, Mass: Ballinger.
Hirschi, T. (1969) *Causes of Delinquency*, Berkeley: University of California Press.
Hollway, W. and Jefferson, T. (1997)'The risk society in an age of anxiety: situating fear of crime' *British Journal of Sociology* vol. 48, no. 2, pp. 255-66.
Hough, M. and Mayhew, P. (1983) *The 1982 British Crime Survey*, London: HMSO.
Hough, M. and Mayhew, P. (1985) *Taking Account of Crime: Key findings from the 1984*

British Crime Survey, London: HMSO.
Hoyle, C. (1998) *Negotiating Domestic Violence*, Oxford: Clarendon.
Jaggar, A.M. (1983) *Feminist Politics and Human Nature*, Totowa, N.J.: Rowman and Allanfield.
Jefferson, T. (1992) '"Wheelin" and "Stealin"', *Achilles Heel*, no. 13, Summer.
Jefferson, T. (1993) 'Theorising masculine subjectivity'. Plenary address, Masculinities and Crime Conference, University of Brunel, September.
Jefferson, T., Sim, J. and Walklate, S. (1992) 'Europe, the left and criminology in the 1990s: accountability, control and the social construction of the consumer' in D. Farrington and S. Walklate (eds) *Victims and Offenders: Theory and policy*, British Society for Criminology: ISTD.
Johnson, N. (ed) (1985) *Marital Violence*, Sociological Review, Monograph no. 31, Keele: University of Keele Press.
Jones, A. (1985) Editorial, *Policing*, vol. 1, no. 4.
Jones, A. (1990) *Women Who Kill*, London: Victor Gollancz.
Jones, S. (1987) *Policewomen and Equality*, London: Macmillan.
Jones, T., MacLean, B. and Young, J. (1986) *The Islington Crime Survey*, Aldershot: Gower.
Karmen, A. (1990) *Crime Victims: an introduction to victimology*, Pacific Grove, California: Brooks Cole.
Katz, J. (1988) *The Seductions of Crime*, New York: Basic Books.
Kelly, L. (1988) *Surviving Sexual Violence*, Oxford: Polity.
Kendall, K. (1991) 'The politics of premenstrual syndrome: implications for feminist justice', *Journal of Human Justice*, vol. 2, no. 2, Spring.
Kennedy, H. (1992) *Eve Was Framed*, London: Chatto and Windus.
Kinsey, R. (1984) *Merseyside Crime Survey: First Report*, Liverpool: Merseyside Police Authority.
Kinsey, R. (1985) *The Merseyside Crime and Police Surveys: Final Report*, Liverpool: Merseyside Police Authority.
Kirkwood, C. (1993) *Leaving Abusive Partners*. London: Sage.
Lees, S. (1989) 'Blaming the victim', *New Statesman, New Society*, 1 December.
Lees, S. (1989) 'Learning to love' in M. Cain (ed) *Growing Up Good*, London: Sage.
Lees, S. (1997) *Ruling Passions*, London: Sage.
Leonard, E.B. (1982) *A Critique of Criminology Theory: Women, Crime and Society*, London: Longman.
Liddle, M. (1993) 'Gender, desire and child sexual abuse: accounting for the male majority', *Theory, Culture and Society*, vol. 10, pp. 103-126.
Liddle, M. (1993) 'Masculinity, 'male behaviour' and crime: a theoretical investigation of sex differences in delinquency and deviant behaviour', Masculinity and Crime Conference Report, Brunel University: Centre for Criminal Justice Research.
Lombroso, C. and Ferraro, W. (1895) *The Female Offender*, London: T. Fisher Unwin.
London Strategic Policy Unit (1986) *Police Response to Domestic Violence*, London: LPSU.
Lowman, J. (1992) 'Rediscovering crime' in J. Young and R. Matthews (eds) *Rethinking Criminology: The Realist Debate*, London: Sage.
Luhmann, N. (1989) 'Familiarity, confidence, trust: problems and alternatives' in D. Gambetta (ed.) *Trust: Making and breaking co-operative rela-*

tions. London: Blackwell, pp. 94-107.
Lukes, S. (1974) *Power*, London: Macmillan.
Lyng, S. (1990) 'Edgework: A social psychological analysis of voluntary risk taking', *American Journal of Sociology*, vol. 95, no.4.
MacDonald, E (1991) *Shoot the Women First*, London: Fourth Estate.
MacIntyre, A. (1988) *Whose Justice? Which Rationality?*, London: Duckworth.
MacKinnon, C. (1989) *Feminism Unmodified*, Harvard, Conn.: Harvard University Press.
MacKinnon, C. (1989) *Towards a Feminist Theory of the State*. Harvard: Harvard University Press.
McConville, M., Sanders, A. and Long, R. (1991) *The Case for the Prosecution*, London: Routledge.
McMullen, R.J. (1990) *Male Rape: Breaking the silence on the last taboo*, London: Gay Men's Press.
Matthews, R. and Young, J. (eds) (1992) *Issues in Realist Criminology*. London: Sage.
Mawby, R.I. and Walklate, S. (1994) *Critical Victimology*, London: Sage.
Mayhew, P. and Hough, M. (1988) 'The British crime survey: origins and impact' in M. Maguire and J. Pointing (eds) *Victims of Crime*, Milton Keynes: Open University Press.
Mayhew, P., Elliott, D. and Dowds, L. (1989) *The 1988 British Crime Survey*, London: HMSO.
Maxfield, M. (1984) *Fear of Crime in England and Wales*, Research Study, no. 78, London: Home Office.
Messerschmidt, J. (1986) *Capitalism, Patriarchy and Crime: Towards a socialist-feminist criminology*, Totowa, N.J.: Rowman and Littlefield.
Messerschmidt, J. (1993) *Masculinities and Crime*, Maryland: Rowman and Littlefield.
Messerschmidt, J. (1997) *Crime as Structured Action*, London: Sage.
Miers, D. (1978) *Responses to Victimisation*, Abingdon: Professional Books.
Miers, D. (1989) 'Positivist victimology: a critique', *International Review of Victimology*, no. 1, pp. 3-22.
Millman, M. (1975/1982) 'Images of deviant men and women' in M. Evans (ed) *The Woman Question*, London: Fontana.
Mirrless-Black and Aye Maung (1993) *Fear of Crime: Findings from the 1992 British Crime Survey*, Home Office Research and Planning Unit, London: HMSO.
Misztal, B. (1996) *Trust in Modern Societies*, Oxford: Polity.
Mooney, J. (1993) *The North London Domestic Violence Survey*, Middlesex University: Centre for Criminology.
Morgan, D. (1992) *Discovering Men*, London: Routledge.
Morgan, R. (1989) *The Demon Lover*, London: Mandarin.
Morley, R. and Mullender, A. (1991) 'Preventing violence against women in the home: feminist dilemmas concerning recent British developments, paper pre sented to British Criminology Conference, York, July.
Morris, A. (1987) *Women, Crime and Criminal Justice*, Oxford: Blackwell.
Moss Kanter, R. (1977) *Men and Women of the Corporation*, New York: Basic Books.
NACRO (1993) *Women Leaving Prison*, London: NACRO.
Naffine, N. (1987) *Female Crime*, Sydney: Allen and Unwin.
Naffine, N. (1990) *Law and the Sexes*, London: Allen and Unwin.
Naffine, N. (1997) *Feminism and Criminology*, Oxford: Polity.

Nelken, D. (1994) 'Whom can you trust? The future of comparative criminology', in D. Nelken (ed.) *The Futures of Criminology*, London: Sage.
Newburn, T. and Stanko, E.A. (1994) *Just Boys Doing Business*, London: Routledge.
Newton, C. (1994) 'Gender theory and prison sociology: using theories of masculinities to interpret the sociology of prisons for men', *Harvard Journal of Criminal Justice*, vol. 33, no. 3, pp. 193-202.
Pahl, J. (1978) *A Refuge for Battered Women. a study of the role of a women's centre*, London: HMSO.
Painter, K. (1991) *Marriage, Wife Rape and the Law*, University of Manchester: Department of Social Policy.
Parsons, T. (1937) *The Structure of Social Action*, New York: McGraw Hill.
Pearson, G. (1983) *Hooligan: a history of respectable fears*, London: Macmillan.
Pizzey, E. (1973) *Scream Quietly or the Neighbours Will Hear*, Harmondsworth: Penguin.
Policy Studies Institute (1983) Smith, D.J. and Gray, J. *Vol 4: The Police in Action*, London: PSI.
Pollak, O. (1950) *The Criminality of Women*, New York: A.S. Barnes/Perpetua.
Radford, J. (1987) 'Policing male violence, policing women' in J. Hamner and M. Maynard (eds) *Women, Policing and Social Control*, London: Macmillan, pp. 30-45.
Radford, J. and Stanko, B. (1991) 'Violence against women and children: The contradictions of crime control under patriarchy' in K. Stenson and D. Cowell (eds) *The Politics of Crime Control*, London: Sage.
Rafter, N. and Heidensohn, F. (1995) *International Feminist Perspectives in Criminology: Engendering a discipline*. Buckingham: Open University Press.
Reeves Sanday, P. (1981) 'The socio-cultural context of rape', *Journal of Social Issues*, vol. 37, no. 4.
Reiner, R. (1991) *Chief Constables*, Oxford: Clarendon.
Reiner, R. (1992) *The Politics of the Police*, Hemel Hempstead: Harvester Wheatsheaf, 2nd edn.
Roberts, J. (1990) *Sexual Assault Legislation in Canada: An evaluation*, Department of Justice: Ottawa.
Rock, P. (1986) *Helping Victims of Crime*, Oxford: Clarendon.
Roiphe, K. (1994) *The Morning After: Sex, fear and feminism*, London: Hamish Hamilton.
Roshier, B. (1989) *Controlling Crime*, Milton Keynes: Open University Press.
Russell, D. (1990) *Rape in Marriage*, Indiana: Indiana University Press.
Sanders, A. (1987) 'Prosecuting domestic and non-domestic violence'. Paper presented to the British Criminology Conference, Sheffield, July.
Scrapec, C. (1993) 'The female serial killer' in H. Birch (ed) *Moving Targets: Women, murder and representation*, London: Virago.
Scraton, P. (1990) 'Scientific knowledge or masculine discourses? challenging patriarchy in criminology' in L. Gelsthorpe and A. Morris (eds) *Feminist Perspectives in Criminology*, Buckingham: Open University Press.
Scully, D. (1990) *Understanding Sexual Violence*, London: Unwin Hyman.
Scully, D. and Marolla, J. (1993) 'Riding the bull at Gilleys': convicted rapists describe the rewards of rape' in P.B. Bart and E.G. Moran (eds) *Violence Against Women: the bloody footprints*, London: Sage.
Seidler, V. (1994) *Unreasonable Men: Masculinity and social theory*. London:

Routledge.
Shapland, J. and Hobbs, R. (1989) 'Policing priorities on the ground' in R. Morgan and D.J. Smith (eds) *Coming to Terms with Policing*, London: Routledge, pp. 11-30.
Sheehy Report (1993) *Inquiry into Police Responsibilities and Rewards: Executive Summary*.
Sherman, L., Schmidt, J., Regan, D., Gartin, P., and Cohn, E. (1991) 'From initial deterrence to long-term escalation: short custody arrest for ghetto poverty violence', *Criminology*, vol. 29, no. 4, pp. 821-49.
Sim, J. (1990) *Medical Power in Prisons*, Buckingham: Open University Press.
Sim, J. (1993) 'Tougher than the Rest', plenary presentation to Masculinities and Crime Conference, University of Brunel, September.
Skogan, W. (1986) 'The fear of crime and its behavioral implications' in E.A. Fattah (ed) *From Crime Policy to Victim Policy*, London: Macmillan.
Smart, C. (1977) *Women, Crime and Criminology*, London: Routledge and Kegan Paul.
Smart, C. (1989) *Feminism and the Power of Law*, London: Routledge.
Smart, C. (1990) 'Feminist approaches to criminology: or postmodern woman meets atavistic man' in L. Gelsthorpe and A. Morris (eds) *Feminist Perspectives in Criminology*, Buckingham: Open University Press.
Smith, D. (1987) *The Everyday World as Problematic: a feminist sociology*, Milton Keynes: Open University Press.
Smith, D. (1990) 'Whistling women: reason, rationality and objectivity', The Harry Hawthorne Lecture, Canadian Learned Societies 25th Conference, University of Victoria.
Smith, L. (1989) *Domestic Violence*, London: HMSO.
Soothill, K. (1993) 'Policewomen in the news', *The Police Journal*, January.
Sparks, R. (1992) 'Reason and unreason in "left realism": some problems in the constitution of the fear of crime' in R. Matthews and J. Young (eds) *Issues in Realist Criminology*, London: Sage.
Stanko, E. (1985) *Intimate Intrusions: women's experience of male violence*, London: Virago.
Stanko, E. (1987) 'Typical violence, normal precaution: men, women and interpersonal violence in England, Wales, Scotland and the USA' in J. Hanmer and M. Maynard (eds) *Women, Violence and Social Control*, Basingstoke: Macmillan.
Stanko, E. (1988) 'Fear of crime and the myth of the safe home: a feminist critique of criminology' in K. Yllo and M. Bograd (eds) *Feminist Perspectives on Wife Abuse*, London: Sage.
Stanko, E.A. (1989) 'Missing the mark? policing battering' in J. Hamner, J. Radford and E. Stanko (eds) *Women, Policing and Male Violence*, London: Routledge, pp. 58-84.
Stanko, E. (1990) *Everyday Violence*, London: Virago.
Stanko, E.A. (1992) 'Plenary Address', Violence Against Women Conference, Manchester Metropolitan University, May.
Stanko, E. (1993) 'Ordinary fear: women, violence and personal safety' in P. Bart and E. Moran (eds) *Violence Against Women: the bloody footprints*, London: Sage.
Stanko, E.A. (1997) 'Safety talk: conceptualising women's risk assessment as a "technology of the soul"', *Theoretical Criminology* vol. 1 no. 4, pp. 479-99.
Stanko, E.A. and Hobdell, K. (1993) 'Assaults on men: masculinity and male

violence', *British Journal of Criminology*, vol. 33. no. 3.

Steinmetz, S. and Strauss, M. (1974) *Violence in the Family*, New York: Harper Row.

Strauss, M., Gelles, R. and Steinmetz, S. (1980) *Behind Closed Doors: Violence in the American family*, New York: Doubleday.

Sumner, C. (1990) 'Foucault, gender and the censure of deviance' in L. Gelsthorpe and A. Morris (eds) *Feminist Perspectives in Criminology*, Buckingham: Open University Press.

Sutherland, E.H. (1947) *Principles of Criminology*, Philadelphia: Lippencott.

Sydie, R. (1989) *Natural Women, Cultured Men*, Milton Keynes: Open University Press.

Tarling, P. (1993) *Analysing Offending: Data, Models, Interpretations*, London: HMSO.

Taylor, I.R.(1990) 'Introduction: the concept of "social cost" in free market theory and the social effects of free market policies' in I.R. Taylor (ed.) *The Social Effects of Free Market Policies*, Hemel Hempstead: Harvester Wheatsheaf.

Taylor, I. (1995)'Private homes and public others: an analysis of talk about crime in suburban South Manchester in the mid-1990s', *British Journal of Criminology*, vol. 35, no. 2, pp. 263-85.

Taylor, I. (1996) 'Fear of crime, urban fortunes and suburban social movements: some reflections from Manchester', *Sociology* vol. 30, no. 2, pp. 317-37.

Taylor, I. (1997)'Crime, anxiety and locality: responding to the condition of England at the end of the century', *Theoretical Criminology*, vol. 1, no. 1, pp. 53-76.

Taylor, I. (1999) *Crime in Context*, Oxford: Polity.

Taylor, I., Evans, K., and Fraser, P. (1996) *A Tale of Two Cities*. London: Routledge.

Taylor, I., Walton, P. and Young, J. (1973) *The New Criminology*, London: Routledge and Kegan Paul.

Thomas, W.I. (1923) *The Unadjusted Girl*, Boston: Little Brown.

Tolson, A. (1977) *The Limits of Masculinity*, London: Routledge.

Tong, R. (1989) *Feminist Thought: a comprehensive introduction*, London: Unwin Hyman.

Uglow, S. (1988) *Policing Liberal Society*, Oxford: Oxford University Press.

Ursel, J. (1990) 'Victim oriented response to wife abuse', paper presented to Canadian Learned Societies Association, University of Victoria, Canada, June.

Walklate, S. (1989) *Victimology: the victim and the criminal Justice process*, London: Unwin Hyman.

Walklate, S. (1992a) 'Jack and Jill join up at Sun Hill: public images of police officers', *Policing and Society*, vol. 2, pp. 219-232.

Walklate, S. (1992b) *Responding to domestic violence: an evaluation of the work of the "dedicated" unit in D Division. Final Report to Merseyside Police*, University of Salford: Department of Sociology.

Walklate, S. (1993a) 'Policing by women, with women, for women?', *Policing*, vol. 9, Summer.

Walklate, S. (1993b) 'Responding to women as "consumers" of a police service: the UK experience 1980-1990' in J. Vigh and G. Katona (eds) *Social Changes, Crime and Police*, Budapest: Eotuos Lerand University Press.

Walklate, S. (1994) 'Can there be a progressive victimology', *Victimology: an inter national review*, vol.3, no1/2.

Walklate, S. (1997) 'Risk and criminal victimisation: a modernist dilemma?' *British Journal of Criminology*, vol. 37, no. 1, pp. 35-46.

Walklate, S. (forthcoming)'Can there be a feminist victimology?' in Davies. P. and Francis, P. (eds) *Understanding Victimisation*, London: Macmillan.

Walklate, S. and Evans, K. (1999) *Zero Tolerance or Community Tolerance? Managing crime in high crime areas*. Aldershot: Ashgate.

Warr, M. (1985) 'Fear of rape among urban women', *Social Problems*, vol. 32, no. 3.

Weatheritt, M. (1993) 'Measuring police performance: accounting or accountability?' in R. Reiner and S. Spencer (eds) *Accountable Policing: Effectiveness, empowerment and equity*, London: Institute for Public Policy Research.

West, D.J. (ed) (1985) *Sexual Victimisation*, Aldershot: Gower.

Wiles, P. (1993) 'Policing structures, organisational change and personnel manage ment' in R. Dingwall and J. Shapland (eds) *Reforming British Policing: missions and structures*, Sheffield: Faculty of Law.

Wilson, E. (1983) *What Is To Be Done About Violence Against Women?*, Harmondsworth: Penguin.

Wilson, J.O. and Herrnstein, R.J. (1985) *Crime and Human Nature*, New York: Touchstone.

Wilson, M. and Daly, M. (1992) 'Till death us do part' in J. Radford and D. Russell (eds) *Femicide: the politics of woman killing*, Buckingham: Open University Press.

Wolfgang, M.E. (1957/1958) *Patterns in Criminal Homicide*, Philadelphia, Pa.: University of Pennsylvania Press.

Wootton, B. (1959) *Social Science and Social Pathology*, London: George, Allen and Unwin.

Worrall, A. (1990) *Offending Women*, London: Routledge.

Young, A. (1992) 'Feminism and the body of criminology' in D.P. Farrington and S. Walklate (eds) *Offenders and Victims: Theory and policy*. Selected papers from The British Criminology Conference 1991: British Society of Criminology, ISTD.

Young, J. (1986) 'The failure of criminology: the need for a radical realism' in R. Matthews and J. Young (eds) *Confronting Crime*, London: Sage, pp. 4-30.

Young, J. (1987) 'The tasks of a realist criminology', *Contemporary Crises* vol. 2, pp. 337-356.

Zedner, L. (1991) *Women, Crime and Custody in Victorian England*, Oxford: Oxford University Press.

Index